CLOUDS FROM
BOTH SIDES

*An Autobiography
by Julie Tullis*

Sierra Club Books · San Francisco

The Sierra Club, founded in 1892 by John Muir, has devoted itself to the study and protection of the earth's scenic and ecological resources—mountains, wetlands, woodlands, wild shores and rivers, deserts and plains. The publishing program of the Sierra Club offers books to the public as a nonprofit educational service in the hope that they may enlarge the public's understanding of the Club's basic concerns. The point of view expressed in each book, however, does not necessarily represent that of the Club. The Sierra Club has some sixty chapters coast to coast, in Canada, Hawaii, and Alaska. For information about how you may participate in its programs to preserve wilderness and the quality of life, please address inquiries to Sierra Club, 730 Polk Street, San Francisco, CA 94109.

Originally published in 1986 by Grafton Books, a Division of the Collins Publishing Group, 8 Grafton Street, London W1X 3LA.

Library of Congress Cataloging-in-Publication Data

Tullis, Julie, 1939–1986.
Clouds from both sides.

  Reprint. Originally published: London: Grafton, 1986.
  1. Tullis, Julie, 1939–1986. 2. Mountaineers—
Great Britain—Biography. 3. Cinematographers—
Great Britain—Biography. I. Title.
GV199.92.T85A3 1987 796.5'22'0924 [B] 87-4510
ISBN 0-87156-716-4

Jacket design by Gael Towey
Printed in the United States of America by R. R. Donnelley
10 9 8 7 6 5 4 3 2 1

CONTENTS

To Terry, the man who made it possible

❧ ACKNOWLEDGEMENTS ☙

My grateful thanks to my exceptional husband and to Elizabeth Grey, Anne Engel and Janice Robertson for their invaluable advice and support.

The author wishes to give her thanks for permission to quote from the following:

A Man and His Mountains by Norman Croucher published by Kaye & Ward

The Martial Arts by Michael Random published by Octopus Books Limited

Summits and Secrets by Kurt Diemberger published by Hodder & Stoughton

For contract reasons I have told only of my own personal experiences on the 1985 expedition to Everest (Chapter 16). The full story will be told in the official expedition book: *Kingdoms of Experience* by Andrew Greig to be published by Century Hutchinson in 1986.

꩜FOREWORD꩜

Imagine a down-to-earth Englishwoman baking cookies for her children in a cozy rural kitchen. Now picture the same woman, ice dagger and axe poised, steel crampons on her feet, nearing the summit of a precipitous Himalayan peak. These are two sides of Julie Tullis, who was extraordinarily successful in both the realm of the world's highest and most dangerous mountains and the equally demanding world of home, family and community.

After a childhood in war-ravaged London, Julie left school at age seventeen to work in a car dealer's office. She began weekend rock-climbing and, at age twenty, married Terry Tullis, a fellow climber. In the twenty years that followed, she and Terry raised two children and ran a climbing school, where they found particular satisfaction in teaching outdoor skills to children with severe physical and psychological handicaps. Julie's eloquent descriptions of working with these young people show the same sensitivity and joy as her lyric accounts of outstanding climbing.

During these years, Julie gave unstintingly to her family and society, putting her own adventures on the back burner. But once her children were grown, she spread her wings wide and entered the world of international expeditionary mountaineering and film-making. "I had spent many years sheltering under the ideas of others," she writes. "Now that the children didn't rely on me so much, I wanted to think my own thoughts . . . and try out my own ideas." And so she did.

It was in 1980, at age forty-one, that Julie first learned to use a still camera. Only two years later, she joined renowned high-altitude cinematographer Kurt Diemberger in making a film on the fierce, lovely Nanga Parbat (26,660 feet). A dizzying succession of satisfying expeditions to the world's most challenging mountains followed: Mt. Everest, K2, and Nanga Parbat again. These Himalayan peaks are among the fourteen mountains in the world that soar above 8000 meters (26,200 feet). All are coveted prizes for mountaineers. Although attempts to climb them began in the 1800s, the first summit was not achieved until 1950, and the first woman did not climb an 8000-meter peak until 1974. In July 1984, when Julie reached the 26,400-foot summit of Broad Peak, she was the first Englishwoman among a handful of women worldwide to reach an 8000-meter summit.

The special nature of Julie Tullis's accomplishment was the insightful and feeling attitude she brought to the challenges of climbing the world's highest mountains. From the practice of meditation and martial arts, she found the strength to continue on a difficult course when others had given up. Even when she neared the limits of her physical endurance, she found that she could go further by "coordinating mind, body, breathing and spirit." And it is the warmth and generosity of her spirit that sets her experiences apart from other accounts of mountain adventure.

Julie climbed for pleasure, not competition or ambition, "moving freely in harmony with the rock and the person I am climbing with." Camped high above the clouds on K2, the world's second-highest peak, she was deeply happy and contented: "It was like looking at and at the same time being part of a great work of art."

Of all mountains, K2—an elegant ice pyramid that rises to 28,250 feet above the wild Baltoro glacier in remote northern Pakistan—was special to Julie. Julie and Kurt Diemberger filmed and climbed on K2 in 1983, 1984, and 1986. Finally, on August 4, 1986, just before sunset, Julie and Kurt reached the summit of the mountain of their dreams.

Their triumph was sorrowfully short-lived. They began a harrowing descent and were forced to overnight in a shallow snow hole just seven hundred feet below the summit. Back at high camp, their tent collapsed, and after four nights above 8000 meters under increasingly desperate conditions, Julie succumbed to exposure and altitude. Hers was one of thirteen deaths on K2 that tragic summer.

Julie Tullis died at age forty-seven, only five years after she began Himalayan mountaineering. During those busy years, she continued to care for her family, made a series of award-winning documentary films, and took part in six major Himalayan expeditions. And she wrote *Clouds from Both Sides*. This book, like Julie herself, is sensitive, creative, and extraordinarily interesting.

Pondering the loss of thirteen talented individuals on K2 during the summer of 1986, one cannot help questioning the motivation behind the sport of high-altitude mountaineering. Why had Julie chosen this most risky and individualistic endeavor?

In the eloquent chapter entitled "Why?" Julie, as though she knew we might ask, explains, "One in twelve Himalayan climbers dies for their ruling passion. But life is short and there has to be a reason for living beyond purely surviving. . . . There are many occasions when to say 'yes' or 'no' makes a great difference in the future of our lives. I am afraid that . . . I have too much curiosity often to say 'no.'"

And so Julie said 'yes' to the challenge of K2. We must leave her at peace there and thank her for leaving us with *Clouds from Both Sides*.

Arlene Blum

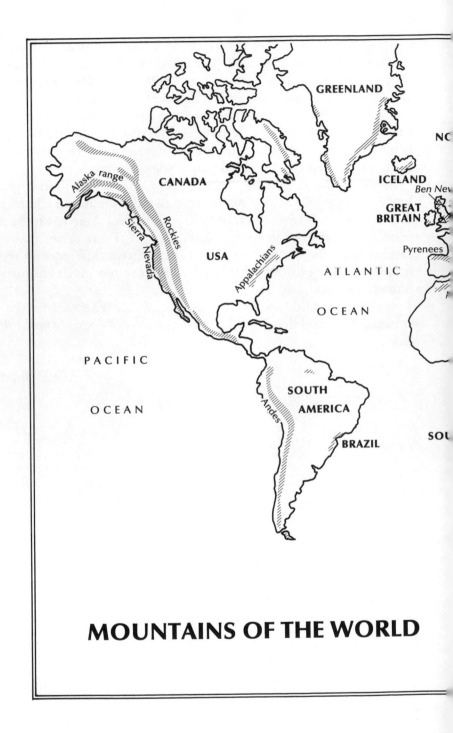

GREENLAND

CANADA

USA

PACIFIC

OCEAN

Alaska range

Sierra Nevada

Rockies

Appalachians

ATLANTIC

OCEAN

SOUTH
AMERICA

Andes

BRAZIL

ICELAND

GREAT
BRITAIN

Ben Nev

Pyrenees

NC

SOU

MOUNTAINS OF THE WORLD

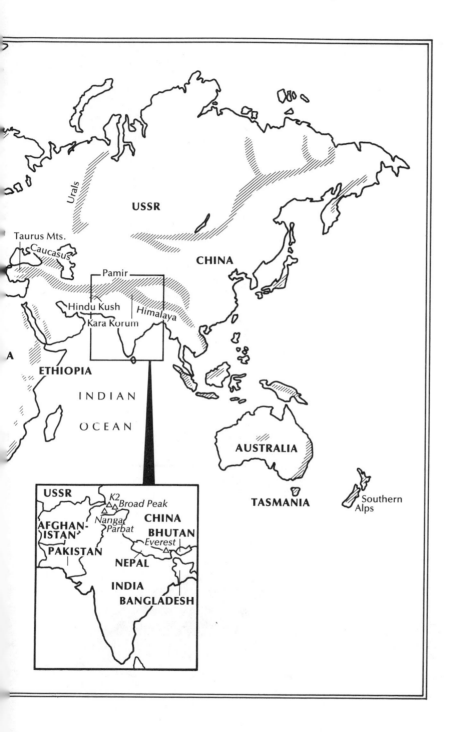

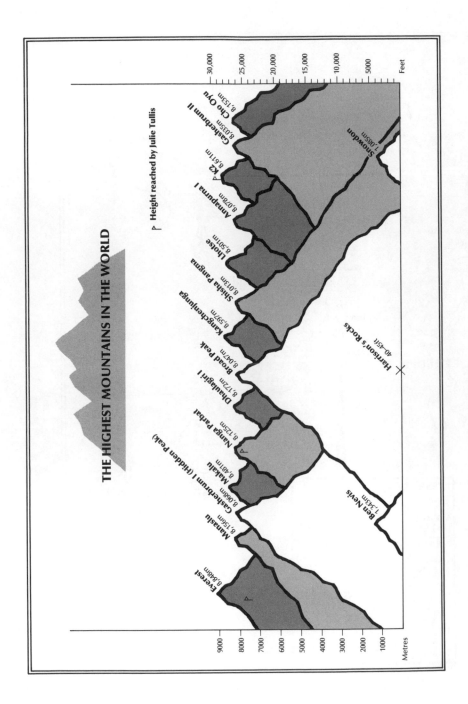

THE HIGHEST MOUNTAINS IN THE WORLD

⊽ Height reached by Julie Tullis

Everest 8,848m
Manaslu 8,156m
Gasherbrum I (Hidden Peak) 8,068m
Makalu 8,481m
Nanga Parbat 8,125m
Dhaulāgiri I 8,172m
Broad Peak 8,047m
Kangchenjunga 8,597m
Shisha Pangma 8,013m
Lhotse 8,501m
Annapurna I 8,078m
K2 8,611m
Gasherbrum II 8,035m
Cho Oyu 8,153m
Snowdon 1,085m
Harrison's Rocks 40–45ft
Ben Nevis 1,343m

Feet
30,000
25,000
20,000
15,000
10,000
5000

Metres
9000
8000
7000
6000
5000
4000
3000
2000
1000

Both Sides Now

Bows and flows of angel hair,
And ice-cream castles in the air,
And feather canyons everywhere:
I've looked at clouds that way.

But now they only block the sun;
They rain and snow on everyone.
So many things I would have done,
But clouds got in my way.

I've looked at clouds from both sides now,
From up and down, and still somehow
It's cloud illusions I recall,
I really don't know clouds at all.

Moons and Junes and ferris wheels,
The dizzy dancing way you feel,
As every fairy tale comes real:
I've looked at love that way.

But now it's just another show;
You leave 'em laughing when you go.
And if you care don't let them know,
Don't give yourself away.

I've looked at love from both sides now,
From give and take, and still somehow
It's love's illusions I recall,
I really don't know love at all.

Tears and fears and feeling proud
To say 'I love you' right out loud,
Dreams and schemes and circus crowds:
I've looked at life that way.

But now old friends are acting strange;
They shake their heads, they say I've changed.
But something's lost, but something's gained
In living every day.

I've looked at life from both sides now,
From win and lose, and still somehow
It's life's illusions I recall,
I really don't know life at all.

Joni Mitchell

❧INTRODUCTION❧

'I've looked at clouds from both sides now . . .'

BROAD PEAK, JULY 1984

There was a whoosh . . . then a dull thud!

My instincts told me that something was happening: something I should be aware of. I struggled for a moment, trying to regain consciousness from the deep sleep that engulfed me after the enormous exertions of the previous days, but my heavy eyelids just would not obey my brain's instructions to open and I gave up trying. I felt Kurt moving, trying to free himself from the strait-jacket restriction of the tiny one-man bivouac tent into which we were both tightly squeezed, and took the opportunity to stretch my cramped limbs into a more comfortable position, snuggling deeper into my warm sleeping bag, and gave in to the over-powering urge to sleep.

'Julie, Julie! Wake up!' The urgent panic in Kurt's voice woke me instantly. I had assumed that he had rushed out to answer a call of nature, but his tone made it obvious that all was not well, and immediately cleared all thoughts of sleep from my mind.

'What is it?', I started to ask, but another 'whoosh' and 'thud' on the front of the tent answered my question most graphically. Avalanche!

The front part of the tent where an integral extension housed our rucksacks went dark and flat. I heard Kurt moving frantically outside. Finally the doorway was clear again and I could see the grey-white of the snow storm outside.

'Quick, Julie, my boots. It must have snowed very heavily after our descent last night, and now . . . God, we must be very fast!' I found one of his heavy double boots and passed it out of the tent, but the other one? I could not see it. Kurt's empty sleeping

1

bag covered all the spare space in the tiny tent. I managed the difficult cramped manoeuvre to reach the tapered far end where the tent was only eight inches high [it was only three foot wide and 24 inches high at the front end]. I felt around but his second boot was not there, then returned to the entrance gasping from my exertions and the lack of oxygen in the thin mountain air. This was Broad Peak in the Himalayan mountains, and a height of 25,000 feet was no place for such contortions. Frantically I dug at the fresh snow deposited by the avalanche in the entrance. To lose a boot at such an altitude on one of the world's highest mountains meant disaster for both of us, and there was no one else on the mountain. I had to find it if we were to survive. I dug more frantically still into the cold wet snow. I unearthed a torch, and some rubbish, and then ... I almost cried with relief ... Kurt's other boot! I passed it out to him and dived to the end of the tent again to get my own boots.

The next minutes were filled with frenzied activity. My boot would not go on over the normal two pairs of socks. In the early morning my feet were swollen from sleeping at altitude, one pair would have to do. I hoped it would not be too cold. It would be ironic to get frostbite now after returning unscathed in the night from the summit.

I was about to stick my foot into the second boot when Kurt shouted, 'Here comes another avalanche!' and I bent my head forward between my knees. Again he worked to free the front of the tent, his arms thrashing like windmills trying to divide the force of the snow, sending some down the steep slope on the outside of the tent and the rest into a deep crevasse on the outer edge of which we were camping – the only flat place we had found to put our final assault camp. Thank goodness he had reacted to the first avalanche while I slept on, otherwise we might have been buried alive in our refuge. I lifted my head and looked at my poised boot. Hell, it was full of soft wet snow. Well, perhaps frostbite was better than dying! With fumbling fingers I struggled with the laces and my snow gaiters.

Once outside the tent Kurt's eyes and the weather quickly conveyed the full seriousness of our position to me. The avalanches were funnelling down from the high summit ridge rocks above. Worse, we could not just retreat straight down the mountain as the steep snowfield ended in an abrupt drop some nine thousand feet to the Godwin Austen Glacier far, far below. We would have to make a long traverse underneath these avalanche prone rocks, and with so much fresh snow and more silently falling all the time, our chances of reaching the safety of the lower camps were not at all good.

Almost mechanically we had put on our double boots, snow gaiters, helmets, snow goggles and gloves, a well practised drill, and hurriedly thrust our sleeping bags, a stove, matches, some tea and food, spare socks and a torch into our rucksacks. We unburied our crampons, ice axes and ski sticks from under the deep snow outside the tent and, last of all, with cold numbed fingers, had struggled to untie our safety rope, which, thankfully, we had used to secure our tiny refuge to the mountainside.

I glanced at my watch. 5.45 am, only fifteen minutes since Kurt had woken me. Usually at altitude one's movements are painfully slow, especially first thing in the morning. I could never have been ready so fast at Base Camp where we normally allowed at least an hour for dressing and packing. We had hardly spoken during our preparations; we were both experienced enough to understand what a very serious situation we were in, and muffled in our bulky down jackets, helmets and big snow goggles, heads bent under the heavily falling snow, conversation was a great effort.

We each tied one end of the short 50-foot rope to our harnesses. Kurt gave me a quick hug and a thumbs-up before turning round and moving slowly forward, his body leaning into the storm. Carefully he probed for hidden crevasses with his ski stick, and slowly placed each foot, sometimes sinking up to his crutch where the snow had filled a hollow. I waited until the slack rope between us was stretched clear of the snow, and with adrenalin flowing forcefully through my body, stepped with exaggerated carefulness into his footsteps.

I knew I must be calm and stay in control of my mind and movements. To try to rush to safety was pointless, we would just become exhausted in no time at all, and probably then lose our sense either of reason or of balance. One of the rules for movement at altitude is to start off slowly and give the heart and lungs time to adjust to the exertion. I began consciously to control my breathing in time to my steps. One, foot forward . . . breathe in! Two, weight forward . . . hold the breath! Three, next foot forward . . . breathe out! In the almost white-out conditions Kurt's form, just fifteen feet ahead was a ghostly shadow and the floating white flakes blanketed our movements in a deathly silence.

I can't remember whether I heard it first, or simply felt it. It was only about twenty minutes after we had left the avalanched tent. Kurt had stopped for a short, much needed rest, and I had gone up close to him. He was just three feet away from me and I tried to shout a warning to him.

'It's an avalanche . . .' but my words were lost as my feet slid away with the snow. I had the sensation of being in a fast lift, my stomach went up as my body went swiftly down and the snow engulfed me with such force that I felt as if I were trapped inside a waterfall. Somehow I knew that I was falling the right way up and that gave me comfort. I was also very aware that I must get some air, or I would suffocate, and I punched out strongly with my right arm as I had done so often in my martial arts practice. Amazingly a hole appeared and I could see that I was slowing down. I had almost stopped. What a relief! It had only been a small avalanche. I was upright and I had air.

No sooner had these thoughts gone from my mind than I felt a strong jerk and I was falling again — but this time it was very different! I was being thrown over and over, completely out of control. Everything was black; heavy wet snow encased me. Unconsciously I had crossed my arms tightly across my chest, gripping my ice axe. Snow crystals blocked my open mouth . . . I couldn't breathe . . . I was suffocating . . . choking . . . drowning . . . falling, falling . . . never survive . . . pain . . . must breathe . . . must breathe . . .

The stop was as sudden as the beginning. I dug furiously with my fingers at the snow which was blocking my mouth in a panic of choking and coughing. The snow was very wet and composed of large ice crystals which had packed tightly together at the back of my throat, and I retched as my fingers probed to free the blockage. I gasped the air into my lungs and lay still, panting for a few moments to recover.

Where was Kurt? Was he alive? He certainly would have fallen too as we were joined together by the rope. *Please* let him be alive and uninjured, I prayed silently. I started to check my body. The last moments of the fall had been full of pain. Surely something must be broken? Where *was* Kurt?

'Julie! Julie! Are you all right?' It was Kurt's voice anxiously calling me from somewhere above. I couldn't see anything. I felt for my eyes and lifted my snow goggles. I could see again! My goggles had filled with snow in the fall, as had my nose, ears and all my clothing.

I took stock of my position. I was lying in the snow about thirty feet below Kurt, on my back, head first down a snow slope. I tried moving my legs . . . yes, the feet moved, and the knees bent but my left thigh was very painful. I tried to get up, but it was impossible. 'I think I'm OK, but I can't move,' I shouted back to Kurt. 'Are you damaged?'

'No, I don't think so,' came his comforting reply.

He came slowly down to join me and looked at me in concern. 'Are you sure you are all right?' he queried. Although I did not realise it at the time, I had wet my pants, a symptom of a broken pelvis, but luckily in my case it was simply caused by the shock. It was my rucksack which was buried in the snow that was preventing me from getting up, but with Kurt's help I was soon, albeit rather shakily, on my feet again. We checked each other for injuries. Kurt had a nasty looking lump above his left eye and had lost his snow goggles, and I had a badly bruised left thigh; otherwise, apart from being generally battered from the fall we were both relatively unscathed.

The weather had cleared momentarily and we looked up to see where we had fallen. High above us loomed the rocks of the summit ridge over which the avalanche had tumbled. It was from the foot of these that we had been swept, first down a long snow slope, then over the 120-foot sheer ice wall of a large serac. At the bottom of the serac was the debris of another big broken ice cliff, and it was down these double-decker-bus size blocks that we had finally fallen, bouncing from one to another until Kurt had finally got jammed between two of them bringing us to a stop. The great saving factor for us had been that most of the snow from the avalanche had filtered in between these blocks, so that we finished up on top rather than entombed underneath what must have been a lot of very unpleasant wet snow.

We also worked out that we must have been in a 'barrel of bricks' situation. I had fallen first underneath the rocks, but when I had almost stopped, Kurt had been carried on down, falling past me until, on the broken ice block section, I had overtaken him again. Miraculously, we had fallen more than four hundred feet, higher than St Paul's Cathedral, from 25,000 feet up on a Himalayan mountain, and survived!

I was also very fortunate that my climbing partner was Kurt Diemberger, one of the most experienced Himalayan mountaineers in the world. He is an Austrian who lives in Italy and Salzburg, writes in German, Italian and English and lectures in an even greater variety of tongues. He is a film-maker, a specialist high-altitude director/cameraman. In 1984 I had known him for fourteen years, and we had discovered several years before that in addition to climbing well together, we had a unique joint ability in filming. We formed 'The Highest Film Team in the World' and had already made two full-length expedition films for French and Italian television. During the summer of 1984 we had been with a Swiss expedition to K2, the second highest mountain in the world, to make a film for British Channel 4 that would not only tell the story of the climb, but would also demonstrate my role as a sound recordist and film assistant and show how practising the Japanese martial arts had changed my life and helped me in mountaineering.

But although several of us had reached a height of 26,247 feet, bad weather had prevented anyone reaching K2's summit. When the Swiss decided to pack up and go home, Kurt and I were given leave to tackle the neighbouring mountain of Broad Peak on our own. On 18 July, at the age of 45, I had looked down on the cloud-topped mountains of China and Pakistan on each side of my first 8,000-metre summit.

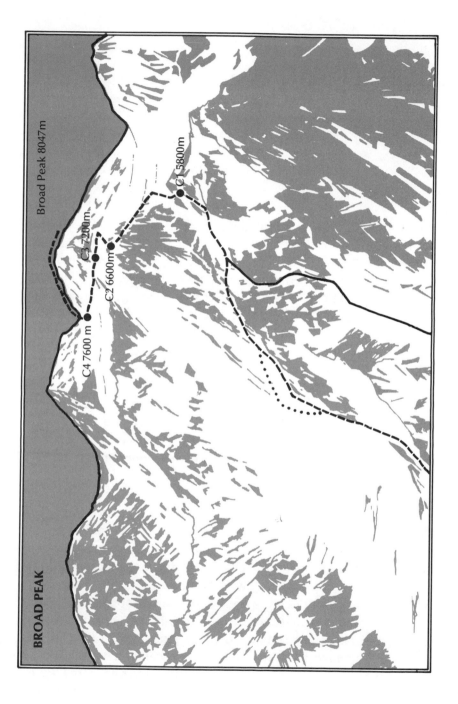

BROAD PEAK

Broad Peak 8047m

C1 5800m

C2 6600m

C3 7200m

C4 7600 m

❧1❧

First steps

It was my sister Zita who introduced me to climbing. She used to go occasionally to North Wales with a boyfriend. When their relationship broke up, she was keen to continue her mountaineering and in 1954 joined the Regent Street Polytechnic Climbing Club. They planned a meet during the Easter holidays to the Ogwen Valley in North Wales, but two days before, someone dropped out.

'Why don't you come with us?' Zita asked me.

I had planned to spend the holiday conscientiously revising for my O Level exams, but to visit Snowdonia seemed far more appealing. 'I don't think I want to climb though,' I said, not sure of what it might involve. 'I'll stay in the valley and get on with my studying.' I had never seen any British mountains and the musical names of the Welsh hills stirred my imagination; Tryfan, Moel Siabod, Pen y role-wen, so I went along.

Nor had I lived in a barn before – it was pretty basic. My bed was a couple of blankets on top of the hay, there were few sleeping bags around in those days. There were spiders in the roof and mice scurried around at night searching for the crumbs of food we had dropped on the floor. Willy's barn was well down in a depression below the Ogwen Youth Hostel, and I found the rugged Welsh mountains towering above very impressive.

On the first day I dutifully took my books onto the grass outside the barn and settled down to study until the climbers returned. Someone had fallen off a climb called Tennis Shoe on the Idwal Slabs, and their lady second had bad rope burns across both her hands. She was very brave as they patched up her painful wounds in the dusty barn, and I understood, for the first time, that climbing was a serious sport.

The following day I was talked into putting on my hefty, fur-lined shoes – I didn't own any boots – and I joined the rest of the group. We were to help Jo Douglas and Pete Murray make a little film for the popular television programme, *Six Five Special,* and they needed as many extras as possible. We didn't do any special climbing that day, but scrambled about on the rain-soaked mountainside. It was enough to inspire me to greater things. I did no more studying that trip. I was hooked. Climbing and the mountains were for me!

The others were all paired off with climbing partners, but a climbing 'bum' had attached himself to our party and was scrounging free bed and board in return for recounting lurid stories in the evenings. We called the young, tousled-haired youth Charlie, because that is what he was . . . a Charlie! He made up in enthusiasm for what he lacked in brain. The first climb that he chose for his new and totally innocent climbing partner was Holly Tree Wall, a Hard Severe route on the impressive Idwal Slabs, not really a fifteen-year-old girl beginner's climb. However, as I only got stuck once on that, we went on to even greater things, the names and grades of which I now forget. Climbing in the fifties was very different from modern climbing. We only had heavy hemp ropes, which became impossible to manage when they were soaked by the inevitable rain; an occasional sling, placed a little hopefully around a convenient rock spike as a runner, and tennis shoes and my school gaberdine raincoat were my climbing gear. It was not easy to be a mountaineer in those days! But it was an unforgettable experience. I vowed to myself that I would do a lot more in the future . . . and I did.

Zita and I were born in Selsdon in Surrey almost three years apart and were totally different in both build and character. I was born on the Ides of March in 1939, the year the Second World War began.

'But she's such an ugly baby!' my poor father had confided to a friend after making his first acquaintance with his second-born daughter, and I certainly was no beauty; my tiny red screwed-up face was totally dominated by an enormous nose. My sister had been a pretty baby and grew into a small-boned graceful child who loved ballet dancing, while I grew tall and awkward with over-size feet.

My father, Francis Palau, had come to England from Spain in 1924. He had worked his way north learning the restaurant trade in some of the most prestigious hotels in the south of France and Paris on the way. My mother, Erica, was actually born in Germany, but her family moved to Geneva when she was nine years old. My parents met when they were both working at Selsdon Park Hotel near Croydon in Surrey. My father was the Restaurant Manager, and mother lady's maid to Mrs Sanderson, the owner's wife. As neither spoke good English at that time they conducted their courtship in their only common language, French. Ancestors on both sides of the family have roots in France, one used to make the incredible journey regularly from Luneville to St Petersburg in Russia, as personal dentist to the Imperial Family. So I come from a very European background – perhaps the basic reason for my wanderlust.

Despite her dainty appearance Zita was a tomboy, and she always had ideas for crazy or dangerous games (for which I usually got the blame when things went wrong). When I was three my parents bought a restaurant called The Basque in Knightsbridge and we all moved to London. As the business kept them so busy we were sent to a private school in the Gloucester Road. The lessons were formal even for my age group, and I can still remember the French lessons about a mouse and his family and the weekly dancing lessons at Madam Vacani's studio close to Harrods, where the bored little boys would tease us by pulling our hair and flicking up our skirts to look at our knickers. Even the dancing teacher of two generations of royal children failed to make me more graceful and co-ordinated.

I can also clearly recall being locked in the tall-ceilinged Victorian lavatory, with its shiny brown mahogany bench seat, and the headmaster's annoyance when they had to break the well-polished brass lock in order to free me – frightened and loudly wailing.

In 1943, to escape the bombing of London, the school was

evacuated to Cambridge and we became boarders. Because I was only four years old I was put into the same dormitory as Zita and her contemporaries.

Every night before going to sleep one of the girls in our room would suggest a game. When it was Zita's turn she suggested that we bite the rubber buttons off our nighties and stick them up our noses! Don't ask me why but to a four-year-old trying to keep up with the 'big' girls it seemed a good idea at the time. Inevitably my button got stuck. We tried everything from poking to thumps on the back until finally, as a crescendo of sobs of pain and panic welled from me, they called the teacher and the doctor was sent for.

There was no National Health Service then. The doctor had a difficult journey to the school with all the black-out restrictions. He was not pleased, and neither was the headmaster – his visit was expensive and I was marked as a troublemaker.

My final undoing was a see-saw. Every evening, if it was fine, we were taken out to play in a large garden. As a special treat each child was given a short turn, first on a see-saw and then on the swing. Our little group had all been on the see-saw and were queueing for their turn on the swing. I sat on the down-end of the empty see-saw and drifted far away into daydreams. With a typical thoughtless childish sense of humour someone pushed down hard on the up-end and I was catapulted into the air. When I landed in a heap on the ground I had a broken wrist. The next morning, with just a bandage wrapped around the injury, I was put on the train back to London, together with my sister and the teacher who had been in charge of us. I had been expelled from my first school at the tender age of four.

I can still remember my poor mother's worried face when she met us at King's Cross Station. The bombings were getting more frequent and she had the added problem now of taking me to hospital for treatment as well as working long hours running the restaurant.

However we proved to be very adaptable children and enjoyed living between the spacious top floor flat of a house opposite the Natural History Museum in the Cromwell Road and the 'shelter' cellar of a new restaurant father was planning to open just behind

South Kensington Station. Everything was ready for the opening – even the tinned food was in the store, but he just could not get the food licence. In fact he never succeeded and finally sold his projected new business in despair.

One night a bomb fell nearby and burst the water main, flooding our cellar. Tins of food floated past our beds and we were having great fun fishing them out onto our 'boat' beds when mother came to rescue us. After that we were taken to the communal shelter in the basement of a nearby large house as soon as the sirens sounded.

Some nights later mother had to leave us to collect something from the flat and asked another woman to keep an eye on us. As Zita and I lay together on one bottom bunk poking with our little inquisitive fingers at the wall, we discovered an old fireplace covered by a piece of peeling wallpaper. We had great fun playing with the velvety black soot. We painted each other's faces, made hand marks all over our clean white nighties, and by the time mother returned only the whites of our eyes gleamed in the dim candlelight. We paid for our fun with sore bottoms and hard scrubbed faces, which had to be cleaned under a barely dripping cold water tap.

It must have been a terrible responsibility to bring up small active children in war-torn London. No routine was possible with the constant day and night-time air raids disrupting everything. To make life even more difficult I started to suffer from frightening asthma attacks and often wet the bed at night. After a couple of months our parents took the only logical solution – evacuation.

I don't remember the goodbyes, perhaps my mother deliberately did not tell us what was going to happen in case the idea of leaving home again upset us. We had our gas masks and we went to a Centre to have a medical, but so had hundreds of others and this did nothing to arouse our suspicions. I hated the strong rubber smell of the gas mask, but liked the monster-like appearance of it, sitting, glass eyes uppermost, in its square cardboard box like a jack-in-the-box.

Liverpool Street Station was an exciting place. The steam from the engines rose high into the glass vaulted roof, and the general hustle and bustle, mixed with the powerful hissing and chuffing of the majestic engines, took all my attention. We stood waiting on the platform for a long time, luggage labels tied to our coat fronts, clutching our gas masks. Our train finally pulled in. It had been held up by an air raid for one and a half hours. My poor mother! We were totally unaware of what she was going through. She stood there chatting and smiling trying to create a holiday atmosphere for her two small daughters, fully realising that she might never see us again. For security reasons parents were not told even to which part of the country their children were going.

Just before we climbed in mother looked very serious. 'Now remember – Zita, it's up to you as the eldest – in your suitcase are two envelopes addressed to Daddy and me. In one envelope it says "YES", and in the other "NO". I don't know the people you will be staying with, so as soon as you get there I want you to send me the "YES" envelope if you like them, or the "NO" envelope if you don't. If you send the "NO" I will come and fetch you immediately!' Poor, poor mother, her children, just six and four years old were about to disappear up the railway line to God knows where.

Zita and I liked the train ride. We had not often travelled this way, and to go by ourselves made us feel very grown-up. Of course, we were not by ourselves, but most of the other children had at least one of their parents with them, usually Mum. Hour after hour the countryside rolled slowly by. Wartime trains were very slow, bomb-damage to the lines and air-raids turned a four-hour journey into an epic. We got hungry, and then starving. Finally someone gave us a small bar of chocolate each, and someone else played a game with us to make it last as long as possible. It was very sweet and terribly sticky chocolate and made me feel a little sick.

Our little group arrived at Ellingham Station at 1.30 in the morning. It was a tiny village about 14 miles from Norwich in East Anglia. A bumpy bus collected us and drove us through the pitch black night to the little schoolhouse where sleepily we lined up in the classroom. At the front of the queue they were asked, 'How many?' and then the call went out to the unfortunates waiting for their billeted evacuees – 'accommodation for three, one adult two children, ten and eight.' Gradually everyone was allocated places except Zita and me. No one wanted the responsibility of two tired scruffy little girls who threatened to scream the place down if they were separated, especially as I still had my arm in plaster, would need further medical attention and, worse, was an asthma sufferer and a bed wetter.

Suddenly the hall was empty except for us and a man in a cloth cap. 'I'd better take you along home with me then,' he said a little resignedly, and he pushed us, one sitting on the saddle, the other on the cross-bar of his bike, for two miles along the tiny Norfolk country lanes back to his cottage. The Red House was tiny, but at half past two in the morning it was too dark to see what it looked like.

His wife was up to welcome us and bustled to make us cups of cocoa and tell us about the chickens at the end of the garden. We looked around the warm friendly room and nodded to each other. 'We have to write to our mother . . . we promised that we would the moment we arrived,' Zita told them and with the honesty of children we explained about the two envelopes.

'All right, dears, we'll send it first thing in the morning,' they told us reassuringly.

'No, we're sorry, it must be now, we gave our faithful promise,' we insisted. 'Our mummy and daddy will worry.'

So we sorted out the envelopes, put some kisses on the bottom and posted the 'YES' one out through the front door. Our hosts had children of their own and knew how to get round this sort of problem. We snuggled happily down in a big double bed with a soft feather mattress, content that our parents would know we had found nice people to live with.

Ellingham was the ideal place for children. Everyone, of course, knew everyone else, so any naughtiness was quickly reported, but the houses were very spread out with plenty of countryside in between to explore. Cars were almost unheard of in the tiny lanes and there was one bus a week to Bungay, the nearest small town.

We settled in immediately and loved our foster parents dearly. George and Mary Burcham had borne three sons, but tragically all had been killed, two in the war and one in a motor-bike accident. Their daughter Alma was fifteen and very grown up in our little eyes.

Paunt (derived from Aunt) and Punk (from Uncle) had hoped to foster two boys, but were happy enough when they discovered they had acquired two tomboys. Just how marvellous they were I only really appreciated as my own children grew up. We were certainly not easy to cope with, especially in such an isolated and basic little house. The Red House had just four tiny rooms and was half a mile from the main road. Water had to be pumped up from a well in the boiler house, a tiny ivy-covered shed which housed the stone clothes boiler, heated by a wood fire, and next door was an earth closet with a broad scrubbed wooden seat. I hated this lavatory; it was, for my small legs, an interminable distance from the house and it was full of spiders. I could not stand spiders, and these were the big-bodied, hairy long-legged spiders that feature as monsters in children's fairy stories. Paunt and Punk liked spiders and would never move them from the house. I would lie in the big bed which I shared with Zita staring for hours at one on the ceiling just in case it dropped down and ran across the bed. Finally I would fall asleep so heavily that even calls of nature would not wake me up. I am sure that the outside loo and the spiders were the reasons my bed-wetting did not improve; there was certainly no shortage of security and love, and Paunt and Punk were very patient about my problem.

Water for washing oneself came from a water butt outside the kitchen door. This was always fascinating as it was full of little creatures and Zita and I vied to get the most 'wrigglers' in each pan we collected. On Sundays we used the special covered butt at the front of the house, and the water from this certainly did feel different, it was a little softer and a prettier green colour. There was no electricity and at night the house was lit by oil lamps and candles, and Paunt did all her cooking on oil stoves. Once a week she would have a baking session and we were banned from the minute corrugated roofed kitchen, because to open any door allowed the heat to escape and that could ruin the cakes – and what wonderful cakes they were, made with fresh eggs from Paunt's chickens and milk from the farm next door.

The farm was a second home for Zita and me, it was just a

field away over the garden fence. Big shire horses ploughed the fields and brought in the harvest, cows were collected twice a day for milking, goats and dogs ran around and cats and kittens lived in the sheds and the rambling house. Best of all there were the children to play with, five of them.

Time has no meaning for young children, either each day or by the month. Seasons became important though, in the country. Autumn was harvest time and we would all go into the fields and help stack the prickly sheaves, shout to the guns if we saw a rabbit run as the windmill blades of the harvester cut through the wheat; stand for hours watching the mighty threshing machine separate the wheat from the chaff; eat too many apples and get stomach ache and make squirrel stores of cob nuts from the tree at the end of the garden in obscure places and then forget where we had hidden them. Winter was a time for playing in the snow and sliding on the frozen puddles, and Christmas, remembered not so much for the presents, as during the War there was not much to give, but for the village community gatherings which were full of warmth and colour. Spring was the lambs' time and primrosing, and in summer we spent long hours fishing with flour bags for tiddlers in the streams and lying in the sweet smelling hay. The War for us was a long way away. Only twice was an air raid siren sounded, and we all hid under the table in the living room, but there was nothing worth bombing for miles around and I think the Germans knew that!

We hadn't been in the safety of Norfolk long when I again became a casualty of another of Zita's good ideas. The lane outside the Red House had been newly patched with small circles of tarred stones. On our way to fetch the milk can from another farm we played 'islands', jumping from one 'safe' place to another. Inevitably, clumsily, I tripped and fell cutting my knee on a stone. I had to be taken to the doctor for the deep cut to be stitched, and my movements were severely restricted.

At last it was time for the stitches to come out. This meant a bike ride to the doctor's three miles away. Punk tied a cushion to his cross bar, sat me astride it and off we set. We were negotiating a corner just three minutes from the house, when I slipped sideways and my foot went into the spokes of the front wheel

16

bringing us to an abrupt halt. We both flew through the air in a graceful arc, straight over a stone wall into a field. Luckily our landing was softened by a pile of dung. (Forty years later I went back to Norfolk and the well-matured dung heap was still there.) We managed to limp home pushing the rather bent bicycle, and the doctor came to visit us, prescribing four days' bed rest for us both.

The only time I was damaged by Zita directly was purely accidental. We had been building an ambitious tree house at the end of the garden. 'Hold the pole while I fix this end,' Zita ordered. Just as I reached up to full stretch to push my end into position she dropped hers and the hefty pole hit me straight in my open mouth, breaking off one of my newly acquired front teeth. Far from being sympathetic she threatened me with dire consequences if I 'told'. The pain was agonising and I went in to lunch with my mouth tightly shut.

'Drink your hot milk dear,' Paunt insisted. The heat of the liquid sent a shooting pain right up through my brain and I surreptitiously swapped my cup for Zita's empty one. The next week was spent carefully avoiding extremes of temperature and gradually the tooth settled down. Nobody noticed a thing. Ironically several years later Zita unintentionally knocked me into a wall in the school playground and broke my other front tooth, so now I have a matching pair. The cold mountain air occasionally makes me close my lips a little sharply even now.

However, whatever the mishaps our loyalty to each other was total and we would never tolerate criticism from outsiders. During our long months in Norfolk we learnt not only how to explore further and further afield but also how to find our way back home, and so much about the countryside. It was our first real introduction to birth and death, in the form of many practical lessons in the farmyard.

Eventually Zita was sent to the local primary school. I got very lonely by myself and decided to go and find out what it was like. I sneaked out of the house when Paunt was busy and walked with the group of children heading for the school two miles away. I went in with them unnoticed and even managed the assembly, enjoying the communal singing, before someone spotted me. There were no telephones then and as nobody was free to take me back home I was allowed to stay, but found it a little boring when it came to arithmetic and spelling.

Each day except Sunday was governed by light, dark and hunger pangs. Sundays were very different. Sunday school started the day, followed by church with Punk who would feed us on peppermints to keep us quiet during the lengthy sermon – Paunt stayed home to cook the Sunday roast which took a long time on the oil stove. Sunday afternoons were spent visiting relatives for tea or entertaining at home. Either way we had to watch our Ps and Qs, as Punk would remind us, and keep ourselves clean and tidy at Paunt's request.

The months rolled so happily by that it was rather a nasty shock when the War ended and mother came to take us home to London. Now we had to learn to 'speak properly' again (we had grown to love our broad Norfolk accents), and adapt to the new house my parents had moved into off the Old Brompton Road in Kensington. It was large enough to accommodate a dozen Red Houses – one room alone was the size of the whole ground floor of the Ellingham cottage, but the garden was the size of a pocket handkerchief.

I was still suffering from bad attacks of asthma. These were distressing for Zita too as they often occurred during the night, and in this house mother slept four floors down. 'Breathe, Julie please breathe,' she would implore as I lay in my bed helplessly gasping like a goldfish out of water. When I was able to draw air into my lungs it sounded equally scary in the still hours of darkness as the rasping wheezing filled our attic bedroom. In addition I had to go to full-time school.

But our time in Norfolk had given us an insatiable taste for freedom and adventure. Climbing trees, jumping off haystacks and playing in streams was replaced by exploring bombed buildings or debris-filled water tanks.

Five of us formed a gang. The others were eight or nine years old and I was getting on for six. It was the time for 'dares'. 'I dare you to walk along that wall.' The fact that the wall was tottering and twelve feet high was inconsequential. We had no sense of danger.

Dares to explore bomb damaged cellars, jump down from great heights onto brick rubble and cross water tanks of unknown depth [none of us could swim] were normal after school fun. We would play hide-and-seek in half demolished houses, Tarzan swing on broken electricity cables, play cops and robbers, rushing up staircases to escape our pursuers only to find they finished abruptly with an airy drop to the ground floor. Another favourite sport was riding in the tiny food lifts of the tall empty houses. Being the smallest and lightest, I was pushed in first – to see if it would take the heavier weights – whilst the others pulled on the ropes sending me up and down the dark shaft. How we survived those times I shall never know, we must have had a very special guardian angel.

Another game, which was perhaps my first real climbing experience, was midnight feasts on the roof of our 60-foot-high house. Our bedroom was in the attic and access to the roof was through a tiny window, which required awkward contortions even for us to get through. Outside was a narrow ledge with a foot-high wall and then the slates sloped steeply to the apex of the roof.

Once you started to climb you had to keep going, as the slates were slippery and quite often moved out of position. Coming down you turned on your tummy and slid till your feet touched the narrow flat ledge inside the low wall. We would picnic sitting on the wall with our feet dangling into space – until one day a neighbour spotted us and told mother.

It took quite a few years before we became civilised city dwellers, and I have a lot of time and sympathy for youngsters from large towns who now come to us to learn to climb. When Zita and I were old enough to ride bicycles our inquisitive energies were rediverted, but I think I had the best education any child could have, learning to live first in the country and then in London.

Every weekend mother and father would take us somewhere. 'Choose any bus you like and let's go to the terminus and see what it's like,' mother would say. Names on the front of buses became real places, sometimes disappointing, other times better than we expected – Hackney Wick, Roehampton, Wimbledon,

Kingston on Thames – and then there was Kew, Wisley, Hampton Court, Chessington Zoo. From London the possibilities were endless, and during the holidays we spent days wandering round the museums, the zoo and London's historic buildings.

Both my parents had tremendous energy. Father was working in the West End of London as Head Waiter at Quaglino's, and his knowledge of wines earned him a high reputation with both other sommeliers and connoisseurs. His job involved very unsociable hours, as he was on duty from twelve until four for lunch and for dinner from seven into the early hours of the morning. During the times of the thick pea-soup smogs in London he would often have to walk home from St James's near Piccadilly after being on his feet all day but he never seemed to tire. Mother rented out bed-sits in our many-roomed house and used her skills as a dressmaker to make some extra funds for our summer holiday travels.

Each year from the time I was eleven, mother would scour London for an old car to buy to take us abroad on holiday. At that time there were four- to six-year waiting lists for new cars and even a 1937 Ford Eight would be snapped up immediately it came onto the market. But somehow mother always worked a miracle, and we would load up the roofrack with jerry cans of petrol, sleeping bags, tents and tinned foods and set off for the endless undulating tree-lined roads of France, heading for our grandparents in the beautiful pine woods of the Black Forest in Germany.

We loved seeing our grandparents and as we went every summer had many young friends in Pforzheim, the town where they lived. In the early fifties it was still under occupation by the Americans and little of the massive devastation of the war had been repaired, but gradually over the years it was rebuilt into a very modern, clean town, famous for its many jewellery factories.

Grandfather was an artist who designed precious gold and silver ornaments, and Zita and I would spend hours browsing through his files of delicate, life-sized paintings, which looked so real, choosing which necklace, ring or bracelet we would buy if we were rich enough. Grandmother was round and bustling in contrast to her placid husband, she was an excellent cook and

20

spoilt us outrageously. Living in Germany and Switzerland my grandparents and mother had the mountains in their blood, and had shared many happy days during her youth skiing and walking in the Alps. During our holidays we would make many excursions into the local gentle pine-covered hills, and then mother would drive us on into the higher snow-capped peaks of Austria, Switzerland, France and Italy.

I loved to see the mountains. Today I cannot imagine how mother drove all those thousands of miles in the little bone-shaker cars laden to the limit with camping gear, over bumpy war-damaged or, worse still, cobbled roads. Sometimes father would join us and then it was a terrible squash to fit us all in, but he did not enjoy camping so generally opted out.

When I was 17 I started work. I was an office junior at Offord & Sons in the Gloucester Road – a company selling motor cars, mainly to the rich. The showroom always smelt of fresh car polish and usually housed Rolls Royces, Bentleys and occasionally something exotic like the Thunderbird ordered by John Osborne, the playwright. Offords also looked after the upkeep of some of the royal coaches.

I was glad to leave the rules and regulations of my single-sex grammar school in Hammersmith. I had been happy at Godolphin and Latymer but was ready to spread my wings. The work was varied enough to teach me all aspects of office routine, and under the slightly stern, motherly wing of Mrs Brown, the Managing Director's secretary, I learnt how to cope with paperwork and people, even the cleaner who was a persistent Jehovah's Witness and tried constantly to lure me into his basement to convert me. I did not live riotously on my £5 per week salary, and all my spare money was saved to buy my dream – a Vespa scooter. I had a whisky bottle into which I put every threepenny bit I could scrape up, and I spent many hours counting and re-counting them over the months. I needed a £30 deposit.

At last the great day arrived. I warned the little garage that I had saved enough. On Saturday, 12 October 1956 at approximately 1 pm, I would be round to take delivery. I couldn't wait to escape from the dusty confines of my little office with its ever-demanding, blinking-eyed switchboard, and at five past twelve I dashed to the bank on the next corner, but in my great hurry I tripped up the steps and all my precious threepenny bits burst out of their paper bags and scattered in every direction. My cheeks burnt as I scrabbled around the busy pavement between the legs of passers-by. I gathered my precious savings together in my skirt and must have looked a very strange figure hobbling into the bank. Nor was the clerk delighted to have 2,400 threepenny bits dumped in disarray on his counter a few minutes before closing time.

At the garage pure joy engulfed me. My wings of freedom had been specially sprayed for me in dark blue and silver. 'Look, I have to get my lunch,' the garage owner said, 'and then there's an important football match. I'll show you quickly what to do, then you can practise round the back streets here and at half time I'll come out and see how you're getting on. This is the brake, here is the throttle and to engage the clutch you pull this in and twist this. Off you go, good luck!'

I set off cautiously in first gear, a little wobbly, gained a little confidence and changed into second. Suddenly a crossroads loomed up, I had to stop! I pushed hard down on the brake, but the engine drove the machine forward; my garage owner had explained about pulling in the clutch to engage the gears but not that I had to disengage it in order to stop. A car was coming across my path and it seemed that my scootering career was going to be a very short one. I had no choice – I baled out. My beautiful scooter lay on its side on the gravelled road, roared at top revs for a second and then died. I struggled to pick it up, tears of frustration and disappointment running down my cheeks. The shiny chrome crash bars on the front and the engine cowling over the back wheel were scratched but other than this it seemed to have remained intact. Luckily there was one other person in London not watching the match and he came to my aid. He knew all about scooters and within ten minutes I was riding competently round and round the block.

I spent every spare moment driving around on my Vespa. It was wonderful to feel so independent and free and there were so many interesting places to explore.

* * *

Zita wanted to go climbing on a sandstone outcrop 40 miles away near Tunbridge Wells called High Rocks. 'Why don't you join me?' she suggested. Always glad of an excuse for a journey on my scooter, I agreed to meet her and her future husband Ron at the pub opposite the rocks. Zita and Ron were travelling down by train.

It was my first night driving after a month of scooter ownership, and I soon discovered that my single six-volt headlamp was no match for the stronger car headlights. I had just turned a sharp corner and came eye to eye with a car its lights on full beam. Blinded with the dazzle, I lost all sense of direction and plunged into the hedge. I disentangled myself and the bike, luckily we were both unscathed, and continued, far more slowly and cautiously, on my way. It was a bitterly cold November night and High Rocks Hotel was just closing when I finally pulled up outside.

I should explain that I had not been there before and that this pub is in the middle of the countryside, two miles from Tunbridge Wells and four from Groombridge. There are not even any houses close to it, and it was not until I tried to unwind my fingers from the throttle grip that I realized how cold I had become. The small crowd emerging from the hostelry went to their cars without sparing me a glance, yet I longed for a warm drink, or just a friendly smile. I had no idea what time Zita would arrive, where I should go or what I should do. The pub's lights were being switched off as I stiffly forced myself to a standing position.

Suddenly the door opened again and a figure emerged. A tall, slim young man with a beard came towards me.

'You look cold,' he said, stating the obvious.

Through chattering teeth I explained about my sister.

'I think you'd better come with me and have a cup of cocoa,' he said kindly. 'Come on, this way.' He led me to the entrance to the Rocks across the road opposite the pub, up some steps, through a lift-type metal gate and into the woods. It was very dark. I was too cold and tired to be worried about his motives. 'Hold my hand, or you're bound to fall over.'

Even I hesitated at that one!

'My name is Terry. Don't worry, I'll see that you don't come to any harm,' he added reassuringly, and I stumbled along beside him until we came to an enormous bonfire.

Oh, the joy of getting warm again. A mug of steaming hot cocoa was pushed into my hands and introductions were made to the little group sitting around the dancing flames. I had quite forgotten about Zita until suddenly there was a bellow from the surrounding inky blackness. 'Julie, where the bloody hell are you?' My worried and irate sister had arrived.

That was the start of regular visits to these impressive sandstone rocks, with their deep steep-sided chimneys, high challenging faces and playground of smaller boulders. As I usually had to work on Saturday mornings, the amount of free time that I could spend there at weekends was short – but so enjoyable after being cooped up in a small windowless office for five and a half days a week. Although I still enjoyed my work as an office junior, I also needed to play.

My camping equipment consisted of an ex-army paratrooper's jumping bag, in which the soldiers sat to keep warm in the unheated, draughty planes *en route* to the jumping zone. It was bulky and weighed about ten pounds, but it was cosy. Together with Terry and his three friends, John, Gerry and Ray, I would sleep out under the stars, protected from the rain and, later, in winter, the snow, by the projecting overhangs of rock.

The days were spent struggling with the wide variety of climbing problems that this imposing rock outcrop offered. When we became tired of climbing we would hold abseiling competitions, to see who could slide fastest down the rope, from the top to the bottom of the rocks. We did not use the conventional methods of wrapping the rope around the body to build up friction for control, or the metal figure-of-eight mechanical device. The 'sandstone' method was simply to hold the rope across your back, letting it run through your hands as you moved sideways down the rock. It amounted to a hardly controlled jump, and as we were launching ourselves off one of the loftiest points, around forty feet high, it took a degree of nerve. The other diversion was 'chimney descents'. For this we wore big boots and heavy combat jackets. You simply jumped sideways into the narrow gap between two steep walls, braking against the sides with your feet, knees and elbows to slow yourself down.

In the dark of night we would play 'follow my leader' around the scrambles and climbs, when we would 'solo' everything without the protection of safety ropes. Good training, but not very safe as sandstone is a soft rock and holds easily break off. One night Terry was leading the way up Stalactite Wall [a far more delicate climb in the 1950s than it is today] when a handhold broke and he suddenly disappeared into the darkness below. For a few seconds there was absolute silence as we groped about trying to find him. We feared that he might have killed himself. Suddenly an awful gasping noise echoed through the woods. He had landed on a small boulder and winded himself.

We became friendly with the other rock climbers, some of whom were very skilled, and our techniques and ability extended with our circle of friends. However, not everyone was greeted enthusiastically. At the sight of a certain young lad of fifteen, we would groan and hide away our store of food. Young Martin Boysen was an unkempt youth; his seemingly off-hand manner upset everyone, and he was always on the scrounge for something to eat. But it was only a rebellious teenage phase. Martin grew up to become one of Britain's most talented climbers, a thoroughly nice person and now a much valued friend.

My family had moved to a house in Streatham in 1957, and by coincidence, Terry lived only two miles away from us, in Clapham Park. The whole group would often meet during the week for a chat and a pint, but almost every weekend we headed for High Rocks. It took just over an hour to drive to Tunbridge Wells. It was never a very comfortable or warm journey on my always overladen Vespa, or in Terry's ex-army jeep – his first love.

Whenever we could afford it we would travel with a special climbers' coach to the mountains of North Wales. The bus would leave London's Baker Street at seven at night on Friday, arriving in Snowdonia via the narrow, twisting A5 at about 2 am. We would sleep in a friendly farmer's barn and go climbing all day Saturday and Sunday, returning late on Sunday night and often arriving back in London just in time for work on Monday.

25

These trips were big adventures, and although the climbs we did were far from noteworthy by today's high standards, they were minor epics for us with only a rather tatty rope and almost no knowledge of climbing techniques, how to protect ourselves properly with the rope, or even which climb we were on. But we enjoyed ourselves and learnt the hard way, by experience. Not a way I would advocate – we were very lucky to survive – but in those days there were no organised 'schools of mountaineering' where you could learn the proper way to do things, and in any case we could never have afforded them.

During the late fifties when we were climbing at Harrison's Rocks and in Wales, Terry and I did not have a very close personal relationship. Although we were not unfriendly, we didn't really like each other. In fact I always thought that when Terry came to our house it was to see my sister, and if he had arrived alone, would keep out of the way. Neither of us can remember when the situation changed, but a year later we had fallen in love.

In 1959 Terry and I were married. Our Wedding Day on 7 November was particularly memorable as by the evening a thick pea-soup fog had ground all forms of transport in London to a halt. As a result we had to share our wedding night at our flat in Streatham with twenty-five of our marooned guests.

2

'From win and lose and still somehow . . .'

During our first year of marriage, another rock outcrop near Tunbridge Wells, Bowles Rocks, was put up for sale. The original asking price was £400, low enough for us to put in an offer, but we were substantially outbid by a businessman from Sevenoaks who wanted to develop an Outdoor Pursuits Centre on the site. The local blacksmith, who owned it, had built and stocked up a pig farm on the land, intending that his son should run it. However, the son ran away with a woman he loved after a short while, and the father had no heart to continue the project by himself. Over the years the weeds took over until head-high brambles covered the property.

Together with other members of the Sandstone Climbing Club from High Rocks, we had helped the new owner John Walters to clear the rocks for several months. In return we were allowed to explore the climbs as we uncovered them. The rock at Bowles faces due south. The light-coloured dry, clean sandstone is very different from the dark, always damp and greasy High Rocks.

'How would you like to come and work for me full time?' John suggested to Terry one hot summer evening. 'You could supervise the rest of the cleaning-up and the building projects and then run the Centre when it's operational. I'll build you a house here and pay you a thousand pounds a year.'

We could not believe our luck! A chance to live and work where we could also climb every day, and have the excitement of being so closely involved with what was for those days, in 1961, a very revolutionary project. Terry was working as Assistant Manager in Thomas Black & Son, a long-established company selling camping and climbing equipment. It was an interesting job. There were then still many corners of the world unspoilt by jet travel and unvisited by civilised men, and he met many intrepid travellers and explorers. A lot of his customers became our friends, and we would spend fascinating evenings in our little flat listening to tales of distant mountains and epic climbs and adventures. But we had both had enough of London, the hassle of travelling to work in the rush hour and the long hours that our respective jobs kept us apart.

A month later we packed the contents of our flat onto a friend's lorry and excitedly drove down to Sussex. John had promised to find some sort of temporary accommodation for us while the house was being constructed, and this turned out to be a sixteen foot by eight foot chicken shed sitting beside a little stream. Although it had been used for the purpose for which it was designed, it had been well cleaned out and the inside was lined with newly painted hardboard.

We moved in a carpet, double bed, dining room table and chairs, sideboard and studio couch to join the little black-leaded solid fuel stove and completely unoperational sink unit. There was little room left to move around, but it had a snug atmosphere. A minor discomfort were the four crossbeams which supported the roof, as they were a little lower than Terry's height. He had to learn to develop a repetitive ducking movement as he walked from the bed at the far end to the door at the front. Drinking water had to be collected from John's house in Crowborough three miles away, and our lavatory was a hole dug behind a convenient bush.

It was a very abrupt change from the sophistication of London, but we found that we did not miss the mod-cons and that life in the country suited us both very well.

Terry set to, battling enthusiastically against the brambles and stinging nettles which hid beneath them the many other problems. Old pig pens constructed of heavy concrete blocks and corrugated iron housed revolting messes. Huge heaps of what appeared to be old intestines, writhing with maggots, were lying around, and the nauseating smell when these were disturbed made you gag.

To complete his Herculean task of moving the old pig sties, Terry was given a spade, a shovel and a wheelbarrow. All the

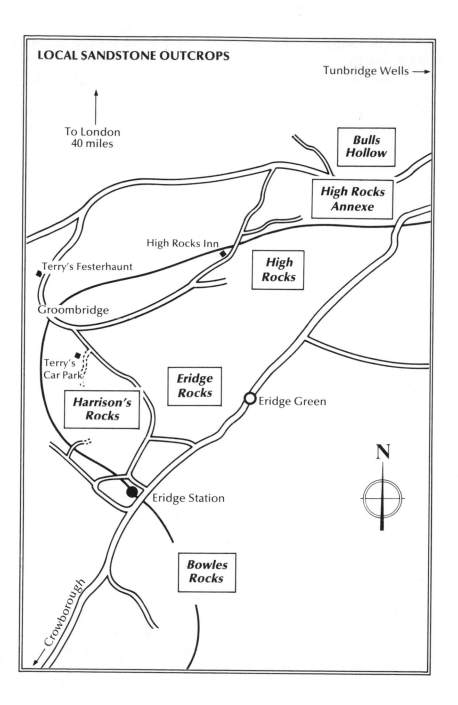

LOCAL SANDSTONE OUTCROPS

Tunbridge Wells →

To London
40 miles

Bulls Hollow

High Rocks Annexe

High Rocks Inn

Terry's Festerhaunt

High Rocks

Groombridge

Terry's
Car Park

Eridge Rocks

Harrison's Rocks

Eridge Green

N

Eridge Station

Crowborough

Bowles Rocks

debris, including hundreds of old concrete tank trap blocks, which weighed around two hundredweight each, had to be wheeled four hundred yards to be dumped underneath what would later become the car park for the Centre. John kept promising help in both manual and mechanical form but it never materialised. A neighbouring farmer offered Terry an old Fordson van for £5. It was a bit battered, but the engine started at the first press of the button and kept on going. He cut out the soft-top roof and removed the back doors, and it was converted into a very useful and willing workhorse. The difference it made in terms of time and effort was enormous, but John did not approve and refused either to buy the van or to pay for the petrol to run it.

John was a design engineer, a man in his forties, of solid, bullish build with a bald head, but he had tremendous charisma. It was very strange, but when he spoke to me I felt a warm glow inside, uplifted, I suppose you could say. Both Terry and I experienced this but had never known such a feeling to emanate from another human being before. This aura impressed us both.

The weeks passed and Terry continued to expect that someone else would be employed to help him with his mammoth task. I helped him with the brambles; I loved the thrill of uncovering something unexpected, like a waterfall we discovered on a steep bank one day, but I could not bear to go near the decomposing pig pens.

One morning after breakfast I was violently sick. We had been living at Bowles for four months. When the same thing happened the following two mornings, I went to see the doctor, who confirmed that I was indeed pregnant. It is wonderful to know that a new life is growing inside you. Somehow, living so close to nature in the simplicity of our chicken shed made me feel that this baby was having a very special start to life.

Christopher was born in October 1962. My only regret was that Terry could not share his arrival into the world because the delivery room at the local hospital was too small. He was a smiling contented baby with tremendous energy and watching him grow gave each day an extra importance and a new meaning.

When a few extra hands were finally employed to help with the building and landscaping we became increasingly worried. Several incidents made us wonder if everything was developing as it should be with the project. The final straw came when John insisted on building a chapel. Terry just could not agree to help to construct something which would be so rarely used when the Centre still lacked many things which were really necessary and would be needed every day – like flush toilets to replace the primitive chemical ones. John was not interested in discussing the correct priorities, and the situation was made more difficult by his choice of site. The chapel was to be constructed on the side of a bank made of soft sand! He wanted to build a replica of the chapel by the lake below the Matterhorn – a mountain that he had a fixation about. He also had a strong faith and when money was short would always tell us not to worry: the good Lord would provide. However, where the chapel was concerned, Terry did worry. The good Lord might provide, but he would not have to dig the foundations by hand!

We lived at Bowles for two years and enjoyed sorting out the initial landscaping and building projects. We finally moved into the lovely wooden house built by the entrance three weeks before Christopher was born and during our second year there the Outdoor Pursuits Centre became operational, but only for rock climbing.

Both Terry and I thoroughly enjoyed meeting the people from all walks of life and helping them to gain satisfaction and skill from our favourite sport. However, after two years we felt restricted by the limited boundaries of the narrow strip of land that formed the Centre. It took all our time and energy and we had no chance to get to the high hills. Mountaineers cannot accept such limitations for long, and as Terry and John were no longer seeing eye to eye over many things we bought a house in Tunbridge Wells and moved on.

What we did not realise was the serious amount of unemployment in early 1963. Being a very adaptable person, Terry had felt sure that he could find some way to earn a living without difficulty but his illusions were swiftly shattered. He found himself joining long queues of people hopefully waiting for interviews, and all too often by the time he heard about a possible job, the position had already been filled.

Our savings dwindled and we became desperate. Terry even became a coalman for a short time, but we soon discovered that it cost a high percentage of his wages to keep him clean. Nevertheless, those hard times were an education that did us no harm, and made us appreciate each other and the good times when they returned.

It was not until the autumn of 1963 that Terry found a permanent job which he really enjoyed. It was with a woodworm and dry rot eradication company and took him into many fascinating old houses in Kent and Sussex and often involved quite intricate carpentry. He also went to college on two evenings a week, and I was very proud when he managed to pass his exams in Wood Science and Timber Technology in two years instead of the normal three.

Our beautiful daughter, Lindsay, was born in July 1964. When she was two years old we came to another major decision. We were getting into a rut. Terry was going off to work at eight o'clock each morning, returning home around six. With the restriction of young children to baby-sit, we fell into the boring routine of watching television every evening and then going to bed. Our lives needed something more. Things had to be changed!

We decided to sell the house; that would force the issue, make something happen. We instructed an estate agent to put the property on the market, and just two days later a couple came to look at our desirable residence. The following day they returned. 'We'll buy it,' the husband said, 'providing that we can take possession in six weeks' time.'

Terry and I looked at each other. We were about to go on a month's holiday, touring Europe. Six weeks would give us a week on either side. 'What the hell,' said Terry. 'We wanted to liven things up. Yes, we agree.'

It was a good holiday. Christopher, now an energetic three-year-old, not only had the thrill of seeing his first Alpine mountains but walked on his little legs up to a mountain hut and spent the night there, at 11,000 feet.

Contracts for the sale of the house were exchanged, and we arranged to store our furniture. 'But where are we going to live?' I asked Terry. We had two days to go before we had to move out.

'Don't worry,' he said reassuringly. 'I'll think of something.'

I was worried. We had two young children, two cars and a lively boxer dog and very soon would have nowhere to park any of them.

Inspiration came in the late afternoon, and we drove to a caravan showroom. 'I think this one will do for us,' Terry said, pointing at a green and white caravan which was not much bigger than our kitchen.

I peered inside. It would certainly save a lot of time doing the housework, but how long would we have to live in it? Summer was over and the mists and chills of autumn were already in the air.

We packed our remaining belongings into our new home. It felt as if we were embarking on a timeless holiday. Terry had not changed his job and had a house to treat for woodworm by the sea, at Camber Sands in Sussex. 'Absolutely perfect,' he said. 'The job will take a week and there's a caravan site just nearby, right behind the beach. The children will love it.'

We all did. The sun shone every day. Unfettered by not having so many possessions or a rigid timetable, we laughed and played together, and we did not feel at all restricted by the limited size of our twelve-foot home.

From September until the following March we camped in our caravan. Living in the corner of a field with no rent to pay meant that Terry could give up his job and stay with us during the daytime too. We had made quite a good profit on the sale of our house and our simple lifestyle did not cost a lot. Lindsay and Christopher loved the country life, fetching milk from the farm still warm from the cows, watching the charcoal burner in the wood with his glowing slow burning fires, splashing in puddles, exploring, running, jumping, playing. We wanted our children to be free spirits, especially before the age of self-consciousness, and in those wonderful months, like young animals, they learnt to live with nature through all five of their senses.

But good though such a life is, it cannot go on for ever, and we started looking for a more permanent place to live. We wanted somewhere where we could work together, to start a business selling climbing equipment.

A general store was on the market in Groombridge, the small village close to Harrison's Rocks, now the most popular climbing centre in the area, and we went to have a look at it. Behind the shop was a tiny tea room used by climbers on their weekend visits to the Rocks. It was not ideal but it would certainly be a start – so we bought it.

We had no idea what running a general store involved and a very rude awakening followed when we took over Saxby's Store. The tiny twelve-foot-square shop was a jumbled mess. The first days were hell. There were no proper display shelves, and nothing was priced. We sold hundreds of different items from potatoes to lighter flints. The girl who had worked for the previous owners said she would stay on to help us but was lured away to a shop down the road, and we were left to cope with the chaos of moving in and opening the shop all by ourselves.

As we were open from eight in the morning until nine o'clock at night, six and a half days a week, we had to reorganise and price every item on our first half-day closing. We shut the door promptly at one o'clock and started emptying the rickety shelves. Terry took the children to the woodyard to buy some timber to build some more substantial new ones, and I started to clear out the refrigerated counter which housed all the butter, margarine and fats. We wanted to move this to the other side of the room to create more space. The floor was littered with cigarettes and tobacco, tins, bottles and boxes and the contents of the display window, including a hanging glass shelf.

After a while I stood up to stretch my cramped limbs and, without looking, stepped back. There was a resounding crack and I fell over as the thick plate glass of the shelf broke under my weight. I looked down expecting to see a pool of blood, but there was nothing. I stood up with a sigh of relief, and then saw with horror a great flap of skin hanging from below my knee, exposing the bone of my kneecap below.

When Terry and the children arrived back, the shop was in

worse chaos than ever, and I was being loaded into an ambulance. But it is an ill wind, as they say, and when the news of my thirty-seven stitches got around, help soon arrived in the form of plump, jolly, fresh-faced Heather. She was a gem. She had worked in the shop before and knew the customers and prices. She was quick and efficient and had a happy likeable personality.

We enjoyed running the shop. It was hard work but it was interesting to build up custom, gradually adding new lines like more adventurous vegetables and a selection of delicatessen meats and cheeses, which always smelt so good. In two years we were turning over £20,000 per year, not bad for a small village shop, especially as the most expensive thing we sold was a seven-and-four-penny (37p) tin of tobacco! We had also made alterations to the tea room and were getting busy there too.

We were lucky. We had been accepted by the villagers very quickly. In those days a new estate of commuter houses had resulted in newcomers being regarded as 'foreigners' who were often kept at a distance for quite a long time.

One young man with whom we became involved was Dick, a good-looking, red-haired, Clint Eastwood look-alike. Dick was twenty-two years old and the first of our 'waifs and strays' that we have semi-adopted over the years. He was the second eldest of five brothers and when he was sixteen had developed a mysterious stomach complaint. He would have fits of stomach cramps and vomiting which left him feeling so weak that he often could not go to his job on a farm or out with his friends in the evenings. The insecurity of not knowing when an attack might start affected his self-confidence and he opted out of much of the teenage life in the village. His contemporaries became attached to regular girlfriends, and sadly, by the time he was nineteen the pairing-off system had left him out.

When I had been in the little Norfolk village during the war, the children were given anticipated marriage partners almost from birth. Of course, they did have a choice when they got older, but not a very open one as strong influence from the families and the lack of other unattached members of the opposite sex made swopping around difficult. In Groombridge in the 1960s things were easier, but still, if you were not engaged to be married by the time you were twenty-five you were destined for the shelf.

Dick drifted gradually into our lives, usually arriving at the shop as we were closing, when he would help us to clean and tidy up ready for the next busy day. His illness was going through a particularly bad patch. The doctor was not very constructive, telling Dick that his problem was psychological and that he should pull himself together. I am sure that in part it was true, but only because the initial problem had never been cured. It took several more years before a correct diagnosis was made and the offending kidney was treated.

Dick was unhappy. Because of his uncertain attendance, he was in danger of losing his job. To take some pressure away, we suggested that he might like to help us with the shop. He could arrive whenever he felt well enough and stock the shelves, collect supplies from the local Cash and Carry and make the house deliveries. All these things could be done as and when he felt well enough.

What a tremendous help he was! While he had been working on the farm he had developed an adaptability to cope with any job quickly and efficiently, and had learnt to accept responsibility without asking a million questions. Better still, he had a lot of common sense. Our delivery customers looked forward to his visits, and coming from a large family himself, he was very good with Christopher and Lindsay. Without the anxiety of schedules governing his life, he became more relaxed, and although his problem did not disappear altogether, it certainly got much better.

Because of the extra help, Terry and I were able to start occasionally teaching rock climbing again, a welcome break from working such long hours in the confines of the shop. It was good to be out in the fresh air, climbing on Harrison's Rocks just a half-hour walk away. Kent County Council had started to give their schools the opportunity to include various outdoor pursuits such as sailing, canoeing and rock climbing in their sports curriculum and were employing experienced visiting coaches part time to instruct. The idea soon caught on and we were being offered more work than we could cope with in our limited spare time. It was decision time again.

'I think we've developed the shop to its full potential. It's time for a change of direction' Terry said after several months of careful thought.

He was echoing my feelings. Neither of us fancied being grocers for the rest of our lives. 'Let's sell the shop and try our luck as freelance climbing instructors.'

It was a difficult time to sell, particularly a leasehold property. An economic squeeze made mortgage loans difficult to acquire. A couple from Cornwall in their fifties wanted to buy the Stores but could not raise all the money. Having taken the decision to move on we were impatient to start our new life. They seemed genuine people, and as the shop was now on such a sound footing with a substantial regular turnover, we agreed to loan them the money that they could not raise. They would repay us at the rate of £7 per week. Although this was not a great amount even in 1967, it would provide a regular income for us, sufficient to buy the weekly groceries for the family.

The next problem was to find somewhere to live. During the years at the Stores we had not only acquired Dick, who now lived with us, but also a donkey. I had always longed to have a pet donkey. When we were on holiday in Spain one year I almost bought one. 'He eez very little, mucho sympatico . . . and very cheap,' I repeated the Spaniard's sales jargon to my sceptical husband, all set to bring him back to England on the back seat of our little Mini, but Terry could not be convinced that it was a good idea and I reluctantly gave up the negotiations.

Later, as the shop took up more and more of our days, we had found that we were not spending enough time talking and playing with the children. The solution arrived in the form of this long-eared, nimble footed little donkey called Puff. With Terry's normal dislike for pre-planning, he arranged for her to be delivered before he had organised where she would live, and she was unloaded from the horse-box into the shop. She spent her first afternoon with us in the little garden behind the store shed while Terry looked for suitable grazing. At least she had arrived on early closing day. Every lunchtime we would pile the children into the car and drive over to her field, have a picnic with her, or take her out for a walk.

It was one of our customers who came up with a temporary solution to our housing problem. He had an empty cottage which we could borrow for six months and there was even a field for Puff. We went to have a look at it. The cottage was built along one side of a large walled garden. It was a very unusual shape, a little like a railway carriage, a hundred feet long and just ten feet wide.

Inside the walls and kitchen sink were splattered with blood. In recent years it had only been used for plucking and drawing Christmas turkeys. I looked forward to the challenge of scrubbing it out and clothing it in a new coat of paint.

But it was the whole estate that excited us. It had been designed by the well-known Victorian architect Norman Shaw in 1869, for his cousin, a shipping magnate of the Shaw Savill line. In the early days it had been completely self-sufficient, relying on the outside world for nothing. It had its own gas works, brewery and water supply which was pumped up into a storage tank beneath the roof of a tower which gave a castle-like appearance to the big main house. There was a coach house with stables for the horses, and a big barn for schooling the horses with angled walls to prevent the riders from knocking their knees if they went too close while training their mounts. There was also a dairy, dog kennels, the main gardener's house and the Bothy: the cottage we were to borrow. This had at one time housed fourteen gardeners in dormitories. A lodge house at the end of the half-mile drive completed the estate – together with the farm and very extensive farmland. During the war it had been used as a hospital by the Canadian Army. In the early fifties it was bought by a city businessman who was a part-time property speculator. Ian Simpson loved old buildings and took great pleasure in converting large country houses which had become unmanageable because of their size into smaller but still gracious family mansions. This estate had such a special atmosphere, however, that he and his wife Ursula decided that they wanted to live there themselves.

I did not realise how much I had missed the freedom to be with Terry and the childen whenever I wanted to. To have time to think my own thoughts and be able to peacefully finish the washing or the ironing without constant interruptions to serve in the shop or deal with a salesman was a real luxury. Life in the Bothy was idyllic. Ian and his wife and family were extremely nice people as were our neighbours; an interesting collection of writers, artists, a sculptor, two Mayfair hairdressers and the then President of the Royal Academy, Sir Thomas Monnington and his wife. The children had plenty of countryside to roam and even Puff had a pleasanter life as she shared a field with two jack donkeys.

We had several family holidays in Wales, Derbyshire, Scotland and the Lake District about this time. The children enjoyed walking, being in the mountains and doing short climbs. However, Terry and I found that we could no longer climb together. It seemed that we had developed a psychological barrier after the children were born, and if one of us could not make a certain move the other also found it impossible. I think we each had respect for the other's ability and if Terry could not get up a difficult manoeuvre I almost gave in before trying. It was the thought of what would happen to the children if we were both injured or killed that restricted us. I also felt very strongly that one adult should not undertake a serious climb with a child. If anything happened to the grown-up the child would be in the terrifying position of having to cope alone with an injured person possibly halfway up a rock face or miles from anywhere. The nine-year-old son of a friend of ours had the shattering experience of watching his father fall and die at his feet.

A perfect place for the children to develop their climbing skills was in the jumble of sandstone boulders surrounding Fontainebleau just forty miles from Paris. It had been an annual Easter event, during the time that we lived in Tunbridge Wells, to hire a mini-bus, fill it with friends and spend the holiday camping in the sandy pine forests in which this French climbing playground sits. Before we were married we had also ventured abroad to the Alps. With our limited earnings we had usually managed to save only £10 or £15 for the two-week holiday so that we endured many disastrous hitch-hiking journeys and often had to live on bread and plonk. But in retrospect these were often the best trips.

But I digress. After we moved into the Bothy Terry had been doing a number of different jobs to supplement our somewhat irregular earnings from teaching rock climbing. In the autumn of 1969 he and Dick were working for a landscape gardening company, preparing the gardens of a newly-built housing estate in Purley for turfing and planting.

One sunny October day I had just finished the hoovering when I heard a car pull up outside. It was Dick. He looked ashen and very tense, and I hurried him inside assuming that he was having another bad turn. He took me totally by surprise when he said, 'Julie, you must come with me at once. Terry's had a terrible accident!'

The journey to Croydon was interminable and nerveracking. As we drove through the village a woman on a bicycle suddenly cut across our path, swerved violently out of the way, and fell off into the hedge. Thank goodness she was unhurt, but we were shaken and had wasted precious minutes. The other motorists seemed to dither about deliberately in front of us, and traffic lights always changed to red just as we reached them. By the time we pulled up outside the hospital, my legs were shaking.

During the drive Dick had explained what had happened. Terry had been using a brand new rotavator to plough up the hard clay soil of one of the front gardens. The ground was full of builder's debris; discarded bricks and other rubble was being thrown forward by the machine towards the double-glazed window of the house. They decided to change the rotating digging tines for a different C-shaped variety so that all the projectiles would be hurled against the thick rubber protective mat at the back of the rotavator, and Terry continued with his work.

The lawn-to-be was on a bank which sloped steeply down to the pavement, and as Terry turned at the top of the hill the heavy machine hit a brick, jumped out of control and headed downhill, with Terry hanging on, trying frantically to turn it. It flipped over and he fell on top of it, the tines still turning. One metal spike stabbed into his leg just below the knee and the powerful motor drove it on through bone and flesh. Terry was fully conscious, but could not reach the 'off' switch. The few people near enough to help had been petrified into immobility. Eventually he managed to stop it and lay unable to move as petrol gushed out all around him. The spike of the tine had re-emerged through the front of his thigh and he was trapped, impaled on its long metal tooth.

An Irish labourer came rushing over, sparks flying from his metal-tipped boots, cigarette in hand. 'Let me help yeh,' he started, but Terry's mind was still alert enough to tell him, in no uncertain terms, to go a long way away. He was not dead yet and did not fancy being incinerated by the pool of petrol that surrounded him. He had helped to unbolt the tine from the machine to free his leg, and by the time the ambulance arrived had bandaged the horrible sight with an old sack.

When the doctor saw the wound he suggested amputation, but Terry said, very firmly, no! On the operating table they had great difficulty in removing the hooked tine, which had carried with it the material of his jeans right through from one side of his leg to the other. They were frightened that the femoral artery might rupture during the removal and cause massive internal bleeding.

The leg was a mess. All three bones, the femur, tibia and fibula, were badly fractured, and muscles, nerves and ligaments on both sides of his knee were torn away.

After the first operation he lay on his back with his leg strung up in traction. Those days in Mayday Hospital in Croydon were a nightmare for us all. For Terry the pain and suffering with his leg was acute. Although most of the nurses were kind and effficient, the facilities, and more importantly the food, left a lot to be desired. 'I had a fish cake, fifteen peas and a dessertspoon of potato on my plate tonight!' he grumbled at visiting time, and despite the many tempting delicacies which my wonderful mother took him to supplement the meagre hospital diet, he lost over three stone during those weeks.

I had different problems. London was a four-hour eighty-mile round trip away, so the only visiting time I could manage was the hour every evening. Sister only allowed the children on the ward to visit their father on Sunday afternoons and it was impossible for me to arrange or afford a babysitter every time I wanted to visit Terry during the week. Visiting also meant that I hardly saw the children after school. If I took them with me, now seven and five years old, they either had to stay alone in the car on a very dark car park or sit on a bench on the dimly-lit landing outside the ward by a flight of steep stone stairs. The regulations would not even allow them to stand at the end of the ward where I could at least see them.

I also had financial worries. Until recently we had been self-employed and so we did not qualify for help with travelling expenses, and I could not get Mayday Hospital to transfer Terry to a more local hospital. Today I would not allow such a situation to continue, but in those days I was still rather shy and did not know how to start dealing with the intricacies of officialdom.

My finances got tighter and tighter as I was having to manage on my single earnings with a lot of extra expense. The couple who had taken over the goodwill of the shop had been very erratic over our loan repayments and I kept asking them to let me have the £7 per week so that I could feed the children and buy petrol to visit Terry, but they always made excuses. A few weeks later they informed me that they would soon go bankrupt. I could not believe it and begged them to let me take over the shop again and build up the custom, but they refused.

The great day at last arrived when Terry was to be taken off traction, have an operation to screw the two ends of the femur together and be put into a plaster cast. At midday the phone rang. It was the hospital. 'Are you coming to see your husband today?' the sister who was so strict about visiting asked over the telephone. 'You can come whenever you like,' she added quickly, and panic began to rise in me.

'What's wrong?' I queried, trying to keep my voice steady.

'It's probably delayed shock,' she said. 'He was so controlled after the accident, the operation today has most likely triggered it off. He's not at all well.'

I collected the children from school early and set off for town, her last words ringing in my ears.

The curtains were drawn around his bed when I arrived. Terry, lying uncovered on the bed, looked emaciated and his pale skin was cold and clammy to the touch. I was shocked by his appearance; it was the first time I had seen him naked since he had been admitted to hospital. 'Here, hold this while I get some clean sheets,' a nurse thrust a urine bottle into my hand. Terry moved his hand indicating that he wanted to use it and I pushed his limp penis inside. He started to urinate and the bottle began to fill. He must stop soon, I thought; they must make these bottles big enough to cover all eventualities . . .

'You'll have to stop!' I ordered my semi-conscious husband. 'The bottle's full, must get another one.' I looked frantically for someone to help, but the bed curtains cut me off from the ward. 'STOP!' I commanded and removed the already overflowing container and put it under the bed. I rushed out and grabbed another one from his neighbour's locker and by the time the nurse returned with the now much needed clean sheets, Terry had half filled that one too.

Another three weeks passed and I kept pushing Mayday to get Terry transferred to a local hospital, but with no success. Finally in desperation I rang my GP.

'It's not ethical, you know,' he told me. 'It's up to the London hospital to arrange the transfer; they won't like it if you interfere.'

I felt like crying. All the weeks of worry, financial hardship and inhuman separation were the responsibility of some faceless person I could never find. Did we who were suffering have no say in the matter?

'Look,' the doctor said 'all I can do is find out if there is a free bed at Crowborough hospital, and then you can tell Mayday that we have room for him. It might help a bit.'

That day I managed the lunchtime visiting hour. I told the sister that our local hospital would have a free bed for Terry.

'Well, he's due to have his plaster changed this afternoon,' she said, looking doubtful. She understood our problems and wanted to help. 'He shouldn't be moved until it has set properly and the doctor's checked the leg again. That's probably another three days.'

I was quite happy with that arrangement as Crowborough did not have a free bed until Monday. It was now Friday, perfect.

'I'll ask the doctor what he thinks,' sister said. 'You can wait if you like until your husband comes back from the plaster room.'

Two hours later Terry was wheeled back into the ward. He was followed by a young doctor. 'I understand that you have arranged for your husband to be accepted by another hospital,' he said disapprovingly. 'Well, you'd better arrange transport.'

I looked at him. 'When can he be moved?' I asked.

'Now, today. At once!' He stalked out.

I couldn't believe it. What about the plaster setting, the doctor's check? 'Will you arrange an ambulance to bring him down,' I asked a nurse. Terry had not been out of bed for six weeks, not even to sit in a chair until that day.

'Oh no, that's not possible, but we could put him on a train,' she said. 'Do trains take stretchers?' I asked naively.

'I don't think so,' she replied. 'No, he'd probably have to go in a normal carriage.'

Was she serious? Would they really put someone so unwell on an ordinary train, to be jolted and jostled? How would he get up and down the stairs? It was crazy. I had to get him out of that place even if he could not go into Crowborough until after the weekend. I would nurse him at home.

'I'll be back in an hour, try to rest,' I told Terry and drove the short distance to my parents' home in Streatham.

My mother helped me fit out the back of our old Renault van with a mattress and blankets and I drove back to the hospital. Even the journey in the wheelchair from the ward down to the car had exhausted Terry, and although I drove very slowly and carefully he was finished by the time I had got him into bed at home.

It was an emotional weekend of laughter and tears, moments of panic trying to keep the excited children and our overjoyed boxer dog from jumping on the bed. A stern warning came from our doctor. As I had accepted Terry home, the local hospital might not now admit him, even though he still needed specialist care.

But on Monday an ambulance did arrive to take him to Crowborough. Fortunately I followed it in the van, because halfway down a small country lane a herd of mooing, frisky escapee cows blocked the road and I had to chase them quite a distance before I could finally shut them in another field and let the ambulance through.

It was five months before Terry was well enough to start work again and by then the couple in the shop had been declared bankrupt.

* * *

'. . . and I would like to give you the first option on the Lease.' The letter was unexpected, but it could not have come at a better time. The landlord was offering us the shop back; now, with all the stock and saleable items removed by the Official Receiver, just an empty shell. We thought about it carefully. We could just about raise enough money to get the café going again, opening only at weekends. Apart from anything else, we had to show the village that we had not sold the previous owners a 'pup'. If we could make a go of it on these terms, people would soon understand that any such accusations could only be grossly unfair.

Three months later things at Terry's Festerhaunt ['fester' is the word used by climbers when they are sitting around and only climbing verbally] were going well. I made the flans, cakes, sausage and onion pies, and bread pudding myself, and we laid it all out on the large counter. It looked like attractive party food and the ravenous climbers helped themselves to well piled plates. It was fun food and not expensive to prepare so that we could afford to sell it for a reasonable price and still make a profit. We also started to sell climbing equipment. We had no stock at first, we simply had no money to buy it. Everything was ordered by the climbers and paid for in advance. We just took a straight ten per cent on the deal. Every penny we made was saved to buy more stock, and gradually we built up a well-stocked and renowned climbing shop. Terry's Festerhaunt was a success.

News of its good value food spread and many of our original customers from the grocer-shop days were pressurising us to open during the week, but with climbing courses I did not have the time. A friend suggested that his sister, who was just recovering from a serious case of anorexia nervosa, might be just the person to help, and so Marion came into our lives.

She was still very thin from her illness – her weight had dropped to just over five stone, and when she was admitted to hospital she was close to dying. Dark-haired and attractive, she had a great zest for life and was a talented and resourceful cook who produced incredible inventions which not only tasted delicious but looked and smelt good as well. The friendly café was the ideal place for her to pick up the threads of life again.

☙3☙

World's end to a new horizon

'You look absolutely worn out', one of our Festerhaunt customers told me, concern in his voice. 'What you need is a rest. Why don't you come climbing with me? I know the perfect place to revitalise you.' He looked at me over his half glasses, his clear blue eyes twinkling. He always had an air of quiet calmness about him which I found sympathetic.

Dennis Kemp had been popping into the café on odd occasions for several years. Like many of our customers he would help clear the tables, wash up and even do some of the cooking if we were very busy. There were often three to four hundred climbers at the Rocks at weekends.

I certainly was feeling tired. Terry's terrible accident, getting the business going again after all the worry of the bankruptcy, the house and two lively children had all gradually sapped my energies. But it was not so easy just to go off and leave Terry to cope and I had been reluctant to expose myself to unnecessary risks while the children were very young. Besides, I enjoyed being a mother, sharing the adventure of discovering life through the children's eyes. But now our offspring were becoming independent; they were ten and twelve years old. I did not feel guilty about leaving them for a short while.

'Look Julie, I'd prefer you to have a week's holiday now than be ill for far longer. Of course you must go,' my wonderfully understanding husband insisted. 'It's time you started climbing for pleasure again, anyway.'

'So I'll meet you at World's End next Monday night.' Dennis reminded me as he left. 'Just turn right out of Llangollen, and you'll see the limestone edge up on the hill. I'll meet you by the river bridge at six o'clock.'

World's End sounded the perfect place to recover my enthusiasm for the chores of everyday life. Just how perfect it was I didn't realise until I arrrived. High in the gentle moorland covered hills above the pretty musical town of Llangollen in Wales, a river falls over jumbled blocks, tumbling and splashing down to a picturesque stone bridge. Here Dennis met me, precisely on schedule.

That evening we climbed on the warm limestone rock until the sun disappeared below a golden horizon. Limestone is my favourite rock – it is relaxing to climb on and I find its warm silky texture exciting to touch, to caress rather than cling to, and its exposed steepness is so enjoyable. To hang in the air, moving freely, to a bump, a small depression, a sharp-edged hole, foothold by foothold, hands following the dance, all the senses aware. I was alive again.

In the early morning Dennis went to work in Connah's Quay, thirty miles away on the banks of the Mersey river. He had an interesting job teaching a variety of subjects, all linked to photography, tape recording and audio-visual skills. His artistry in putting together pictures and sound is not only beautiful to see but he has the special ability to stimulate others to look and listen to what is around them.

I spent the day wandering for miles through the sweet smelling purple heather of the vast moorland which covered the whole area above the cliff face on which we had been climbing. I seemed to have the whole place to myself. My inhibitions left me and I ran into the bracing wind and then threw myself onto a thick bed of springy heather. The wind rocked me gently as I lay there watching the fluffy clouds scurrying by overhead. I felt sad that other people with mental pressures were limited to the palliative of pills, or a rest in a hospital or institution. How much quicker they would be revitalised if they could have their bodies relaxed by the warm sun and troubles blown away by the refreshing breeze, release their tensions by running . . . jumping . . . shouting . . . unrestricted by walls and other people. Up on the wild moors I felt cleansed and my *joie de vivre* had returned.

47

It was during those days that I discovered what a truly special person Dennis was. I knew nothing about his past until he told me he had been injured during the last weeks of the war in Germany. It was a sniper's bullet, that hit him in the groin. The wound was horrifying – his scrotum and half his penis had been shot away. He was just twenty-one years old. It was a miracle that he had survived such an extensive damage and the shock which accompanies it.

After extensive surgery Dennis recovered enough to be sent to Switzerland to convalesce, and was captivated by the beauty and grandeur of the Alps. He wanted to return and get to know these breathtaking snow-covered mountains.

One day in 1949 he was browsing through a copy of *The Times* and came across a small ad for a climbing school in the Dauphiné Alps. It was there that he discovered the joys of climbing, a sport he previously was not aware existed. But once discovered it became a passion which did much to keep him sane while he came to terms with his life-shattering disability. As he could not have children, Dennis took the decision not to marry, even though he had fallen in love, but he certainly did not become reclusive or bitter. You can see in his superb photography his love of life and joy of living. He is a man with a lot of love to give and has not allowed his war wound to prevent him from sharing it.

In the 1950s he was one of six people who collectively bought Harrison's Rocks, the sandstone outcrop closest to our Fester-haunt. Feeling that it was unjust for the ownership of such an important climbing area to be in the hands of a small group of people, they put the rocks into trust for all climbers. However, the British Mountaineering Council, the obvious ideal adminis-trators for the Trust, were not empowered to hold land, so that task was handed on to the Central Council for Physical Rec-reation. Several years later the CCPR became defunct and the newly formed Sports Council took over their job. But Harrison's Rocks, with which in later years we were to become so involved, was originally bought by climbers and placed for perpetuity into trust for all other climbers, in the hope that they would care enough about the outcrop to look after it voluntarily for future generations. But more of that later . . .

Dennis is an extremely competent climber, and still seems to get better every year. He has an easy sense of humour, and a strong feeling for honesty. Despite his sixty years it is his tremendous enthusiasm and drive for life, especially where climbing and adventure are involved, that is so contagious and inspiring. He is an inveterate traveller – mountaineering is a wonderful excuse to peregrinate about the world – and his amusing and graphically descriptive letters are fascinating to read. Australia, the Himalayas, Yosemite, Scotland or skiing in the Alps, you never know where he will turn up next.

It was Den's influence that stimulated me so much in my return to personal climbing. Although I had been teaching both at Harrison's and in the British mountains, my performance was rarely pushed above what the students could manage. After that first visit to Llangollen in 1974, whenever I could meet Dennis for a few days' climbing, I could always be sure that we would achieve a lot of good routes. We would be on the rock from morning till night, even if it meant moving around to find some good weather.

To most other climbers we were an unusual older climbing team. Dennis was in his fifties when I climbed with him at World's End and at thirty-four I was surprised and elated to find myself enjoyably swarming up far more routes in a weekend than I would have tackled in a week or longer in my younger days. I was determined not to waste a second of the precious time that Terry so generously gave me. I fully realised what a great sacrifice it was on his part, especially as his leg still prevented him from walking any distance over rough ground. As a minor compensation I was usually able to phone him every evening with a healthy list of climbs we had achieved.

On one occasion, to extend the day still more, we decided to tackle Diagonal (a Hard Very Severe route) on Dinas Mot before breakfast. We climbed up from our little tent site at Ynys Ettws and arrived at the foot of the climb by 7 o'clock. It gave the climb a special flavour to start in the freshness of a new day and to be able to look down on the tents of all the other still-sleeping mountaineers in the Llanberis valley far below; a peaceful contrast to the normal scene with climbers swarming up and down the surrounding cliffs, and climbing calls and oaths from both sides of the valley echoing through the air.

It was delicate, airy climbing on clear grey granite, and all too soon we had arrived at the final pitch. Dennis led on up to the top. I gazed down this impressive valley towards the sea at Caernarvon. When I am seconding I do not like to watch the leader, unless he is likely to fall off. I prefer to tackle the moves in my own way, uninfluenced by his technique. My head was full of mouthwatering bacon and eggs, washed down by cups of aromatic coffee, and I called up to Dennis who was now safely belayed, 'What a great idea this was. It'll make breakfast taste like it never has tasted before!' And then I started to climb – or at least I tried to. I just could not make the first moves. I tried my right foot in the crack, then my left foot; wriggling; struggling; pushing; pulling. It just would not work. It was crazy. I had made the crux move of the climb with no effort at all. After twenty minutes of scrabbling, it didn't seem possible! Now that I had mentioned the succulent breakfast back at the tent, Dennis's stomach was reminding him how hungry a couple of hours' exercise had made him, and his jocular calls of encouragement became demands for action. Suddenly I found the right combination and popped over the top like a cork out of a bottle. I had really begun to think that this 'extra' route might cost us our climbing for the rest of the day.

I also enjoyed climbing with Dennis because he did not restrict his routes to a specific grade. Some of the easier routes can offer special qualities that are as interesting as the challenge and delicacy of the harder grades. Many climbers make an orderly progress up the grades and will only climb within their present standard or try harder routes. This puts pressures and restrictions not only on them but also on their climbing companions.

Many times in climbers' pubs you will also hear lengthy discussions and post mortems on what went wrong. For me, climbing is recreation, and must, first and foremost, be fun. I want to remember the routes with enjoyment, for the thrill of moving freely in harmony with the rock and the person I am climbing with. Obviously there are moments of panic, of struggle, they are part of the challenge of climbing, but I personally do not want them as constant companions.

Between the visit to World's End and my later climbing, something else happened which was to change my life. John, a young friend of ours, was the studious type who took life fairly seriously. The family lived in a country lane, remote from public transport, so as soon as he was sixteen he bought a small motorbike. He was quietly driving along a road one afternoon when, from a minor side road, a fire engine came bearing down on him, knocked him off his bike and into the gutter. 'Sorry mate,' the driver said, as he lay in a haze of pain. 'I put my foot on the brake, but nothing happened!'

Terry was asked by John's parents to take some photographs of the scene of the accident, which he did. Then he went in search of the fire engine to record the damage that it had sustained – but it was nowhere to be found. Neither the fire brigade nor the police wanted to help, and the police refused to bring a prosecution against the fire brigade.

So John lay in his hospital bed, labelled as just another silly kid who had fallen off his motorbike. He had been badly injured. His right wrist and left femur were broken and his right knee was smashed. He also had facial cuts and a lot of bruising. But when I went to visit him, it was his attitude that intrigued me. There was no bitterness at the injustice that he was suffering, just a calm determination to get better. Many teenagers would have been destroyed by the suffering and unfairness of such a situation, but John's attitude was very positive; as a consequence his recovery was surprisingly rapid.

Before the accident, John had often invited me to visit his traditional martial arts club. 'I know you'd be interested in what we do,' he had insisted and, when I protested that I didn't like violent sports, had added, 'it's not like you think.' But I kept putting it off. When I saw how he coped with the accident, I wanted to see for myself what had helped him so much, so I went along to his local club in Tunbridge Wells to watch a class.

It was so different from what I had imagined; graceful and

flowing; fascinating to watch the total commitment of the students; yet there was an incredible aura of peacefulness. It was certainly not the group of macho sweaty men beating hell out of each other that I had expected.

However, my excitement over what I had seen was not for myself. It was beautiful and exciting to watch, but I had no desire to participate. I rushed home to Terry. 'You said that you wanted to find a physical activity that you could take up. Well, I've just seen the perfect thing. It's so right for you, the strength, precise movements, the grace. I've told the teacher about your damaged leg, and he thinks that it wouldn't be a problem. Please come and see for yourself.'

Terry watched the class with interest. 'Well, I'd like to have a go, but I'll only join if you do.' I hesitated. It did arouse my curiosity, but there were no other women practising and I did have inhibitions left over from my childhood when I was always so clumsy. I had also developed ugly bunions on my feet, about which I was very self-conscious, and always tried to keep them hidden. Three weeks later I was no longer worried about such trivialities.

The classes were run on very traditional lines; even the instructions were given in Japanese. The discipline was strict. From the moment the students stepped onto the mat until the class was over, roughly two hours later, they did not speak unless the teacher (the Sensei) spoke to them, and then only to say *'hai'* or 'yes' to confirm that they understood. You will never hear a student use the word 'no' in the *dojo* (the Practice Hall).

We learnt in the simplest way, as very small children do, by watching and then copying. Children learn and absorb so much during their first four years of life, and acquire many skills: to walk, talk, feed themselves, and appreciate the dimensions and pleasures of the world around them. And all this is done before a child understands how to reason academically, and have doubts.

The Sensei would demonstrate a technique with one student while the rest of the class sat on their heels and watched, giving their full attention to what was being taught. The more I tried mentally to capture the movements, however simple, the more confused I became. '. . . right leg forward, left hand takes right wrist, left leg steps behind ...' I would try to memorise his movements but by the end of the sequence had forgotten how it began. The higher-grade students would try to lead me in the right direction but I felt pretty stupid, and my embarrassment made me awkward and stilted. I was still shy and, at thirty-seven, unused to being the pupil and having my movements scrutinised and corrected. But both Terry and I enjoyed the classes and after a few weeks Lindsay and Christopher joined in too.

The art of watching and copying took a long time to master, but it is so useful for many things in everyday life. I used to practise by mimicking the movement of people on television and this helped me get over the feeling of self-consciousness. Soon I lost the restriction of thinking 'I'll never be able to do that' and my fear of failure.

But the first thing I had to learn was to relax and breathe properly. It seems amazing that we can go through life not understanding this basic function. We did many breathing exercises, really filling and emptying our lungs, drawing breath from the lower abdomen as opera singers do, using our diaphragms for control. It is from the very pit of the stomach that the *kiai* – or shout – in karate comes. This is not just to intimidate but helps to add strength by a unity of breath and relaxed movement. The mere action of breathing out makes you relax; it is very difficult to run forward or even laugh if you hold your breath.

The best example of this is when we try to push a car. With feet firmly planted, arms extended, we shout 'OK, I'm ready,' and take a deep breath in and hold it. The tummy muscles tighten; arm muscles go stiff; and we go red in the face. It is only with brute strength and ignorance that we get the thing finally to move. It is far easier to take a deep breath and let it go when you need to push or lift anything heavy.

John's martial arts club 'Budokan' is fairly unusual. But then David Passmore, the chief instructor, is a very unusual man. He emanates an atmosphere which demands respect, but which, at the same time, makes you feel free. Like big mountains do. He is totally dedicated to the martial arts and a superb exponent and teacher. And 'arts' are what they are, requiring the search for perfection which that word implies. I was once told by a psychiatrist friend that we should never strive for perfection. It creates too many frustrations, he said. I think that it is our egos that we need to lose, then there is no problem.

David, a 6th Dan Black Belt, teaches budo, the bringing together of many of the disciplines. Karate teaches you to go forward and attack, to punch and kick, block and defend, but only using hard strength for the moment when it is really needed. Defence should be without conflict, using body movement to create space. A strong punch or kick can be avoided or deflected at the right distance with a flick of the wrist. Learning to get this right can be painful, but achieving harmony is never easy. With graceful flowing aikido you lead your attacker off balance using his own body movement, then throw him. But again the goal is harmony: 'conflict no conflict'. Jo-do and jo-jitsu involve defensive and attacking movements using a simple wooden pole. During the year 1588 the ruling Shogunate in Japan, Hideyoshi, banned the peasants from owning swords and other weapons. As a consequence they learnt to protect themselves with whatever they had, rice flails and stout sticks which could be effective even against a samurai sword. Bokken techniques, using a wooden sword, are perhaps the most interesting of all, as the martial arts draw their roots from the movement of the sword.

Black belts in the club also practise iaido, the art of drawing the sword using a metal blade. This takes great concentration and control of *ki*, the energy force which stems from the Centre, or *hara*, a point about two inches below the navel. It is quite difficult to keep this Centre steady and calm in all movements, but it is important that the flow of body and mind in harmony come from this point smoothly, giving a solid base for balance and energy.

All these different arts can be mixed together and greater understanding of one can grow from all of the others. Most martial arts clubs tend to separate each discipline and concentrate purely on karate, aikido, kendo or iaido, and there are many different styles, some competitive, of each one. I particularly love the subtlety and flexibility of budo.

In the martial arts it is the basis of any practice to harmonise mind, body and spirit. Normally we tend to waste a lot of our energy, spilling it out in many directions from our bodies, like heat escaping from an uninsulated house. Learning to control and direct energy could benefit everyone in so many ways, but is something which is not considered even in sport. Just as we regrettably no longer use our basic senses to their full potential, so we ignore a capability that we all have and which could save so much effort and stress. This control, which has enabled me to be strong enough to cope with so many hardships in my mountaineering and continue when others have given up, I gained mainly through sitting absolutely still in meditation.

One of the easiest ways to explain about directing energy is to rest an extended arm on someone's shoulder and ask them to use all their strength to bend it. If you try to maintain a straight arm by muscular power you will soon tire. However, if you relax and concentrate on letting the energy flow smoothly out from the Centre (or *hara*) along the arm out through the tips of the fingers, like water from a hose, it is impossible for the arm to be bent. I demonstrated this to a group of medical students in Pakistan and they were so impressed they nicknamed me 'Superwoman'! But after five minutes they could do it too.

Unfortunately body and mind are generally treated as two entirely separate entities, and yet the mind controls the body. If the mind says 'You can't go on,' the body will respond by not trying. But the mind gives in more easily than the body, and from my own experience in the mountains I know that even when I have felt that I have reached the limits of my endurance I could go on for a long time by co-ordinating mind, body, breathing and spirit. Using this harmonised energy in a controlled directed way makes wonderful things possible. This is how frail old masters of the martial arts are able to perform incredible feats of strength. Kurt has experienced this harmonisation too, when climbing at high altitude in the Himalayas. I realise more and more that he has come to understand many things during his life in the mountains that I have discovered in the *dojo*.

The famous breaking techniques are done by focusing this force on the object to be demolished. Normally we do not practise these, but I have broken bricks and house tiles for fun. Strangely there is no jarring at the moment of impact; on the contrary it is a 'soft action' as you do not concentrate on hitting the top of the object, as when hitting a nail with a hammer, but on a movement which goes through to the other side of the target.

Keeping the stillness of body and mind is one of the hardest things to maintain, especially when you first start doing *zazen*, or sitting meditation. It is an absolute quietness of body and mind that you strive for, total relaxation with full awareness – not easy when niggling discomforts and tickles make you lose concentration. Then you need to retreat to your *hara*. It is tremendous to sit in meditation in the peace of the mountains, or any wild place, or in a spot where a past civilisation has existed and you can feel and absorb the atmosphere of its history: places like Death Valley or Monument Valley National Park in America, Machu Picchu in Peru or the slate mines of North Wales. We get little time to sit totally peacefully in our lives, and it is a beautiful experience, especially when shared with others.

I have practised in many different countries when I have been on climbing trips abroad, in Europe, America and Asia, and have always been made welcome and made many friends. Traditional practice is universal.

My life has certainly opened up since I went to find out what helped John so much to recover from his accident and I have seen many other students change the quality of their lives as a result of their practice. Budokan has members from all walks of life and every student, young or old, who reaches a certain grade will be expected to teach, however lucid or literate, shy or retiring they may be. I have never known a bad teacher to evolve. Given the right encouragement and motivation people can do many things they never thought possible with great benefit to others. At the start of every class the students and teacher ask each other to 'Please teach me', and it certainly does go full circle. Through teaching you learn. I started to teach first within a normal class, then at a youth club when I was a Green Belt, 3rd Kyu. A year later I ran an Adult Education course before starting my own club within Budokan for adults and children in Crowborough. I particularly loved the junior class which included youngsters from five to fifteen years of age. It was an exciting group which had as much dedication and control as the adults' class.

Several parents were worried at first that their children might become aggressive and bully others as a result of their training, but in actual fact it has the opposite effect. The students learn respect for others and to understand pain and how easy it is to injure. My own son, who practised for two years, maintains that the martial arts not only taught him to control his temper but how to avoid being provoked in the first place, and many teachers have remarked on the improved concentration and behaviour of our young students. Even if youngsters drift away from the *dojo* to take up another interest, tasting many experiences is a necessary part of childhood, what they have learnt continues to help them: being able to copy movments, concentrate on one thing at a time and commit themselves to doing it without allowing inhibiting feelings to hold them back. This goes for students of all ages. As well as being an excellent form of exercise the martial arts can help people to widen the spectrum of their lives, like a camera lens opening up from a small aperture to see all around like a wide-angled fish eye.

David has a deep understanding of the philosophy and history of the martial arts and its practical aspects from karate competitions he took part in over a period of eight years in his younger days. However, he came to realise that such competitive practice was limited. His present traditional classes open doors to people of all ages and, as the belief is that you do not reach a true understanding until you are in the maturity of old age, give purpose to the present and great hope for the future.

When he developed cancer in 1982, after a particularly traumatic business period in his life, David's beliefs and teachings were well tested on a personal level. He took the brave decision to refuse the doctors' treatments after the growths were surgically removed, as the side effects would inhibit his life. Apart from a few days' break for the actual operations he has continued his martial arts practice without interruption, made a remarkable recovery and four years later is as strong and active as ever. I was lucky to find such a good teacher, who himself continues to extend his own knowledge through other good teachers.

However although Budokan classes are dynamic and physically demanding the martial arts are not just for the super fit; the various disciplines provide something for everybody, just as there are many facets to mountaineering. The basic philosophy is the same. Nevertheless the martial arts do derive from the arts of war, and their true reality remains a question of life and death. The present philosophy is well explained in Michael Random's beautifully illustrated book *The Martial Arts*. 'In the Meiji era (1868–1912) all forms of martial arts, beginning to lose their offensive character, took the name Budo – thus relating them to the traditional teaching of Japanese arts associated with peace and serenity. *Do* meaning the way or harmony, Budo means the martial arts (from *bu* meaning war and *do*, Way), or better still the "Way of the Warrior" in the chivalrous sense. In other words it gives a humanist significance to the martial arts.'

But for high grades that reality must have a meaning in the total commitment of the attacks and the precision of the defensive counters. Whether you are working with others or by yourself with an imaginary opponent, as in iaido or kata, the challenge is to stay in harmony with your opponent and yourself: to use the flow of the other's energy to create space, think as he does to anticipate his next moves, breathe in his rhythm. The one that loses that harmony loses the battle. Of course, as in life, there can be no continuous harmony, but the moments when it does happen are worth all the hard work of practice, and trying to achieve it again is what makes these arts so addictive.

Martial arts practice is like a bottomless pool; the deeper you look the more you want to see.

In a foreword to Michael Random's book Jean-Lucien Jazarin wrote: 'The martial arts cannot be practised as a form of entertainment or distraction. You cannot approach them tentatively with your fingertips, with a mere touch of the lips, or with superficial layers of thought or heart. It would be better never to become involved but if you do, it is essential to carry on to the end, until one's being is regenerated to the point of being made man again – a real man.'

That for me epitomises mountaineering too.

After I had been practising for a few months I realised that my approach to many things in life, and especially my climbing, had changed. A lot of things I had learnt in the *dojo* could also be used to improve my climbing and, even more important, the way in which I taught climbing. I made myself and my students breathe out when making a strenuous move and to relax. I understood far more about how muscles and joints worked. Warming-up exercises were explained and done in a logical sequence. Much emphasis is placed on developing a supple spine, and ankles, wrists, fingers and toes, parts often neglected in normal keep-fit classes. Practising slow controlled movements improved my balance and co-ordination. Moving from the Centre makes everything easier, and understanding that tiredness and pain do not mean one has to give up, the body can go on, has saved my life on several occasions.

Best of all I was enjoying my climbing more than ever before. It was fascinating to find two activities which complemented each other so well.

Dennis Kemp saw the change, and while he was on a climbing trip in Australia, he wrote me a poem.

First Poem

I will climb quietly, today

Today, the camp is empty,
I have no partner to climb with,
So, I go to Syrinx, to solo.

To solo, yes, but not to climb alone.
I shall be with Julie today;
Julie, nine sun-hours away;
150° of longitude;
Ten thousand miles of black-crow flight;
Julie, Black Belt,
will be with my every move
spiritually to encourage me
teach me, guide me,
to better integration of self and surroundings,
her Aikido way:

I stand under Tiger Wall,
200 metres of orange and grey craggy steepness,

massive red overhangs on high.
Syrinx; grade 10 the guidebook says
and a three-star route: highly recommended.
An English 'Diff', say; the rock is good,
well within my competence to climb.

I will climb quietly today,
Planning the moves first in my mind
then placing foot and hand with precision.
Layback; bridge; jam;
pull up to the next ledge
and rest
aware of my breath,
of the response of my heart.
I look at the grey lichen
curling at the edges in the heat and the dry;
I enjoy the company of a minute shrub,
only a stem and a dozen serrated leaves,
rooted in the narrowest of cracks.
Hang in there, my friend. That crack is your life
and the rockface beyond you offers me
hand-sized cracks for contemplation.
Should I go that way? The first moves will be easy,
but what beyond?
Look ahead! There is scant room for errors, soloing.
Faulty judgement or performance
could receive harsh sentence.

All is going well.
The rock hugs my fingers,
warm to the touch, and warm in colour:
I feel the breeze on my cheek;
a plant scents the air,
a fly buzzes my ear,
I concentrate; on body awareness
balance
movement.
Ah! that foot placement was inexact –
it had an element of shuffle in it.
There is no-one to see me,
To say 'Could that be better?'
But I know it could be better
for Julie is at my elbow
inspiring me to strive for excellence.

Why should her black belt
influence me here in Australia?

World's end to a new horizon

It is not the award,
but the manner of the giving,
that influences me so strongly.

The view unfolds, the sky draws nearer —
the half-moon is a minute white smudge in the blue of the east.
A falcon towers on a column of air
the greybird calls in the descent gully,
rockwalls echoing the notes.

The climb is finished.
No heroics, no drama,
no desperate moments.
No-one was watching; simply
a very personal awareness; experience.

Thank you, David,
for extending my world
through your pupil
and friend.

Dennis Kemp
Arapiles
November 1981

4

Harrison's and handicaps

In early 1978, eight years after we had taken back the Festerhaunt, we sold it again. Although we were very sad to lose the regular contact with our many customers, we knew we would see them climbing at the Rocks and many of them had become such good friends that they came to the house to see us. Administratively the climbing shop and café had ceased to be fun. The delivery of equipment from the manufacturers had become totally unpredictable and we were constantly having to apologise to customers when tents, sleeping bags, jackets, etc. did not arrive for several weeks. Cheap substantial attractive food became increasingly expensive to produce, and the complicated book-keeping that became necessary with the introduction of Value Added Tax became a hassle I could well live without.

We had built up the Festerhaunt from nothing to a business which had become world famous amongst climbers. Our Visitor's Book looked like an international *Who's Who* of the climbing fraternity, and our takings compared with many of the London climbing shops. It would have made a perfect extension to one of the larger chains of camping-climbing retailers, but at that time none of them had the finance or staff to take it on. A private buyer bought the business, and although he said that he wanted to continue it as we had run it, in a couple of years he sold it and the new owner got permission to convert the building to a private house. For five years it stood empty, looking unkempt and forlorn, but in 1985 it changed hands again and is being resurrected as a café.

While Terry and I had been teaching rock climbing during the week on a part-time basis when we still had the Festerhaunt,

Marion had looked after it very efficiently. However, she eventually decided to go back to teaching, and a year later surprised us by marrying Dick. The only members of our semi-adopted family so far to fall in love, they now have a family of their own.

When Marion left we reverted to opening only at weekends, which was when the bulk of the climbers came to the Rocks. Our climbing instruction commitments increased with the extension of the school-leaving age from fifteen to sixteen, until we were working quite a hectic seven-day week. Another reason why we sold the Festerhaunt.

We teach mainly at Harrison's Rocks. This is a sandstone edge on one side of a river valley, extending for 650 yards and offering a very wide variety of climbing problems. Chimneys, face climbs, cracks and overhangs of all grades. The very hard routes offer some extremely difficult technical climbing, and it is possible to practise climbing to a very high standard safely on all the local outcrops as we use a top-roping system. In the mountains, climbs are done in a series of pitches, or rope lengths. The lead climber must take up the rope, towing it behind him until he finds a suitable 'stance' or place where he can stop and tie himself onto the rock. This is called a 'belay'. He then brings up the second on the other end of the rope, and when he is securely tied on, the leader continues up the next pitch. To safeguard himself between belays he places runners, which are points of attachment to the rock through which the rope runs, so that if he falls off at any point he, hopefully, will only fall as far as the top runner plus that distance again, providing it remains in place. Runners nowadays are made of different sized shapes of metal which jam into cracks or small holes in the rocks. Climbing ethics have changed and anything that scars the rock is no longer acceptable. They have a short sling attached and the climbing rope runs through a metal snaplink or 'carabiner' which is clipped into this sling. Placing these properly is an interesting part of the climbing as they must be able to take a shock loading in the correct direction in the event of a fall. It is not just the mechanics of placing these nuts and chocks which is a skill, but doing so whilst hanging on with one hand with your feet perched on minute holds or almost invisible depressions in the rock. Taking them out again is quite an art and the job of the second as he climbs up. Heaven help him if he does not retrieve them all; they are very expensive to replace.

At Harrison's we simply go to the top of the rocks and tie a long sling to a suitable tree. The climbing rope is clipped through a carabiner and both ends are dropped to the foot of the climb. The climber ties onto one end and the second takes in the other as he goes up, so that should the climber fall he will only drop as far as the rope stretches. With the danger of falling for long distances removed, and as the climbs are never longer than forty feet, it is possible to practise climbing to a very high standard fairly quickly. Heavy usage of the soft sandstone makes many of the holds erode rapidly and become downward sloping without sharp edges. Using these soon builds up strong fingers and forearms.

Many climbers visit these rocks from all over the world. Harrison's must be the smallest climbing ground with the highest usage anywhere.

I mentioned earlier that Dennis Kemp and some friends had bought Harrison's in the 1950s and placed them into trust. During the seventies thousands of people a year were visiting them and it became necessary to build a car park as the road verges were being destroyed by the hundreds of cars. The Sports Council kindly stepped in with a grant and organised the building of a large car park and handsome sandstone-faced toilet block. For several years the management of Bowles Rocks, now also a trust, looked after the car park on a part-time basis, but it soon became apparent that it would be an advantage to have someone more permanently involved: someone whom climbers would recognise and relate to and would see as a climber as well as an authoritarian figure. Terry fitted the bill perfectly, and the job was ideal for our lifestyle too. Five years ago he became the Warden of Harrison's Car Park. But this is a strange *Clochemerle* situation. The car park and toilet block cost so much money to build that the Sports Council had to give them an official title and designated them a National Centre, on a par with the National Mountaineering Centre at Plas Y Brenin in North Wales and Crystal Palace, the National Sports Centre. Terry is paid a management fee for looking after this facility but not for the Rocks themselves, which he wardens on a purely voluntary basis. He can lay claim to several titles: Manager of a National Centre, Warden of Harrison's Rocks, or just a car park and lavatory attendant – a diversity which his sense of humour enjoys.

He has become well respected over the years. His large bearded figure is easily recognisable, and being a climber himself and understanding that the climbing fraternity are rather anarchistic and do not appreciate rules and regulations (which at Harrison's are kept to a minimum) he appeals to the climbers' common sense if they do anything which could be detrimental to others or the Rocks. Usually his sense of humour wins them over; otherwise his well-built presence deters them from arguing. The toilet block, which stands in a remote woodland half a mile from the outcrop, must be the most unvandalised set of public lavatories in Britain.

Over the years Terry and I have become well known as climbing instructors and he has been able to adapt to the limited use of his left leg. He can still rock climb very competently, but negotiating rough ground over long distances can be a problem for him. Most of the time we make a reasonable living from our teaching although periods of bad weather are a problem. Nowadays people seem less tough than they were ten years ago, and many groups will cancel if it is raining. If they do, we do not get paid, one of the penalties of being self-employed.

Somehow in the early days we scraped through these thin times by borrowing, selling things and living very frugally. It was a great relief when Terry started to earn a regular fee from the Sports Council. Today we can afford to save money to see us through those 'rainy days'. Over the years we have sacrificed quite a lot financially to enjoy the lifestyle we have chosen, but no money could possibly buy the adventures and pleasure we have had. I certainly have no regrets.

Rock climbing and mountaineering are activities very akin to the martial arts in that you can be shown the way but most of the discovering you must do for yourself. This is what makes both extremely exciting to teach. A very wide variety of people come to our courses: the Police, Army, Fire Brigade, Scouts and Guides, youth groups, Adult Education courses and many odd individuals like stunt men and actors. When we help with filming, we often meet terrified actors who have absolutely no knowledge of climbing but have told the casting director that they are budding Boningtons in order to get the job.

Sandstone is technically in a class of its own, and many excellent climbers from granite or limestone areas have difficulty when they visit our Rocks. Getting off the ground is often the hardest part. Over the years the ground at Harrison's has eroded away at the foot of the rocks making the first holds more and more difficult to reach. Often Terry and I have to act as stand-ins because the actors find the climbing too difficult.

One such occasion was during the filming of a commercial for wool. Paul arrived on location wearing pristine white wool trousers which left nothing to the imagination and showed off his well-developed leg muscles perfectly. On his top half he wore a tartan wool shirt. He strutted around puffing out his chest and flexing his muscles. I was impressed by his physique. When he tried to climb the chosen route, however, he failed miserably – he had obviously never climbed on sandstone before.

After a lot of struggling and grunting from poor Paul, Terry was asked to stand in. He was not as tall or apparently as well-built as Paul, and he opted out of wearing the revealing white leotard-type trousers. He did put on the tartan shirt though and was calmly stepping forward to pick up the climbing rope when . . . ping! All the buttons flew off. The embarrassed actor looked as if he wanted to crawl into a hole. Not only had he failed to perform on the rocks, but all his body-building training had been negated when Terry took a normal breath!

The main part of our teaching is with older school children from Kent, Sussex and the Inner London Education Authority. This is interesting work as the children come from all types of educational establishments, from single sex public schools to those for the educationally subnormal. We are given a totally free hand to decide what to include in a session and if the weather, mood or ability of the group is not right for rock climbing we can set up an adventurous river crossing, mystery map reading walk or a lesson in search and rescue and first aid. General information about the animal and plant life around the Rocks falls naturally into every course, and we encourage the regular groups to involve themselves in the voluntary upkeep of the area, usually rewarding their efforts with a bonfire and baked potatoes. We have a very informal relationship with our students and the first session always includes a lot of easy scrambles without ropes to build up their confidence in us and in their own abilities. As well as rock faces to climb up, we have tunnels to crawl through, slabs to slide down and a mud-slide to get them really dirty. Despite our advice to wear old clothes many children turn up in their best jeans and jackets, which they use as an excuse to opt out of the action if they are a little uncertain about their capabilities as rock climbers. Once they are dirty they can start to relax and have fun. 'My mum could never do that,' is a regular comment that I get from pupils, but I am sure that many parents would love to have the opportunity to shatter their kids' illusions. I hope too that my example gives them hope for their own futures, and that at forty and fifty they will be out climbing and letting their hair down with their own children.

Climbing is one of the few non-competitive sports taught in schools and I think it is very important for young people to learn to extend themselves without the constant pressure of competition. Luckily it is not always the most athletic who become the most successful. It always pleases me greatly if the underdog of a group (because of build or lack of academic intelligence) gradually evolves as the most skilled. It happens fairly often and a great deal of much-needed self-confidence is gained at one end with lessons in humility and respect for the less fortunate at the other.

One of the good things about rock climbing locally is that it is easy to continue after leaving school. All that is necessary is a rope and pair of plimsolls or training shoes. You can always find someone to climb with at the rocks. Terry and I have been teaching for over twenty years and to our delight often meet pupils from the past climbing with their own families.

We also have groups from the Intermediate Treatment scheme which helps young people who have committed minor misdemeanours to find new outlets for their energies. Some youngsters turn to crimes, such as stealing cars, shoplifting and disturbing the peace to bring more excitement into their lives. After appearing in Court they may be committed to attend a centre where they are introduced to new activities and, it is hoped, also develop a stronger social conscience from the new experiences and their leaders. If the unit is well run it is an excellent scheme and a good alternative to our other corrective methods such as preventive detention, but sometimes the social workers are weak and allow the children to rule them. I am all for a kinder form of reformatory training, but it is during our youth that we learn life's social boundaries and are constantly testing to find out how far we can go. Young people (and many older ones) often need an adult to tell them when enough is enough.

Unfortunately when people have been categorised they will try to retain the image they have been labelled with: 'difficult' children will try to be just that, particularly when meeting new people in authority.

The first time I met an Intermediate Treatment group they flatly refused to get out of the minibus.

'F. . . off!' they shouted.

'Don't want to go to your sodding rocks,' said a six-foot Hell's Angel. I soon learnt that tough, aggressive-sounding youngsters are often the most insecure when faced with a previously unexperienced challenge. However, they are usually intelligent enough to realise that not only their safety but also their reputation with the rest of the group lies in the hands of the person instructing them. It would be easy for them to lose face if their ability did not match their mouths. Both Terry and I insist on good behaviour while they are at the Rocks, climbing is too dangerous for messing about and there are other climbers to be considered. Harrison's is owned by climbers for climbers, and they are privileged to be there.

There is no magic formula for maintaining discipline. It is a question of experience. Both Terry and I worked for several months in a Detention Centre as social workers. We wanted to learn more about young offenders and how to help them. I would return home completely worn out by the constant abuse and swearing, and the frustration of not being able to give any positive help in changing their young lives. These were mainly old hands even at fifteen and sixteen and they were already cynical and knew the best way to milk the system. A pair of new jeans would be supplied for a Court appearance; the next day they would have disappeared. 'Someone must have nicked them,' was the usual cry, but we all knew they had been sold for cigarettes. With the new scourge of drug abuse I wonder how they now raise enough money to get a 'fix'. Our penal system is not a great deterrent to crime for young people once they have a record and are no longer worried about their reputations. It is generally very lenient and the often-changing academic theories of how to treat offenders are not always very practical.

I tend to treat all young people in the same way that I brought up my own children, saying 'no' when necessary and meaning it, tempering firmness with love.

One day I joined a particularly noisy IT group at the foot of the Rocks. Immediately I asked them to be quieter and to stop swearing, explaining that people living close to the outcrop had sensitive ears and a right to some peace. I also found it boring to hear the same four-letter words constantly repeated. I looked down at the ground. It was covered with discarded sweet papers. 'Please pick up your litter.' I asked them. 'There is no one employed to clear up after you and it means that people like Terry and I have to do it.' They muttered a bit, but cleaned up the mess.

One lad – his name was Shaun – was sitting on a rock; he had not moved. Slowly he took a sweet out of his pocket and after unwrapping it made a big show of throwing the paper onto the ground.

'Please pick it up!' I asked him, twice.

'Sod off!' was his impolite reply.

The social worker said nothing, but looked worried.

'Pick it up!' I ordered, and flicked at his ear with my fingers.

He rose to his feet, his face flushed with anger. 'Don't you hit me,' he screamed. 'No one does that to me. I break people's arms for things like that.'

I looked at him. He was a slightly built lad of about sixteen. 'Great, go ahead,' I replied. 'But pick up that sweet paper first.' I heard the other lads sniggering behind me. Shaun bent down and, muttering something about killing me, stuffed the wrapper into his pocket. Then he wandered away and sat down by himself.

'Why is he with your corrective unit?' I asked the social worker.'

'He's been convicted of causing actual bodily harm,' he told me. 'He's a real tough nut. This time he was arrested because he stabbed someone.'

I left Shaun alone for a while and then led him round a corner away from the view of the rest of the group. I put my arm round his shoulders and gave him a squeeze. 'What's the problem?' I asked.

All his tough exterior crumpled. 'I'm scared about the climbing,' he whispered.

'Don't worry, I won't ask you to climb anything you're not capable of, but you'll have to trust my judgement.'

For the rest of the afternoon Shaun did not leave my side, and because I had his interest as leader of the group, I had no trouble from the rest.

'D'you think I really could do that?' he would ask me at the foot of each climb, then arrive at the top with a big smile on his face.

'I've never seen him look happy before,' the social worker confided. 'He's normally the one who stirs up all the others, a right little so-and-so.'

Terry and I are not just interested in turning out skilled rock climbers. It is the opportunity to talk to young people about life in general, and show them what is around them and give them ideas for ways to fill their ever-increasing leisure time which is equally important. Rock climbing is a sport which leaves time for conversation. It seems to relax people, perhaps because of the concentrated effort of struggling up a climb and the personal achievement of succeeding. Maybe the youngsters feel that as we have grown-up children ourselves and have been closely involved with teenagers over many years, we have sympathy and experience to listen. At home, too, many young people with temporary problems regard us as second parents. Some have grown up and are now married. At this moment four teenage girls have attached themselves to us – it certainly helps to keep Terry young!

All the young people with whom we have been so closely involved have special qualities, like Peter, the brother of John who introduced me to the martial arts. He was nick-named 'Little Pete' because he was only thirteen when he started to climb many of the very hard routes in North Wales. One climber almost fell off Cemetery Gates when he struggled round the corner to find a little blond boy leading the crux move of this Extreme climb.

Peter had done his first very cautious leading with Christopher on a practice slab just a year earlier when we had a family trip to North Wales. He was a natural and could easily have become one of Britain's top climbers. However, nowadays you have to be very competitive to get to, and stay at, the top and he prefers to keep a low profile. A couple of years ago I climbed Cemetery Gates with Peter, when he was ten years older, and it was a joy to climb with him. One of the pleasures I get from climbing is watching someone moving smoothly and competently on rock; it is a form of vertical ballet and visually very aesthetic. Peter also took up martial arts, for which he also has a natural ability. He is now a 2nd Dan.

Tim is another member of our expanded family. Before we met him he was very overweight – his mother was such a good cook he could not resist her food. His teenage contemporaries teased him so much that he became embarrassed to go out, and when he was eighteen he decided that he must do something about his obesity. He started by not eating so much and exercising with a Bull Worker in his bedroom. When Tim is determined to do something he always succeeds, and in eight months he lost four stone. In recent years he has taken up marathon running and collected more than £3,500 for charity from his efforts. He has also competed in a quadrathon, for which he had to swim two miles in the sea, walk fifty kilometres, cycle one hundred miles and then run a marathon. Unfortunately bad blisters prevented him from running the final marathon section, but for a totally self-motivated young man I find his efforts very impressive.

The most rewarding teaching has to be with children with handicaps. Several years ago we were asked to help with a holiday group. 'We've got two hours and would like them all to do a climb,' one of the well-meaning helpers told us.

I looked at the group. Twenty-two children. All but two were in wheel-chairs and these were pretty girls with stunted growth and no arms – their mothers had taken Thalidomide during pregnancy. One by one we hauled them up a rock face. As many had no speech it was not possible to tell whether they were enjoying it or were terrified.

'Thanks,' the helpers said as they left. 'We can go back and say that everyone did a climb.'

As we drove home I thought about the children. I wondered how many of them had truly benefited from the experience. In future, I swore to myself, I would only teach climbing to handicapped people for their personal needs, at their individual pace and for their own enjoyment.

Not long after I was lucky enough to be asked if I was prepared to instruct a group of children from a school for the blind. Dennis Parker, the sports master, already knew Terry and myself as he had previously taught at one of the other schools which came to the Rocks. As with anyone whom I teach to rock climb, the first priority is to gain their confidence and to build up their own self-assurance. Not many sports really test your physical strength. Rock climbing is very akin to gymnastics, requiring a lot of physical effort until technique is acquired. Girls in particular are very unsure of their arm strength and need to learn right from the start to push with their stronger legs rather than pull away with their arms to gain height.

The blind children were physically very fit and we soon overcame their lack of vision by telling them where the holds were and in which direction to use them. 'There's a pocket hold at two o'clock; put your fingers in and pull to the left;' or 'a ledge is just above your waist, press down with both your hands and walk your feet up.' As they got more used to me and the different problems which the rock offered, we could simply tap on the rock where the next hold was and the sound would direct them, giving them a greater freedom from constant instructions. Of course, not all the children were totally blind, but that often caused more difficulties, as those with partial vision would see holds and distances in a distorted fashion. I discovered that even people with no sight feel the sensation of exposure.

When all the initial problems had been solved, I felt that we could use outdoor pursuits to link these teenagers to those from an able-bodied school. Most of them were boarders at Dorton House, near Sevenoaks, during term time, and although the school is in a magnificent large country mansion in a beautiful setting, they were isolated and their knowledge of what went on in normal teenage life was limited.

I spoke to Dick Boetius, a longstanding friend, who was then teaching at Trinity School in Croydon. He had taught many of his sixth-formers to be competent rock climbers, cavers and canoeists, and one of the places they often visited were the gently rolling mountains of the Brecon Beacons in South Wales. Dick also had the use of a barn which had a camping field outside. It was the ideal place for the blind children to extend themselves further.

The first trip was a great success. Dick, Dennis Parker and I took a step back and watched the sixth-formers make friends with and help their less fortunate contemporaries. The idea was to give the blind youngsters as much freedom as possible to do things for themselves, Dick's boys working on a one-to-one basis with them.

The blind teenagers slept in tents outside the barn, within easy call of help if it was needed but with the feeling that they were on their own. When they put up their tents, Dick's lads stood near and chatted to them. They slipped the odd helpful comment into the conversation when necessary. 'Have you heard that latest single by The Who . . . the tent peg you're looking for is by your right foot . . . it's a really great record.' We had allowed plenty of time so that they could be as independent as possible.

The following day Dick organised a caving trip. I felt as apprehensive as they did as we entered the entrance to the cave. It was actually my first experience of exploring underground. The blind youngsters were at no great disadvantage as they could feel the rock walls of the narrow tunnels, tell which direction they were going in by the flow of the water, and find passages by the sound of side streams or by voice, using the acoustics. Walking along feeling the ground under the river with my feet, crawling on my tummy through narrow tunnels, I shut my eyes. Yes, with the right unobtrusive supervision, caving was ideal for people with limited or no vision.

In the afternoon we emerged into the sunshine and went canoeing. Dick had done a lot of the basic work in the school swimming pool and they were all at home on the water. On the spacious still waters of Llangorse Lake their feeling of freedom was a pleasure to see. For those who wanted a bit of peace to paddle around quietly by themselves this was the ideal place. In the ever-accompanying safety boat the Trinity boys kept quiet if they were watching a solo canoeist, not wanting to disturb his or her tranquillity. For the more lively ones, they organised a game of water borne 'He'.

The next day was spent walking on the green mountains of the Brecon Beacons. On uneven ground, instead of holding Cynthia's arm, I put my hand underneath hers and rested her arm on top of mine. That way I was able to lead her more easily, pointing her this way or that, lifting my hand if she needed to step over a rock on the ground. Spoken instructions did not need to interrupt our interesting conversation. In suitable places I would walk with her shoulder to shoulder. She soon picked up my movements and could feel the angle of the grassy slope. If the terrain was easy enough I could even take one pace away so that she could walk without the feeling of being controlled. She had become suddenly blind at the age of 15, a year earlier, and must have felt horribly restricted.

Future trips followed regularly and more and more adventurous possibilities opened up. Making and sailing hay rafts right across the lake; two-day camping expeditions; more adventurous caving. The best day for me was when Jeremy, a quiet, totally blind boy of sixteen who also happened to be coloured and felt the cold badly, had gained enough confidence to run down the gentle inclines by himself. This time he was the first person to get back to the minibus; usually he was the last.

I backed slowly, and rather reluctantly, out of the work with the blind school, leaving it to Dick and his very able pupils to continue. They no longer needed my help and I wanted to work with other handicapped people. I tried to keep up my contact with them by occasional trips to South Wales, and would try to bring along one of our friends whom I thought would be interesting for the group to meet: people like Dennis Kemp, who told them fascinating stories of his travels round the world.

There are many children with unlabelled handicaps among the groups which come to the Rocks from normal schools. Terry and I can usually spot them fairly quickly and give them the extra attention they need, but a faster method is to watch Pila, our hairy black Briard dog. She is the French version of the Old English Sheepdog, but easier to groom and totally uncomplicated in character.

We meet and introduce ourselves to each new class on the car park at Harrison's and during the half-mile walk through the woods to the Rocks, if Pila walks close to one young person in particular, he or she is the one with problems. Pila is not a dog who worries for attention, she is very self-contained, but perhaps because she came from a broken home herself she is sensitive to people with problems. When she was a puppy she lived with her Briard mother and an Afghan hound, in a family that had two young children. The husband and wife split up and the dogs were put into kennels. When we bought Pila she was six months old and so insecure that she would panic and wet the carpet if we even raised our voices to scold her. Today she is very placid and stable. She is an amazing dog and seems to have a sixth sense when she can be of comfort to someone. One of the blind children told me once that she never minded waiting to be escorted down from the top of the rocks. 'Pila always comes and gives me such a lovely cuddle.'

We have worked with a lot of handicapped people over the years, but the next real challenge came with a group of severely mentally handicapped pupils from Grange School near Maidstone. Many of the children had lived in the adjoining hospital, like David, a happy energetic lad who suffered from Down's Syndrome. He soon became a competent rock climber, but his problem was that he was terrified of dogs. When he first saw Pila he ran back into the safety of the minibus and took a lot of coaxing to come back out. Pila stayed away from him and we showed him how to make her sit by voice and hand command, even from a distance. At the end of that session he sat in the car with Pila, and on future visits his first question would be 'Where's Pila?' After a few more weeks he would clip her onto a long sling and lead her around the rocks, reluctantly giving her back to us when he went back to school. Our work in this field is not a question of turning out rock climbers, but of helping to broaden horizons for young people who are very limited by their disabilities. Some did become competent on the easier routes, but sometimes it took a while before their eyes came to life and we knew they had taken a real step forward.

As our knowledge of how best to help them increased, Marcus Frisby, the very capable master who looked after the physical activities at the school, started to bring down the more severely handicapped children who were not very physically able. Simon was such a case. He was also a victim of Down's Syndrome, but he had only one lung and had difficulty breathing. Simon found it an effort to walk even twenty-five yards and would be forced to sit down gasping to recover his breath. He was very insecure and had to cling on to either someone or something; even carrying the climbing rope gave him comfort. Like many of the severely mentally handicapped children he would stand with his shoulders hunched and his arms crossed tightly across his body, hugging himself.

The first thing that I did was to stroke his fingertips towards me, talking to him reassuringly until he gradually unwound his arms and reached for my hands, which I slowly drew further back. Once his arms were extended I kept brushing his fingertips, drawing him forward but not letting him take hold of my hands. One step, two steps. It was slow progress, but a great achievement for him. Many of these children have never walked on uneven ground before. Their world was restricted to school and hospital corridors and concrete pathways. To have to step over and round different-sized boulders was like an obstacle race for them. We gradually increased the distance and steepness for Simon. First the path beneath the rocks was enough of a challenge, then he graduated to the gulleys, and several months later started to do simple climbs. The progress he made was tremendous, both with his co-ordination and his breathing. One day he ran away for fun and I had trouble keeping up with him. It was quite a relief for me too when he ran out of steam and we both sat on a rock to regain our breath.

Every child that came to the rocks with Marcus gained something, but the most dramatic has to be Mark. His mother had contracted German measles while she was pregnant and he was born almost totally blind and deaf. As he was also very mentally disturbed it was difficult for the doctors to assess the true extent of his disabilities. He lived in a very shut-off world with little expression on his face.

It took a lot of time initially to gain his confidence and get him to co-operate enough to make him realise that he could enjoy the physical activity of climbing. Once he did he was a changed person. We always make the children wear climbing helmets; some have a very poor sense of balance and the majority are epileptics. At first Mark had refused to wear a helmet and would hurl it away in temper if we insisted. Later, when he got pleasure from climbing, the moment he felt its hard dome-shape in his hands he would put it on his head and jump up and down with delight, making it difficult to fasten the strap.

Over the months I began to suspect that he had more vision than we thought and I put my theory to the test. I took his arm and led him towards a large boulder. He avoided it. I moved on to a smaller one. He avoided that one too. I chose smaller and smaller obstacles and he never kicked them with his feet. At the foot of the next climb, instead of tying the rope around his waist, I dropped it in front of him. He saw it fall and bent down and picked it up. He handed it to Marcus who was standing behind him, pulling at Marcus's hands, urging him to tie him on so that he could start climbing. Mark would never see very well, but climbing unlocked something in him. He came to life and started to smile.

Although it is slightly hazardous, it is very rewarding work. Sometimes in a moment of frustration a youngster may bite, or lash out, and many have no sense of fear or danger and can suddenly hurl themselves down on you for no apparent reason. My anticipatory and evasive skills learnt in the *dojo* have been invaluable. This is the only group we teach that always come to the rocks whatever the weather.

All the work that we have done would not have been possible without the background knowledge of the children that Marcus had, or his trust to allow us to push the children to do things that might seem impossible. It is difficult not to be too protective, especially when the youngsters often have no way of telling us themselves how they feel.

'All the children that have attended on a regular basis show a marked improvement in all areas of ability,' Marcus wrote in a report. 'This embraces both physical achievement and mental awareness. A small number are now physically highly competent, but even children who are not as dramatic as this now have immense knowledge of themselves and their environment, due to the availability of exploratory experience, often denied for many reasons.

'Increased mobility, strength, spatial and body awareness are all tangible physical benefits of this activity, but so are the rewards of getting wet in the rain, being allowed to sit in the mud, feeling changes in the seasons, experiencing the many different textures, tastes and noises of outdoor life . . .'

For the past year or so I have had little time for teaching, and I feel particularly sad about this when Terry comes home with stories of how well the children from Grange School are doing. However much enjoyment they get from coming to the Rocks, my pleasure in the time we shared together was greater.

5

A question of fate

We were having dinner at High Rocks Hotel to celebrate Terry's birthday in June 1976. Just as we finished our hors d'oeuvres the waiter came over to our table. 'Excuse me, sir, there's a telephone call for you – a Mr Kurt Diemberger.'

We were surprised. We had not heard from Kurt for over a year. The last time we met, in 1975, he had been in England on a lecture tour. As he had never climbed in this country, and expressed a wish to climb on sea cliffs, Terry had insisted that Dennis and I should meet him in North Wales and show him the delights of Welsh rock.

The first night, at Dennis's house in Cilcain, a small village not far from Mold, Dennis and Kurt had put on a slide show for some of our climbing friends and neighbours. After a while they forgot about the audience and became engrossed in showing each other their pictures. Both are superb photographers, and had often approached a subject in the same way, which was interesting. But what was most fascinating was the creative artistry they both portrayed in their photographs. The images appearing on the screen were more than pretty pictures, they pleased the soul.

The next day we had driven over to Snowdonia. Kurt leapt out of the car and ran most of the way down the Llanberis Pass, his camera clicking furiously to record the dramatic grey granite cliffs, the backdrop to many climbing epics, which give the steep-sided valley such a powerful atmosphere. I was pleasantly surprised that someone who had climbed some of the world's highest mountains was so impressed and excited by our British hills. Later we climbed halfway up Snowdon, to just below the airy traverse of Crib Goch. There Kurt showed me where to find crystals. (It was his hobby as a crystal hunter which had started him climbing.) We found some little ones, but left them to nestle in the hollow of rock which protected them. It was enough to know they were there.

It was a crisp November day with a clear alpine blue sky as Kurt and his attractive wife, Teresa, followed Dennis and me back down the rocky hillside. Patches of ice had spilled over the icicle-hung stream, forming sparkling transparent sheets beneath which the water still flowed in wobbly patterns. There were crystals all around us. It was an invigorating day.

'My feet are hurting very much,' Teresa complained. Her boots were borrowed for this unexpected excursion and did not fit very well. A little farther on she flopped down on the icy grass and started to take off the instruments of her torture. 'You can't take off your boots here, you could get frostbite,' Kurt remonstrated with his young wife, but no amount of vociferous cajoling could persuade her to put them back on. Italian is a noisy language; even a gentle discussion sounds like an argument. It took quite a lot of discussion before Teresa agreed at least to wear a safety rope, in case she fell on the slippery surface of the frozen grass or glassy frozen puddles and started an uncontrollable slide down the long slope. I still chuckle at the vision of this famous Austrian mountain guide leading his rebellious charge down a Welsh mountainside covered in patches of snow and ice, in her socks.

That evening Kurt had lectured to mountaineers in Llanberis until two in the morning – the audience would not let him leave – and the following day we arranged to meet several of our friends at Wen Zawn on the nearby island of Anglesey. Unfortunately we arrived too late in the day for Kurt to climb the impressive route A Dream of White Horses, which traverses the cliff face high above the ever-moving sea. I had already climbed it with Dennis and it was a route which had delighted me.

We separated into ropes of two and each pair chose a different climb. I opted for DDE, an HVS route I had not tried before and, with the smooth-moving Tim Jepson, an Instructor from the National Mountaineering Centre at Plas Y Brenin, as a climbing partner, danced enjoyably from hold to hold.

Kurt was climbing on a parallel route with Rowland Edwards,

a Welsh mountain guide. Wen was their choice, a steep crack leading vertically up the cliff. From a promontory to one side of the zawn, where we had all sat and picnicked before climbing, Wen Slab looks impressively steep and holdless. It does have an angle of 80°. But the sight is made even more dramatic by the clash of rolling waves hitting the base of the cliff. The frothing white spume sprays into the air for twenty to thirty feet, as the force of the North Atlantic ocean smashes against the rock, and then with a thirsty suck draws back to come in again with another resounding booming explosion. You have to abseil down to the start of the climb, over the edge of the sheer cliff towards the hissing, frothing sea.

It was the first time that Kurt had climbed on sea cliffs. I could hear his shouts of pleasure floating across the rock face. As we all neared the top a golden sunset painted the sea, and the mournful sound of the fog horn heralded banks of rolling sea mist drifting across the water from the horizon. We sat on the cliff top and watched the spectacle until the silent mist enveloped us. It was the perfect last scene to the day.

The next morning Teresa had to fly back to Italy to take an important examination – she was studying to be a lawyer. Dennis dropped us all at Liverpool Airport on his way to college. 'See you this evening,' he called to me as he drove off. I had come to the airport as it was my job to make sure that Kurt got to Manchester in time for an important British Mountaineering Council lecture that evening, and because Kurt and I wanted to return across the fabled Mersey ferry to Dennis's house where Kurt had left his lecture slides.

'All flights from this Airport are delayed because of fog,' we were informed over the public address system, first at nine o'clock ... then at ten ... eleven ... mid-day. I grew nervous. It would take at least four hours to pick up Kurt's slides from Dennis's house and ensure that he got to Manchester in time for the lecture. His deadline there was six o'clock that evening. At two o'clock I was really worried; there was still no sign of the flight leaving. 'Kurt, I know you don't want to leave Teresa, but I think we must get the slides. If we hire a car we can just do it and then come back to find out what is happening,' I suggested, and thankfully he agreed.

We drove as fast as I dared. We had to hire the car with Kurt's driving licence as I did not have mine with me, but arrange for me to drive as I knew the way: along the dual carriageway, round roundabouts, and finally into the one-car narrow country lanes that make Cilcain such a desirable lorry-free place to live. We grabbed the slides and Kurt's belongings and sped off again back to Liverpool airport. With relief we learnt that Teresa's flight had finally gone. I drove to the station and Kurt just caught a train which would get him to Manchester with three minutes to spare. He gave me a quick hug. 'Thank you, Julie, it was all a wonderful adventure,' he said before running down the stairs.

The telephone call on Terry's birthday was from Tunbridge Wells Station and I went to fetch Kurt.

'I'm staying at St Katherine's Dock on the Thames in London,' Kurt started his explanation as we resumed our meal. 'My brother-in-law, Herbert Radichnig, has bought a yacht in Denmark, and we have just sailed it to England to have it refitted. It's a very beautiful boat, a two-masted catamaran with sonar equipment and so on; it's quite big – they had to raise Tower Bridge to let it through! But the reason that I'm here is because I want to repay Julie for the beautiful Welsh adventure. The boat has to go to Southampton on Monday to the boatyard. We thought that we would sail it over to France for the weekend and would like you to come with us, Julie.'

I was a little taken aback. The offer attracted me immensely but I hardly knew Kurt. In Wales there had always been a crowd of people around him and the only time I had been alone with him I had been rushing around so fast with my mind full of the problems of the arrangements that it had been a rather superficial acquaintance. To spend a weekend alone on a luxury yacht with two film directors, one I had never met and the other I hardly knew. Well, I wasn't sure.

But there was a far more practical reason why it was not really possible. Dennis had telephoned me the previous week with the disturbing news that he had angina. Of course this was a terrible shock and although he was determined that it would not stop him from climbing, he would have to modify his future mountaineering exertions.

That Saturday I was going to the National Mountaineering Centre at Plas Y Brenin in North Wales with a group of teachers from Kent schools for a How to Teach Rock Climbing course. My job was to liaise between the teachers and the Centre staff, as I knew them all, and ensure that everything went smoothly. I had already arranged to spend Friday and the Saturday morning climbing with Dennis.

'It's the chance of a lifetime, Julie,' Kurt said persuasively. 'You can't turn it down.' It was unlikely that Herbert would ever bring the boat back to England again.

'Of course it is,' Terry encouraged. 'You could take a night train up from Dover and be with the course for Monday morning. They won't be doing anything too serious until then ... just ring the Centre and explain. They're mountaineers, they'll understand that such opportunities are not to be missed!' But in my heart I knew that Dennis needed a friend to help him through the initial acceptance of his illness, particularly as it affected his mountaineering, so, despite Kurt's persuasive arguing and insistence that I should go sailing, I stuck to my original plans.

A day later Terry and I dropped Kurt at Tunbridge Wells Station. As he left I felt a little sad. He was quite disappointed and understandably upset, and our goodbyes were rather formal. Several years later, when we became honest friends, he told me that he'd had such a strong feeling that I should have gone on the boat that he was really quite angry that I had not shared his conviction. Not only was it to be an outstanding adventure, but he had discovered that sailing held the same excitements as climbing, and wanted me to experience it too. Strangely, it was not only out of loyalty to Dennis that I refused; deep inside I had a very strong feeling – call it intuition if you like – that I should not go, that this was not the time to get to know Kurt better.

Dennis was far from downhearted when I met him the following evening. We did some good climbs at Craig y Forwyn the next day before driving over to Snowdonia. Dennis was climbing with his normal good form – the angina was not affecting his spirits or climbing ability. I however had a few nasty moments when I pulled up on a large block. The whole lump of rock slowly detached itself from the cliff. I made a rapid sideways leap and grabbed at a hold, breaking my finger nails in the effort. 'Below,' I shouted frantically in case anyone was underneath as the rock bounced down the cliff face, shattering itself into hundreds of pieces 150 feet lower on the valley floor. It is always the 'what might have happened' thoughts that make you feel nauseous after such near misses, and I did wonder whether I should have gone sailing after all.

The course at the Centre went very well, after an initial setback. 1976 was the year of the long summer drought, and the weather was more than perfect; even boggy Moel Siabod was dry. It was during the first day's climbing that I had to cope with a mini-revolution. The course aims had been explained in a brochure, which all the teachers had read but not taken seriously. 'To rethink and improve your teaching skills when teaching rock climbing' was the theme, and the instructors at the National Centre had given much time and thought to the course's structure and content.

The morning of Day One was spent scrambling up boulders revising basic movement, the groundwork for learning technique and building confidence. I found it very interesting – not so the teachers. 'Julie, you'll have to tell the Instructors that we're wasting our time playing around like this. We want to go climbing on something more serious, otherwise we'll go on strike!'

I explained the situation to the course instructor, who happened to be Tim Jepson, with whom I had climbed on Wen Zawn. He was not pleased either. 'You must explain to them that Kent County Council have asked us to run a course to improve their teaching abilities, not their personal climbing performance. If they're teaching good techniques, it will automatically follow that their own climbing will improve. If they just want to go home with an impressive list of climbs they've knocked off, well, they'll have to do that in their own time.'

After lunch we all met in the minibus. Rather surprisingly the Principal of the Brenin, Big Bill March, himself an excellent climber, was sitting in the driving seat. He turned round and looked sternly at the group. 'I understand that you don't like our course,' he said calmly, 'that you would prefer to be out climbing hard routes . . .'

There was total silence. 'All right', he continued 'this afternoon we'll play it your way. We'll go climbing in the Llanberis Pass.' There was a glint in his eye and I am not sure whether it was his tone or presence that put a look of apprehension rather than delight on the teachers' faces. By that evening Bill had re-established clear communication with a very tired group, and they were prepared to learn to walk first! This was a far more productive progression, and by the end of the week we were all thoroughly enjoying some of the classic climbs on Cloggy. It was not an easy lesson, but one I hope the teachers will not be too proud to pass on to any of their own over-keen pupils.

As the fine dry weather, so unusual for North Wales, continued, I telephoned Terry and asked him if he could cope alone until Monday, allowing me two extra days' climbing. Understanding as ever, he said he could, and on Friday evening Dennis and Mark, a tall American friend, collected me and we drove down to the Llanberis Pass to show Mark the view and point out all the classic routes. A unique assortment of climbing gems are to be found on the steep grey cliffs which decorate the side of the meandering road which twists and turns down from the Snowdon car park to Nant Peris, so many of which I have now climbed. I have walked and driven down the pass on numerous occasions in the past twenty-five years and am always impressed and fascinated by it and its many possibilities.

It was such a beautiful evening that Dennis suggested a quick route. Unfortunately, I had left all my gear at the Brenin and said I would relax in the warm evening sun and watch their exertions. Twenty minutes later I was cursing my luck, for they decided to climb Spectre, a superb Hard Very Severe route on the Grochan on which I had had my eye for quite a while, but without my soft climbing boots I could only watch them enviously.

I was so engrossed that I did not notice a car stop behind Dennis's van, or the driver get out and come to stand next to me. His gentle voice brought me back to reality with a start. It was one of Britain's top rock climbers, Alec Sharp. 'Why aren't you climbing?' the young man asked me, and I explained about the gear. 'Well, how about coming climbing on Cloggy with me tomorrow?' he suggested. I could not believe my ears. Did he really want to climb with me? My climbing was still way below his standard.

I had met Alec at Harrison's a couple of times, and had loved to watch him floating effortlessly up the hardest of climbs. Actually to climb with him on the same rope on the committing Black Cliff, on which he had put up several Extreme first ascents, was beyond my wildest dreams. 'If you drive up the track about halfway, to the little Tea House, we can all bivi together and then make an early start in the morning. Bye, see you later.' He was back in his car and away down the road before I had regained my voice to thank him for the invitation.

I could not wait for Dennis and Mark to finish their climb and tell them the news. We had already planned to go to Cloggy the following day. To climb on this isolated majestic cliff set high on the north-west flank of Snowdon is quite a special experience. It is an imposing, intimidating mass of dark rock which creates a very serious impression even from a distance, well before you set foot or hand on it. If you hear climbers in North Wales discussing routes and they speak with a touch of awe in their voices, you can be sure that the climbs they are discussing are on Cloggy.

The night was cloud-free and I lay restlessly in my sleeping bag under the twinkling stars waiting for the new day to dawn. At first light Alex and I were up, and by 6.30 am were walking quickly with a strange feeling of urgency towards the distant huge black shadow. I always seem to get myself into committing circumstances with semi-strangers, and this was no exception. Of course I had seen the graceful beauty of Alec's climbing, and there was no doubt about his competence; I also felt happy to be in his company . . . but I knew absolutely nothing about him as a person. I do not mind living dangerously, but it is quite nice to know who you are living dangerously with.

By the time we reached the crag we were half-running. We wanted to be the first people there; it had an unspoken importance that we should start our communion with this special rock face alone.

'Let's get tied on,' Alec urged, 'We'll start with a route I know you'll enjoy so much. It's one of my routes. Here, this is it, Jelly Roll.' I looked up the steep, thin crack. A few months before, from the comparative safety of Curving Crack, a modest Very Severe route adjacent, I had seen some climbers struggling and swearing on this Extreme climb. It had passed through my mind then that I would never be competent, or brave enough, to venture out onto the formidable steep central wall of the East Buttress. But suddenly, here I was, supposedly sane enough to be aware of what I was about to do, or at least try to do, and even feeling calm and happy to be there!

As I paid out the rope to Alec, who flowed smoothly from one minute hold to the other, my mind drifted back to the *dojo* and the calmness of sitting relaxed in meditation before a class. It was the same feeling.

'OK Julie,' Alec's shouts came from above and I prepared to climb. The morning stiffness left me within the first few moves. Alec had told me that I would enjoy it, but this was really something else. By the time I joined him on the first stance my heart was singing. The next pitch was even better – was it some special magic that Cloggy produced? I always enjoyed climbing but thought carefully about my technique, the placing of each foot and hand, and loved feeling the intricate mechanics of the stresses and tensions which pulling or pushing from different angles produced before the body came into relaxing balance once again. I would study the rock before moving, plan carefully ahead, try to conserve my limited arm strength in case a strenuous move took me by surprise. First the mind and then the body would move up the rock. This day was different ... it just happened naturally, I was making no conscious effort. At last my martial arts training to bring body and mind into harmony had extended into my climbing, bringing a totally new freedom. By not trying to analyse every move first, my energy could flow out freely through my limbs.

Alec felt my elation and we had a short discussion about my discovery when we met on the next airy stance. I had just gone through the same barrier that I had been pushed through by David in the *dojo*. That time it had been harder. I had been

87

physically driven through it in a suffering of pain and confusion, not wanting to let go of what had been indoctrinated in me all my life. 'Think ... use your head ... why don't you apply your brain ...' These are phrases used time and again when we get things wrong. Everything has to be thought out first. This time it was easy, it just happened.

I felt that this day nothing was impossible, and Alec, feeding on my outgoing enthusiasm, felt the same. (He later experienced martial arts for himself with David Passmore.) We hung in the ropes and talked about all the climbs we would like to do on Cloggy if we had time. We felt we could almost fly! We finished Jelly Roll, and went straight on to another climb which started at the top of the first route. Pinnacle Arete, another Extreme, had been first climbed by Martin Boysen of early High Rocks days, now one of Britain's most talented climbers. It wound its way delicately round a steep pillar, an exposed and intricate problem. Without descending we moved on round the cliff to our third Extreme of the morning, Hand Traverse on Pinnacle East Gully Wall. This fingery, short, but very strenuous climb almost totally lacks any footholds on the traverse section. It is committing for both leader and second as, once you start to hang on your arms over an enormous drop to the bottom of the crag, you have to keep going.

At lunchtime we were back at the foot of the crag, hungrily devouring sandwiches and Dennis's home-made cake. It was a very hot day, but we felt as if we had only just begun. Dennis and Mark joined us and the cheerful American reminded me that I had promised to climb White Slab with him in the afternoon. I was disappointed. I did not want to lose the magic, frightened I might not keep it if I climbed with someone else, but I had promised Mark.

I had done this superb route before with Dennis. It was an easier Extreme, the climbing steep and excellent, but as the afternoon sun heated up the rock we began to sweat profusely and at every stance were enveloped in a cloud of persistent, tickling, buzzing flies. Mark was a competent climber, but his movements were slow and careful and after the flowing dance up the rock in the morning I found the long fly-pestered waits at the stances irritating and looked longingly down to the sparkling waters of Lyn d'ur Addur far, far below, wishing I was down with the happy nude bathers splashing in its sun-warmed depths.

It took us almost four hours to finish the route and then we still had to negotiate the broken rock and the steep path leading back to the foot of the cliff. Perhaps it was good to have the contrast of the slow afternoon climbing after the dreamlike revelation of the morning. It was a day that affected all my climbing, on rock and on snow and ice, for ever. I was ready for any voyage into the unknown now.

Legless in Peru

'Who wants another beer?' Norman shouted above the hubbub.

The waiter hovered, a little bewildered by the disorganised scene, then in typically South American manner shrugged his shoulders and disappeared.

The evening had started quietly, just six of us around the table, but later it seemed that all the other mountaineers in Huaraz, the climbing capital of Peru (the equivalent of Chamonix in the Alps), had joined us and things had got slightly out of hand. Tables had been joined together as French, German, Spanish, Italian, American, Japanese and Peruvian climbers had arrived and our impromptu international party now took up most of the restaurant.

In late November 1977 Terry and I received a most surprising invitation to join an expedition to the Peruvian Andes. It was the final deciding factor in the future of the shop and café. If we wanted to go we would have to contribute £1,000 and selling the shop would be the only way we could finance the trip. This time we did not have the problem of finding somewhere to live as we had been able to buy the home we had come to love so much. The Bothy was just right for us, economical to maintain and run and only a ten-minute walk across the fields from Harrison's Rocks where we did most of our teaching. It was ideal in every way. The whole estate has such an aura of peace and tranquillity rare to find in our hectic modern world, which would have been very hard to leave.

Christopher and Lindsay happily went to stay with friends, and on a rainy Sunday in early July we flew to Lima. Our leader Norman Croucher had rather special mountaineering problems –

he has two artificial legs, the result of an accident with a train when he was nineteen years old (he is now thirty-eight). In Peru word of his disability and amazing exploits had spread and many people wanted to meet him. Once they did his exuberant sense of humour made them reluctant to leave. He was the catalyst. Hearing the fun more people wandered over to the table and were quickly absorbed into the group. With the help of the cheap but drinkable Peruvian beer, the riotous mood of the evening soon broke all communication barriers. Everyone was speaking odd words of a different language; the Germans were translating French into Spanish, the French Spanish into English and sometimes it was necessary to go through several people from various countries to complete a sentence. Jokes were the most complicated to translate, but laughter, gestures, and more beer made them even funnier.

Outside the restaurant the rain lashed down and intermittent brilliant shafts of lightning lit up the little shanty town.

Tonight there was a fiesta in Huaraz, with dancing and fireworks in the streets. Of course we planned to join the locals in their celebrations. 'It never rains at this time of year,' the Peruvians kept insisting, but the downpour went on, drumming noisily on the corrugated iron roofs.

'I'll have another beer, if you can get the waiter to come back.' I was sitting next to Norman and was one of the few who had heard the question. I really had already drunk too much, but what the hell, we had every reason to celebrate. Our expedition had achieved its aim to climb to six thousand metres and to gain publicity, and hopefully more funds, for an unusual outdoor pursuits centre, The Calvert Trust in the Lake District, of which Norman is a Trustee. This well-equipped, peaceful centre set amid the restful green hills of Wordsworth country is the perfect place for people with handicaps of all kinds and their families to explore the possibilities of living a more normal life through sport. It is often easy to adapt equipment or style to allow a partially mobile person to enjoy their chosen sport and join a local club with benefits on both sides. There is no age or specific time when you become handicapped; it can happen to us all, from an accident, or through illness, suddenly, irrevocably; and having disabled friends is the first step to understanding that life does go on; the real person is still there on the inside, however battered the bodywork may be.

We had eight members on the expedition. Apart from Norman there were Dennis Kemp and Denny Moorehouse, who had been a friend of ours for many years. Denny started Clogwyn Climbing Gear and his carabiners, ascendeurs and descendeurs, ice axes and pitons were world famous. Harry Curtis was a friend of Norman's who was a very likeable character, but totally careless about his appearance. Like A. A. Milne's 'bad bear' of the 'Two Little Bears who Lived in the Wood', his shoe laces were always undone, and you could always recognise his clothes as they had toothpaste all over them. But Harry had an amazingly orderly memory for figures, and we appointed him Expedition Account-ant. He kept a record of how much credit each member had left, in his head, and was accurate to the last peso. We had also known Mike Welham for several years. He was a deep sea diver, and on this trip acted as the expedition photographer while his friend Mike O'Shea came along as the expedition base camp manager. Terry and I made up the group.

South America was sultry, noisy, colourful and very exciting. On our arrival in Lima we had the thrill of having tea with the famous mountaineer Walter Bonatti, a man I had always longed to meet. Then from the overcast grey capital we had driven in a bone-shaking bus three hundred kilometres to Huaraz.

I staggered a little as I got out. We had travelled from Lima at sea level to Huaraz at 10,000 feet in ten hours, and the altitude really hit me. I was struggling for breath as we climbed the stairs in the hotel to reach the large dormitory room where most of the mountaineers in this part of the Andes had their base. Norman took up residence on a floor space just opposite the door leading to the staircase. Not perhaps the wisest choice, for the next morning a Frenchman came bouncing into the room and almost fell back down the stairs when he saw Norman's trousered legs and boots parked neatly next to his sleeping bag.

We spent a few days adjusting to living at this new height, and explored the town. Norman describes it perfectly in his book *A Man and his Mountains*:

Legless in Peru

How can Huaras be captured in words? Any attempt must be inadequate but, first, think of straight concreted streets, some of them recently built after earthquake and alluvion damage; an alluvion is a rapidly moving mixture of rock, sand, mud and water spilled by collapse of a lake's morainal dam, or by massive ice avalanches falling into a lake and displacing the water.

Earthquake hazard influences the height of buildings which mostly have no more than two or three floors. Away from the main streets most are single storey, while larger structures of reinforced concrete have been put in the centre. Roofs are made of red tiles or corrugated iron. Some of the living creatures that crowd into the town centre I have already mentioned: barefoot children, women carrying babies in blankets, donkeys, little pigs and street traders. Shoeshine boys and newspaper boys wander everywhere, and ice-cream or drinks vendors pedal their three-wheeled barrows slowly around. In all of the several markets, squatting women sell vegetables, eggs and fruit spread out for display on blankets, and there are stalls, too, for meat, ironmongery, clothes, wool and herbs. Higher up the scale there are bookshops, shoeshops, chemists, dress shops, like anywhere else. So it is a spectrum, from the lady squatted beside a single cake sold slice by slice, through small tattered stalls, through big and well-kept stalls, through small shops to some large ones. Eating out is characterised by a similar spectrum of style and price. You can buy a slice of that cake or some bread from a barrowboy or a stallholder, then there are scruffy cafés and better ones, and a few good restaurants. Wide-eyed adults and children stare in through restaurant windows like they were watching TV. Grubby stalls, grubby feet, grubby children, grubby streets. Bank notes are tatty, begging by children is commonplace, buses are crammed full, fares are cheap, the police are armed, there are lots of rickety, ramshackle cars and gaily painted trucks coming and going. The air is more of activity than bustle, with people going about their business but not rushing. The hills and mountains stand all around but not too close; Huaras does not feel closed in. And usually the sky is bright and blue . . .

I took to Huaraz immediately, it was a place I could easily fit into. The street markets were full of bright colours. Most things lay scattered on blankets or sacks at the side of the dirty lanes. But the brightness of the mounds of coloured cheap plasticware, heaps of fluorescent coloured wool, shining silver tin pots and pans, and so many vegetables and fruits of different hues distracted the eye from the surrounding squalor.

Just shortly after we arrived in Huaraz I developed a strange addiction to bananas. I have always liked them, but suddenly I could not seem to live without them. By good fortune I was put in charge of shopping for the mountain supplies, until the others discovered that they always included a rucksack full of bananas, which turned to a horrible black mush very fast as the result of travelling, and overnight frosts at the base camps. I was like an alchoholic, and tried to keep a secret store, which was not easy in a small tent, as bad bananas do not smell very good. As soon as we returned to the villages from the various mountains I would buy bunches at a time, and eat them all in one go. Terry began to worry, especially as he has had a vasectomy! When we returned to Lima at the end of the expedition I felt that I really must try to do something about my cravings; bananas in England were too expensive to keep up my indulgence.

Like any other addict I did not like to admit to my lack of control over my longings, particularly to a vice as stupid as bananas, and sneaked off by myself to try to effect a cure. I wandered through the grey streets. Bananas are plentiful in Lima, heaps of their lovely yellow curves beckoned me from stalls, shops and vans. At last I found what I was looking for. I stopped the Peruvian pushing his barrow. I held up three fingers and pointed to the most manky, tatty fruits he had. 'No! no! no!' he said and pointed to some large attractive plump ones. 'Si! Si!' I insisted, and again put up three fingers but added, 'Kilos'. He took a lot of persuading to sell me his worst wares, and gave me half for nothing, possibly as a gesture of sympathy to someone too crazy to understand.

I hurried away down the street stuffing one after another of the dry, floury, almost bitter bananas into my mouth. My plan was to make myself sick of these fruits of my temptation, to hate them for evermore. By the time I reached our hotel and headed for the bathroom, I was convinced that it had worked. In fact it put me off eating anything for twenty-four hours, but then, it was as bad again as ever. I gave up. Back in England economics gradually weaned me off them; they did not seem to taste the same anyway. I have never found an explanation for my banana phase and, thank goodness, have not had a compulsive desire for any food in the same way since.

We had climbed two mountains in two weeks in the majestic lofty Andes, and everything had gone well. It was the perfect initiation into big mountains as Peru offers the sort of mountaineering that is a natural step up from the Alps. It is possible to climb many peaks in Alpine style, which means carrying everything up in one go without having to fix ropes or establish and stock camps on the route first. Most base camps were already at above the height of Mont Blanc, Europe's highest mountain at 15,766 feet.

In his normal considerate way, Dennis, who has had previous Himalayan experience, quietly climbed both peaks before Norman tackled them, to check out the problems that he might encounter, but he did not tell anyone that he had been to the summits. The first peak was 16,800 feet high, our acclimatisation climb and a chance for Norman and me to sort out any technical problems before going on to something more demanding. Norman was fantastic – he had already had a lot of Alpine experience – and I felt very confident climbing with him. His technique was excellent and the altitude did not bother him unduly. We had both suffered from headaches first thing in the morning. At the top camp I woke up with such a throbbing head that I could not bear to open my eyes even with sun glasses on, and it was two hours and several aspirins later before I could emerge from the tent, but we reached the summit later that day and I felt fine.

We also had some very wild dreams, as we lay in our sleeping bags in the night. I saw a train coming through the tent, a hallucination possibly triggered off by the noise of avalanches cascading down the surrounding mountainsides, and Norman had a fish which kept swimming into his eyes. I have no explanation for that one!

The second mountain, Pisco, named after a Peruvian fire water, was almost 19,000 feet high. It took us three days to climb. Mike O'Shea stayed at Base Camp to defend it from bandits. There had been several cases when mountaineers had returned to their tents and found that everything had been stolen. People had also been attacked with guns and knives by local brigands while they were sleeping: a few had been killed or injured just for their watches, radios and cameras. The influx of mountaineers, trekkers and tourists into the remote areas has opened the eyes of the hill people to their own abject poverty, which, due to natural disasters and administrative corruption, has no solution. Luckily as they can grow their own food they are not starving, but they have no material possessions. In the towns it is the children who support the parents, working long hours selling papers, cleaning shoes and doing anything they can find to make a few pesos. Childhood is brief in Peru.

On Pisco Terry helped us by ferrying heavy loads up to Camp 1. He was very strong, but found that he could not bear the pressure of climbing with me, even on these mountains. He discovered on Pisco that he preferred climbing smaller mountains, partly because of his damaged leg which objected with pain to long steep walks, but also because he enjoys more gentle mountaineering. One of the delights of the sport is that it offers so much choice.

It was good to be with Denny and Dennis, who valiantly went ahead to plough a trail through the deep new snow, and Harry and Mike, who were struggling with the tiredness of climbing at altitude. After reaching the summit, Dennis and I went down after the others, going more slowly with Norman, safeguarding him with a rope on the steeper sections.

'I'll be glad when we are over this next bit,' Dennis said to me quietly. 'We have to go quite close to the edge of the slope, and there's a hell of a cornice overhanging the valley. Difficult to say where the solid bit ends!'

Norman went down using his unusual sideways but practical technique. I quickly followed, sliding down the furrow which his body had made in the soft snow, anxious to get back to the tent before darkness hit the glacier.

Suddenly I was out of control, a bump had flung me out of the shallow groove in the snow and I was sliding towards the cornice that Dennis had just warned me about. Everything seemed to slow down. 'This is silly. Do something or it will be too late!' I ordered myself, and rolled over onto my ice axe. 'Keep your feet in the air, you're wearing crampons which could flip you out of control,' was the next thing that went through my mind. How much time I had to think as I was sliding towards disaster and possible demise. I pushed down hard on the ice axe and it bit into the snow and braked me to a halt.

I looked up at Dennis, forty feet above me, and saw what I thought was extreme disapproval on his face. Later he told me that he was just stunned. He had been wondering how he could possibly tell Terry of my death! I lay very still. Supposing I was lying on the curving overhang of the cornice, my weight could break it at any moment and I had no safety rope. Slowly, carefully, inch by inch I moved sideways back to the security of Norman's groove. That night as I lay in the tent I began to shake as the shock of my narrow escape hit me.

The others in the restaurant were busy discussing their plans; they wanted to spend the last days in this captivating country as tourists. There was so much to see, remote valleys, the Inca ruins, Lake Titicaca, the highest lake in the world. They wanted to taste the full flavour of the country.

Norman and I looked at each other. After just one day back in Huaraz we were already suffering withdrawal symptoms from the incredible, beautiful mountains that were so near and yet so far away. Given luck with the weather and a lot of understanding from Terry, we could surely manage just one more, and still make a flying visit to Machu Picchu to fulfil his ambition to visit and photograph the mysterious Inca ruins set high on the mountainside above the leafy jungle of the Urubamba valley.

But which mountain could we tackle, and who else would want to join us? They all had other plans.

Another half glass of beer, and we giggled like conspirators. We had said it simultaneously, half as a joke. 'Why not Huascaran?' The beer made everything a possibility, even Peru's highest mountain – the disastrous mountain of horrific avalanches that had killed thousands of people over the years.

One terrible avalanche in May 1970, actuated by an earthquake, had travelled seven miles on its catastrophic journey. The huge ice blocks which were dislodged ruptured a moraine dam in their path, releasing sand, mud and water in a devastating cascade down to the Rio de Shacsha, flooding it, washing away villages in its path. However, even more disastrously, part of it swept up over a small hill, became airborne, and fell in a deadly suffocating cloud onto the town of Yungay where 17,000 people perished. Ironically, only the cemetery hillock remained untouched.

Even in our present silly state, we knew that the rain that was drowning the celebrations in Huaraz would be falling as snow on the high slopes of Huascaran, making conditions difficult and the risk of avalanches even higher than usual.

'I'll just pop over to that group of Austrians to ask what they know of the route. They're intending to climb Huascaran in the next few days.' In Peru in 1978 there were no maps available, and our English guidebooks, maps and descriptions were very rudimentary.

'Excuse me, are you going to Huascaran . . .?' I began. Their leader looked up from his plate. 'Ve do not take vimen on ze mountain,' he said sternly before I could continue. 'Suit yourself,' I thought. 'But I don't want to go with you . . . I only want some information . . . for my friend,' I added a little ambiguously, and got the details we needed.

We managed to talk Harry into joining us. He was the most easygoing, if desperately absent-minded member of the party.

A few days later we were sitting on top of a very overloaded potato lorry heading towards our mountain. 'Christ, it looks enormous!' said Norman, voicing our thoughts. The closer we got, the bigger it grew. It is one thing to sit comfortably in a restaurant and choose a peak, buoyed up by alcohol, quite another suddenly to be so close to such a mountain that it towers into the sky. Should we admit it was all really a joke and go back to Huaraz?

We had reached our lorry's destination, and there were the Austrians who had 'read' the weather the same way as we had. They were looking very pleased as they had arranged for a small truck to carry them up the mountain track to the donkey station. Well, we couldn't lose face by turning back now!

'You want a truck?' asked a tatty but smiling Peruvian who had appeared from nowhere.

'Sure,' we said.

It is strange but sometimes it is possible to upset people

ABOVE: Zita and me, tidied up for Madame Vacani's dancing class
RIGHT: With Paunt outside the Red House in Ilingham
BELOW: Zita, father and me with one of our summer holiday cars – a 1938 Ford 8, which took us 3,000 miles across Europe

LEFT: A family group: mother, me, Zita and father in Germany when I was eleven
RIGHT: Even on our early scrambles by the side of an Alpine footpath, Zita looked more like being the natural climber

LEFT: Terry abseiling High Rock-
style with the rope just running
under his arms (*John Topham
Picture Library*)
ABOVE: Terry teaching on
Salamander Slab at Bowles, where
the sandstone is usually dry and
clean (*John Topham Picture
Library*)
BELOW: Cloggy (Clogwyn Du'r
Arddu), near Snowdon. A travers
Bow Shaped Slab showing clearly
how chocks and runners work

ABOVE: John, Ray and Gerry camping under an overhang at High Rocks in 1958, with Terry's first love – his jeep
RIGHT: In November 1959 Terry and I were married
BELOW: A rather battered photograph of our children, Christopher and Lindsay, which has been with me on several expeditions

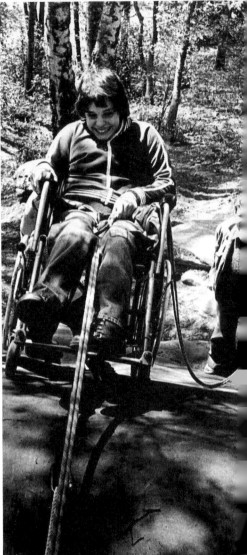

ABOVE LEFT: He led me to the entrance to the Rocks. 'I think y should hold my hand . . . my na is Terry.' We have been holding hands for twenty-seven years (N *Charnick*)

ABOVE RIGHT: Doing normal th like abseiling in a wheelchair is great fun, especially if you're in control yourself

LEFT: Leading Nicky to have th confidence to go downhill by himself

ABOVE: David Passmore demonstrates how to use energy from the centre, with Peter at a children's class
LEFT: The movement of the sword is the basis for all martial arts practice, with or without the weapon

LEFT: Kurt and me renewing our acquaintance at the Trento Film Festival in 1979. 'I think you should come and climb with me in the Alps,' he said

BELOW LEFT: We had the thrill of having tea in Lima with the legendary mountaineer Walter Bonatti

BELOW RIGHT: Dennis Kemp – he looked at me over his half-glasses, his clear blue eyes twinkling

FOOT: Pierre Mazeaud being tidied up by his nephew, Jeff, our Nanga Parbat doctor. Keeping up appearances is important for expedition leaders and politicians. Michel Affanasieff looks on slightly perplexed

RIGHT: Despite its
appearance from above, the
bed of the Shaksgam river
was completely dry when
we reached it after crossing
the famous Aghil Pass in
China on the way to K2.
The camel train just below
the centre of the photo
shows the scale

BELOW: The side glacier to
the foot of Broad Peak was
tightly packed with mini ice
mountains. We spent many
hours climbing up and
down their steep sides
trying to find a way through

LEFT: Kurt coming up t
the summit of Afternoc
Peak. The long evening
shadows make him loo
30 feet tall. Not really
suitable terrain for my
ten-year-old bendy boo
BELOW: Exploring the
river gorge near the
Gasherbrum glacier
(China), we tried to ke
our feet dry jumping fr
boulder to boulder, bu
the gorge narrowed m
boulders disappeared
underneath the icy wa

continually with absolutely no intention of doing so. Our driver must have sensed a feeling of competition from the Austrians, and by a miracle and a lot of nerve, overtook their truck on the narrow track. Their driver had slowed down to negotiate a large hole in the road, showing concern for his passengers; ours trusted to mountaineers having a strong grip, and went across at full speed.

We arrived dusty and shaken up at the cluster of mud houses at the end of the bumpy hairpinned road and were given the first, and only, donkeys. The unhappy Austrians had to wait three more hours in the clammy mid-day heat for some more to be found. We were drinking tea, our Base Camp established, when they arrived, harassed, sweating and swearing.

The next morning, by the time we had roused ourselves from our sleeping bags, they had long gone, and after a relaxed English breakfast we set off for our next camp, leaving Manuel, our Peruvian base camp guardian, to protect our possessions.

Above our base camp the long broken glacier had to be climbed. Norman's crampons kept falling off on the hard uneven ice, and he was, understandably, getting very fed up. His tin legs have no articulation at the ankle, and as he cannot get frostbite he wears lightweight bendy boots; all this places extra stresses on his crampon bindings and they constantly came undone.

'Shit! If they come off again I'm going back,' he shouted with frustration as the metal spikes twisted away from the sole of his boot yet again. We were all sweating profusely from the heat, but Norman had to make so much extra effort for every movement. His metal artificial legs are the old-fashioned heavy type; the modern ones do not stand up to the rigours of mountaineering. Keeping his balance on the hard surface of the sloping broken glacier while moving these heavy limbs demanded the utmost concentration and effort. However, if you did not know about his disability, from the way he moved on the mountain, and his cheerful banter, you would never guess that he had more than a limp. He is a man of overwhelming courage. Another purpose of this expedition was to find out what special problems Norman would encounter at higher altitudes and whether he could integrate with normal able-bodied expeditions to the world's highest mountains. He did not want the restriction of having to run his own expeditions, a costly and time-consuming job to organise.

He has always lived frugally, working full-time to help other handicapped people. Giving really constructive personal help has meant a lot of sacrifices for both him and his devoted wife Judy, who has supported him in all that he does with great love and loyalty.

'There's no way you're going down simply because your crampons keep falling off,' I said. It seemed a crazy reason to have to give up. 'I think I have the answer,' and I tied them firmly to his boots with thin cord. 'You'll have to leave them on all the time now.' I told him; and indeed, the problem was solved – every night Norman would remove his boots and crampons still attached to his legs and trousers and store the whole lot in a polythene bag outside the tent.

We joined the Austrians at the next camp late in the afternoon. When moving on less steep snow Norman uses adjustable crutches as other people use ski sticks. The poor organised Austrians were confused by our strange little group; the woman, a somewhat scruffy man and Norman with his crutches, walking slightly awkwardly.

They could not contain their curiosity. 'Your friend has a bad leg?' one of them asked me, somewhat bewildered.

The explanation in German rolls easily off the tongue, 'Er hat keine Beine!' He has no legs!

Their worst fears were confirmed – we were quite mad and definitely to be kept at a very safe distance. They returned to their comparatively palatial tent and firmly closed the door.

The following day we really worked hard on the mountain. We were getting high and a very satisfying day was spoilt only by the filthy campsite at 20,000 feet. Rubbish and excreta littered the only possible flat place for our little tent and we felt very sad that our fellow mountaineers had so little regard for the beauty of the mountain, or for those to come after them. It was difficult for us to find a clean space just six feet by four and we had to go a long way from the tent to get our drinking snow.

Our luck with the weather held and early the next morning we set off for our summit bid. The altitude was affecting Harry and he was tired and slow. After an hour I began to worry; Norman is a fine mountaineer and, despite his handicap, quite fast going up, but unavoidably slower coming down. If we couldn't take advantage of his speed on the ascent we would certainly be caught by the night on the descent – a serious prospect at this altitude.

I had just reached the top of another pitch of the long snow slope and was bringing Norman up when Harry lost one of his crampons. It slid rapidly down the endless section up which he had just so arduously toiled. Before Norman and I could voice our fears our friend called up that he was going back to the tent. We felt sad for, despite his infuriating carelessness, he was an excellent companion and a good solid climber. We were also a little worried as the route back was rather hazardous with deep crevasses to be negotiated. Norman and I looked at each other. Perhaps we should give up and go back with Harry; it was still a very long way to the summit.

Huascaran teases you with its false 'nipple' summit while the true top of this big mountain is a lot farther away. But how could I voice such a thought to this incredibly courageous man? How many future opportunities would he have to reach such heights? No, he was strong and fit and today was his day, the summit should be his. We watched Harry retrieve his crampon, he looked back in control, and gave our concentrated effort to the mountain. Up and up we went, our pace getting slower and breathing more laboured. But the gods were with us – the weather was crystal clear and snow conditions good. Hours later we saw a distant speck moving up below us. Could it be? Impossible! By using porters the Austrians had missed out the top camp and already climbed the mountain and gone down. It had to be Harry. What should we do? To wait for him made the summit, still nearly two hours away, an impossibility for Norman, who had worked and sweated so hard to get to where he was, already higher than any other so severely disabled person in the world. As Harry had reached easier ground and we had left a good trail, we went on, but a lot of our carefree pleasure had been replaced by concern.

Norman reached the summit well ahead of me. When I joined

him we sat together very quietly. I found it difficult to speak, such a strong emotion welled up in me; my throat constricted and my eyes were watery with tears. I think Norman was feeling the same way. 'Cheers Julie,' he said briefly as we looked out over the miles of mountains spread out beneath us.

We could not stay for long as it was already late, but we waited for Harry to reach the summit and took our photographs. I felt very fortunate to be with such lovable friends who had so much determination of spirit.

Norman and I started down and Harry soon caught up with us, but we were too slow and darkness fell before we reached the yawning crevasses which separated us from the camp. The difficulties of negotiating them were exaggerated by our tiredness, the blackness of the night and the freezing cold. We longed to reach the shelter of our little tent and rest our tired limbs, to get warm again and to drink and drink . . . Finally we were there. Our movements were automatic, dreamlike. It took so long to take off our boots, to get organised . . . Our tent was designed for two not three people. Only one of us could make any manoeuvre at a time, so to get into our sleeping bags, heat the snow and generally arrange our equipment took a very long time.

There was to be little sleep for us that night. The wind rose to ferocious strength and rattled and tore at the tent. We sat holding onto the poles, each in our private world. Harry occasionally muttered something about his feet, but refused to move them out of his warm sleeping bag so that we could examine them.

The next morning the wind continued to gust with full force. It was impossible to take down the tent in such a storm – obviously the weather had broken. By noon it abated slightly and we decided to move. A lot of snow had fallen during the night. We came to a snow ridge with deep crevasses on either side and roped up. I was leading with Norman in the middle. There was no way we could walk along the ridge while the wind was gusting so strongly; it caught our packs and hurled us to the ground. We crouched low to the snow and I tried to count the length of the gaps between the gusts, but there was no regular pattern. We would have to trust to luck.

Poor Norman could not get to a standing position very easily and I was frightened that I might pull him off the narrow ridge simply by walking forward while he was still trying to get onto his feet. I could not warn the others when I was about to move because my voice was blown away in the wind and with their heads down they could not see any arm signals. The narrowness of the ridge and force of the wind made it impossible even to turn round to look at my companions. That six hundred feet took us a long time and it was with great relief we dropped down and round the corner out of the unbalancing, buffeting wind. We wasted no time crossing the avalanche field – fresh blocks had already fallen that day – and on down, down, down. We sent prayers of thanks to whoever had placed a few fixed ropes on the steep walls of the terraced section and made good speed to the camp above the glacier, so good that we decided to carry on to the lower camp where our porter would be waiting, hopefully with some tea.

We started to go down the glacier. At first it was easy but then, covered in new snow which obliterated all the tracks and hid some of the smaller crevasses, it became more and more of a maze and several times we had to retrace our tired steps. Jumping crevasses or even making wide steps across them is very hazardous for Norman. Flexible toes, ankles and knees all play an important part in these movements and he does not have the spring required.

For the second time on the mountain our luck ran out. Finding our way had taken too long and suddenly night and its darkness was upon us. We had no choice but to stay just where we were knowing that the end of the glacier where huge ice blocks continually broke away was very close. The creakings, crackings and groanings of the river of ice reminded us of its constant movement downhill. Harry sat down to take off his crampons, but leapt to his feet with a sideways jump as the ice cracked violently under his bottom. I carved out a little seat for us in the hard ice and managed to place ice axe belays to prevent our sliding into any hidden crevasses around. We got into our sleeping bags, boots and all, and wrapped ourselves in the tent, made some tea and ate some sardines.

Crack! It always sounded so close, and we held our breath. Would we suddenly be swallowed up by the glacier and gradually pulverised by the grinding movement of its vast icy walls? How could we sleep in such a nerve-racking situation? But we did and to our amazement it was eight o'clock the following morning when we awoke. We looked down. Yes, we were right. We were just fifteen minutes from the end of the glacier!

Back at Base Camp the euphoria of our success began to surface, but was a little subdued by the sight of Harry's feet. His toes were definitely frostbitten and very, very painful. I bandaged them as best I could, and then carefully and gently manoeuvred the clean sock he had given me over one swollen, painful foot. He was very brave but even so I heaved a sigh of relief as I finally got the second sock into position. I looked at his feet . . . 'Harry,' I said in utter disbelief, 'there's a lump in your sock!' Right down by his instep there was an unidentifiable bulge over which no boot would fit. How could he be so careless to leave something in his sock? 'It will have to come off.' I was angry for his sake. He would have to suffer the slow painful business all over again.

I pulled the sock off as gently as possible, thrust my hand inside and brought out . . . a pair of my knickers! We all had identical socks and knowing that Manuel would look through our gear while he was alone at Base Camp I had hastily shoved my dirty washing out of sight. Poor Harry! Then we all saw the funny side and started to laugh. Even Manuel joined in although he did not really understand why.

Harry, wearing only his outer boots, went down with Manuel the next morning. Norman and I stayed an extra day on the mountain to rest Norman's stumps and to wait for the donkeys.

'Oh, for a beer,' was our constant thought on the long walk down. We arrived hot, tired and dusty at the tiny village to learn that there were no cars to take us down to the valley.

'That's fine,' said Norman, 'we can sit in the shade and drink beer after beer after beer. I have six days' drinking to catch up on.'

I went to the shop and returned with two bottles.

The heat was intensified by a large group of school children who gathered around, probing us with incessant questions and inquisitive fingers, and after sharing only one of the beers we were both in the same inebriated state that had led to the conception of this adventure.

We rested briefly in Huaraz. Harry's feet were so painful that he could not even manage the short walk to the local hospital to get them examined. Terry and I went on ahead to try to spare him the normal lengthy wait. We had a carrier bag full of antibiotics and other drugs which luckily we had not used during the expedition, to donate to their pharmacy.

The squat sun-yellow hospital building was surrounded by a tall iron railing fence and sentries were posted at the closed gates. 'I wonder whether they're to keep the patients in or the relatives out?' Terry pondered as we approached. However, we were allowed through without question and entered the long-corridored building. No one asked us what we wanted. We wandered up and down, peering into doorways, and were just on the point of going outside to try to find someone to help us when a door opened and a white-coated woman stuck her head out.

'Pssst!' I looked at her a little blankly. 'Pssst!' she went again a little more urgently, and beckoned.

'Come on,' I pulled at Terry's arm. 'I think that someone wants to help us,' and dragged him towards the door.

We pushed the door open. Were we really in a hospital? The room was full of white-coated people laughing, talking and drinking . . . champagne! With no questions as to who we were or what we wanted, we were included in the party.

'Where you from?' an attractive Peruvian lady eventually asked shyly in English.

'From England,' we told her.

She passed on this information to the whole room. 'And what you say for this?' She chinked her glass with Terry's.

'Cheers, I suppose,' I replied, still a little amazed by the whole scene.

'OK. Cheers!'

We clinked glasses all round and, in a gesture of friendliness, followed the Peruvians' example and downed the contents in one go. Immediately another glass was pressed into our hands. Of course we had to toast them in return, and we had three attempts at 'Santé' before we got the accent to their satisfaction. By the end of the seventh glass we felt that it was too complicated with slurred speech to try to explain Harry's plight. Far better to wait for him to arrive with Norman in the taxi and simply point at his problem. We did manage to hand over the drugs, and they insisted that we had more champagne to say thank you, then we had to reciprocate our thanks for the hospitality!

Suddenly at 2 pm the party, which we discovered was for a departing doctor, was over and the room became a waiting room once again. Terry and I walked, somewhat unsteadily, outside into the sunshine to wait for our friends. Poor Harry, it was bad enough to entrust himself to the doubtful Peruvian medical system, but to find us sitting in the hospital grounds giggling stupidly, obviously drunk, and be told that we were not the only ones in that condition in the hospital, did nothing to boost his confidence.

Luckily, Pepe, a Peruvian 'Mr Fix-It' friend, had also come along. Whatever you needed, Pepe's stock phrase was 'Eez possible', and somehow, for a price, it always was. 'I go to find a doctor. In zeeze 'ospitals first you find your own doctor,' he explained, and rushed off inside. Fifteen minutes later he was back. 'Eez OK. I have found a very good doctor.' We all looked relieved. 'Yes,' Pepe continued, 'he eez a very good doctor . . . he eez a dentist.' Harry went green, but as he was in no state to run away from all this madness, allowed himself to be half carried to his fate.

The Casualty Department, with good planning, was up two flights of stairs and along several corridors. Many of the doors had small glass windows through which you could catch a glimpse of trays of surgical instruments or very sick-looking people. The doctor, when we found him, was far more interested in Norman than Harry but eventually took his patient into another room and firmly shut the door. Ten minutes later Harry re-emerged, looking very relieved. Amputation would not be necessary, just rest, dilatory drugs and return to England as soon as possible. Two days later he managed to get a flight back home, but was not treated too kindly when he staggered, scruffy and untidy as ever and still wearing his expedition clothes, into a London hospital and announced that he had frost-bite . . . in the middle of a hot July!

106

❧ 7 ❧

Graduation by bicycle and
Eine Kleine Nachtmusik

In April 1979 Terry and I had been asked to go to Trento in northern Italy by the British Mountaineering Council as the British representatives at the Mountain Film Festival, a gathering of film-makers and top mountaineers from all over the world. Although we had no specific role in filming at that time, we were very interested and Terry was also keen to update his library of photo-portraits of mountaineering personalities, so we were delighted to accept the invitation.

When we arrived we discovered that Kurt Diemberger and his wife were staying not only in our hotel but actually in the next room. I had not heard from Kurt since I had rejected his invitation to go sailing on his brother-in-law's yacht three years before, and I wondered how he would react when he saw me again. But immediately he saw me he grabbed me in a bear hug, gabbling in incomprehensible Italian.

Both the films and the social events of the Film Festival were stimulating. Kurt was treated as something of a guru. As a top mountaineer and highly respected film-maker, many people hung on his every word. After lunch one day towards the end of the Festival, while the prizewinners were being chosen, a heated discussion arose. Several exciting films about ski and hang-gliding descents in the Himalayas and Andes had been shown. Now the question earnestly debated was whether it was more creative and exciting, indeed important, to make films of the ascents of mountains or of different and daring ways of coming down. Kurt had listened to the arguments quietly. Then as the coffee cups were refilled there was a brief silence. Suddenly the great man spoke, clearly and in English as most of the debate had been in

107

that language. 'For me, it is like an erection . . . It goes up, and eventually it has to come down!' There was a stunned pause as they contemplated his words, then a burst of laughter as the absurdity of the argument was appreciated, and the subject was changed.

On the last morning I stopped at the Diemberger family's breakfast table to say goodbye. Kurt put down his coffee cup. 'I think you should come and climb with me in the Alps. I will telephone you when I am next in Salzburg.'

I did not know what to say; I had concentrated on rock climbing in what little spare time I had; my ice and snow techniques were very rusty for the technical routes he would want to tackle. Well, most probably he would forget.

In the spring of 1980 I had just driven Terry to Gatwick. He was flying to America to visit Yosemite National Park in California and then travel on to a small but very special town in Colorado to attend their Film Festival. Telluride had been a ghost town since the 1880s when the silver mines had closed but some friends that we had made at Trento had gone there ten years before to start a new life. Bill and Sue Kees were modern pioneers. They had packed all their belongings into an old car and driven east from California looking for a place to settle. In Telluride they found kindred spirits, and the setting was beautiful; it was like a small Alpine town nestling in the Rocky Mountains. They formed a close community as they worked together to rebuild the dilapidated, deserted houses and shops behind the original façade. Bill had to learn to be a carpenter. The bank in Telluride had been raided by Butch Cassidy in the old days; still today the main street has the feeling of an old Western and has been used as a background for Hollywood films. It is this and the community spirit that remains from the original creative pioneers which makes the town so popular and the atmosphere of their Film Festival so special. Bill and Sue had invited us both, but as I was going to spend six weeks climbing with Dennis in Yosemite in June, I elected to stay home and look after the climbing courses.

Half an hour after I had returned from the airport, at 9.30 am, the telephone rang. 'Hello! Here is Kurt speaking.' I was surprised:

it was almost exactly one year since we had last spoken at Trento.

'Where are you?' I asked, expecting him to be in England again. 'I am in Salzburg. I think you should come to the mountains! When will you come?' It was such a direct and simple question that to answer it should not be difficult. I thought rapidly. Today was Thursday and I had a climbing course of Venture Scouts from London, but Friday afternoon, Saturday and Sunday I was not working. From the little I knew of Kurt, I had learnt that he enjoyed sudden challenges and instant adventures. 'I'll come tomorrow!' I said expecting him to be surprised, even to say it was not possible.

Without even a second's hesitation, he calmly said, 'That's fine,' and I was the one left with doubts.

'Well, I'll have to try to get a flight,' I said, hedging a little, 'I'll ring you back when I've fixed it to let you know it's OK.'

'There's no need,' he said, 'just ring me when you arrive in Salzburg and I will come to fetch you.'

I put down the phone slowly. Was I mad? I had planned to have a relaxing weekend, now I was committing myself to some serious climbing in the Alps – something I had not done for twenty years – with one of the world's best Alpinists.

Well, fate was putting me on the line. Four months before, in January, I had won £100 on the Premium Bonds. It was the first time I had ever won anything substantial, but could not decide what to do with the money. £100 was not enough to buy a new washing machine, and too much just to squander on clothes, so I put the money into a Deposit Account until the right thing to spend it on came along. This trip to the Alps had to be it.

I rang the local travel agents. 'How much is a return flight to Munich?' I asked. 'About £160,' the girl told me. 'Thank you,' I said, and put down the phone. There was no way that I could justify spending £160 for a weekend, especially as I was saving to go to Yosemite.

But I did not want to give in so easily. Travel by train and coach were out because of the time they took. I made a cup of coffee and sat down to think. Suddenly I had an inspiration! A couple of months earlier my mother had flown to Germany with a 'bucket' shop ticket I rang her at once. 'Yes, dear, it cost me £80 return,' she told me, and gave me the number.

'Do you have a seat on a flight to Munich tomorrow?' I asked the young man who answered the phone.

I could hear him tapping the keys of a computer. 'Yes, there's space on the 7.30 pm flight,' he said. 'But you must come to the shop to pay and pick up the ticket today.'

Hell, I had just solved one problem to hit another. There was no way I could get to the travel agents in London before they closed – I had to teach at Harrison's Rocks from 10.30 until 5. I rang my mother again. 'Would it be possible for you to pick up the ticket for me from High Steet Kensington?' I asked.

'Don't worry,' she said. 'My neighbour works just along the road. I know that she'll pick it up for you and bring it here. You can drive up this evening and get it.'

Suddenly I found myself laughing. It seemed so crazy. One moment I was enjoying a peaceful life, and the next disrupting it for something I was not totally sure I could handle. Was I really doing the right thing? Apart from anything else, I still hardly knew Kurt. Supposing we did not get on under the pressure which can arise while climbing . . .

Well, I thought to myself, if it makes you laugh it can't be such a bad thing. After all, it was only for a weekend!

During the day I discovered that the Venture Scouts came from Streatham in South London. 'I've got to drive there tonight, to pick up my ticket to Munich,' I told the leader, and his good deed for the day was to arrange for one of the fathers to bring the ticket to the Rocks.

So in a rather complicated but almost predestined way, I found myself at Salzburg station at two in the morning. I went into a telephone box to call Kurt, then hesitated. What an unsocial hour to arrive! The alternative was to sleep on a bench at the station, and I certainly did not fancy that. No, he had been so laid-back about my arrival, why should I suffer, I reasoned, and put my money into the box.

We got on well, right from the moment of meeting.

'Let's go and eat, you must be hungry after your journey,' Kurt suggested, and guided me towards a late night restaurant – not all of Salzburg goes to sleep at night. I felt relaxed as we sat eating our schnitzels and he told me about the book he was writing. My thoughts went to his *Summits and Secrets,* one of the best mountaineering books ever published. It is the sort of book not only to inspire the would-be or already competent climber, but containing beautifully written stories and philosophies is of interest to everyone and has been translated into many languages. It is a book that I constantly dip into, always finding something new that I had not discovered before. *Summits and Secrets* was written when Kurt was in his late thirties, and it had taken him two years to complete. Now at forty-seven he felt inspired to up-date his fascinating life story, but had little time to write and less than a year to complete this second book, due to his many travels.

I slept well for what was left of the night and awoke next morning to the sound of rain beating against the large windows of the flat which Kurt shared for part of the year with his elderly but very active father.

Apart from exploring, climbing and making films all over the world, he has three homes, one in Salzburg, the second with his first wife and two daughters in Varesse in Italy, the third in Bologna where his present wife, Teresa, and little son live; and he lives part-time in them all. I call him the 'Three-Day Man' because he never seems to stay anywhere longer than that.

The weather forecast for the whole of the Alps was bad, and there was no question of going climbing.

'Don't worry,' Kurt said. 'If the weather clears in the afternoon we can go for a bicycle ride, and if it improves tomorrow we'll go the mountains.'

I had read the chapter in his book about his grandfather's 1909 antiquated bicycle and of how he had pedalled hundreds of kilometres all the way from Salzburg to the sheer granite spires of the Dolomites and another time to the snow-covered Matterhorn. That afternoon I found myself embarking on a more minor epic, but as I had not sat on a bicycle since I was twelve years old what we achieved was quite a feat. My steed was a heavy black 1950s model, and I wobbled along the traffic-filled streets of Salzburg trying to keep up with Kurt. The rain stopped at 2 o'clock as he guided me out of the town towards the bordering mountains,

111

and as the gradient increased, I found that I had to stand up on the pedals in order to get enough push to keep me mobile. Kurt sat nonchalantly on his saddle and made no more effort than he had on the flatter part. Every time he glanced round to make sure I was still following I sat down hurriedly, pretending that it was easy for me too. I thought that if I failed the bicycle test he might think that I was not fit enough for the mountaineering. And a test it certainly turned out to be. We pedalled for hours and climbed up and zoomed down three thousand feet that afternoon and evening. We returned to his flat at eleven that night. Later I learnt just what a fitting introduction our outing had been to Kurt's *modus operandi*. He is capable of packing far more action than most people into a day.

But this day was not over. After supper he suggested that I might like to help him write a chapter of the book. 'I have never done this before,' he explained, 'but I think it could work very well,' and he went on to tell me the story that he wanted to relate. But the book was to be written in German. He picked up a tape recorder and started to dictate. My German was reasonably fluent from those teenage summer holidays, and I had spent six weeks alone with my grandparents in the Black Forest when I was sixteen. It seemed quite natural to add my comments so that together we composed the chapter, in both English and German. Sometimes Kurt would correct my English and occasionally I would suggest a different word or sentence in German. We did not notice the time, but dawn was breaking over the fast-flowing Salzach river outside his windows when we finally put down the tape recorder.

'It'll be a pig to translate,' I told him. Kurt's writing involves much subtle use of language, and several dual-purpose words or expressions would not work in translation.

'Don't worry,' he reassured me. 'It will be a good chapter.'

I had gone for a weekend but stayed a week. The weather only improved enough for short climbs on the mountains around Salzburg, but every day we went on some expedition. We even visited Hermann Buhl's widow. Kurt had been with this legendary Austrian mountaineer on the first ascent of Broad Peak in 1957 and was alone with him when he fell to his death on Chogolisa in the Himalayas just afterwards. After the accident in a storm high up on the mountain, Kurt had managed to get down by himself. 'For long indescribable hours of horror,' he wrote, 'during which I, at times, had a feeling that Hermann was still with me – I managed by some miracle, to find my way, onwards, downwards. Then, just before the great ice-falls, my pocket-lamp failed; so I had to bivouac at 18,000 feet. In the first pale light of dawn I made my way down the ice-falls. On and on, endlessly on . . . till 27 hours after Hermann's fall, I tottered into base camp.' Kurt was just twenty-five years old when the accident happened and it was his first Himalayan expedition. It must have been a horrendous experience suddenly to find that his companion had disappeared and that he was totally alone on the huge mountain. I liked Frau Buhl enormously. She had tremendous vitality and saw deep into people. I felt she was a kindred spirit.

Every night we worked on the book, from about ten o'clock, and every morning I saw the sunrise. By the time I left Salzburg six chapters had been roughly completed. I learnt a lot about how a book evolves, and Kurt and I discovered that we had a rare creative rapport which we were later to develop further when we made films together.

It is odd how things work out. Had I turned down Kurt's invitation to climb with him in the Alps (as I did with the sailing boat) I would not have had the chance to work with him on his book and the wonderful adventures of the next few years would never have happened.

Sun dance in Yosemite

'Would you come and join me in Yosemite in the summer?' Dennis asked me. It was Boxing Day 1979 and after sharing a very enjoyable Christmas Day with our family, he had driven us to Heathrow Airport. Terry and I were off to explore Thailand and Malaysia for six weeks – Pila had paid for the trip with a litter of eleven puppies. It was a nostalgic journey for Terry and an intriguing one for me. He had been stationed in Malaya during the Emergency in 1953, while doing his National Service, and I was longing to see the old haunts I had heard so much about. We took no luggage other than Terry's cameras; we were travelling ultra-light and without plans. We went by train, bus and boat wherever the fancy took us, buying the cheap and far more suitable local clothes as we needed them. Most of the time we wound ourselves into cool, brightly coloured cotton sarongs. We had a marvellous time roaming from Bangkok to Singapore in the south, then back up the opposite coast to the little town Chiang Mai on the edge of the jungle in the north of Thailand. Christopher, now 18, was living at the Outdoor Pursuits Centre where he worked and Lindsay went to stay with a friend. It was the first real holiday that Terry and I had taken alone for twenty years and we got a lot of pleasure from each other's company.

Time flew by after our return in February, and on 15 July 1980 I was sitting in San Francisco Airport waiting for Dennis to collect me. We travelled by Amtrak train and coach through the Californian countryside but as the coach went through the gates into Yosemite National Park, paradise opened up. Soaring granite cliffs touching the sky three thousand feet above the valley floor surrounded us. Yosemite is a climbers' Mecca. I had visited it with the family once before, as a tourist. I could not believe that this time I was here purely to climb.

'Come on,' Dennis said as soon as we arrived at the campsite, 'let's go climbing.' I was still a little knocked out by the Californian heat – he had lived there since April and was used to it – but within half an hour of arriving in the Valley we were putting on our rubber-soled climbing boots at the foot of some huge slabs.

I had learnt a long time before never to ask Dennis the grade of a climb before starting. He knows my limitations and I have complete faith in his competence not to put either of us into an unnecessarily dangerous situation by trying something too hard. There is a lot of psychological battling in climbing. Sometimes, if I knew the route was difficult, I would feel negative about tackling it. Now Dennis moved fast and smoothly up and up the steep white granite. Then it was my turn. 'Wuh,' I barked. Dennis and I have evolved our own system of climbing communication calls. Conventionally you call, 'Climb when you're ready,' to your partner when you have safely attached yourself to the rock at the end of the first rope length. 'Climbing,' the second warns the leader when he has untied his own belay and all the slack rope has been taken in, and so on. The problem is that in windy conditions, or when a barrier of solid rock separates you, these calls cannot always be heard. Although a silent system of communication can be worked through the rope, it is not always positive enough. A deep grunt from the pit of the stomach, using the same principle as the 'kiai' – the force-producing shout used in karate – sounds a little like the bark of a hoarse sea-lion but seems always to be heard.

I concentrated on the rock. To my fuzzy, jet-lagged eyes, still unaccustomed to the harsh white sunlight bouncing off the bright reflective granite, the surface looked completely smooth. The rock rose two thousand feet skywards and although the angle was only around forty-five degrees, it looked far steeper. I felt like a beginner again. With every different type of rock you have to vary your technique and approach. Sandstone, limestone, gritstone and granite are all a different challenge, and even within those broad categories the texture of the rock can differ. Yosemite granite was unlike anything I had ever encountered. This climb had a 5.7

start, not even the equivalent of our middle-ranging, Very Severe grade, and I could not see how to get even one foot off the ground!

But there was no comparison to be made with our British grades. We take into account long unprotected run outs. In Yosemite, to climb for 160 feet with no means of placing any 'runners' to lessen the distance in the case of a fall is not unusual. Their classification does not have any regard for the exposed nature of a route. Here exposure is always total: real fly-on-the-wall stuff.

'Look for the small depressions,' Dennis shouted down. I tried hard to focus and saw a smudge of white chalk on a fingernail thick flake. Some previous climber, his fingertips coated with chalk to help his grip, had found some sort of hold there. I reached for it and found that it accommodated, yes, that's right, a fingernail! Below was a slightly rougher spot in the granite which provided a moment of friction for a foot ... and I was away. The next lesson I had to learn is that once you start to move upwards you must not stop. If you hesitate even for a moment your feet start to slide downwards on the smooth slabs and you get a sinking feeling in the stomach. It is also very hard to get going again.

I soon mastered the polar bear pad – hands pushed flat against the warm rock, like a lizard's, with feet busily pedalling up below. By the time I reached Den, I was enjoying it thoroughly.

Yosemite valley is a very special part of the world. America's National Parks are owned by the government, unlike our National Parks where most of the land is privately owned. The Valley covers seven square miles and is dominated by spectacular huge granite cliffs and tall cascading waterfalls. The crystal-clear Merced river flows through fragrant pine forests and rough meadows where wild flowers and animals abound.

There are eight different campsites, some very civilised with tent cabins which have beds with sheets and blankets and restaurant and shower facilities. There are also two hotels, a Visitor's Centre; museums; a replica Indian village with demonstrations of American Indian crafts; a well-stocked general store and good gift shops.

The organisation, education and law enforcement are controlled by Park Rangers, and the Park comes under Federal Law, not California County Law. Fines are charged on the spot for offences like bad parking, feeding wild animals, nude sunbathing, polluting rivers, etc. For more serious crimes such as shoplifting, rape or parachuting off the cliffs without a permit, there is a Court House in the Valley with full federal powers. For the lesser misdemeanours you can work off the fines by cleaning toilets or the streets.

The Rangers run a programme of walks and talks covering many subjects interesting to all age ranges. Yosemite caters for families. Photography, Indian culture, star-gazing, survival in the wilderness, bears, flora and fauna – even the sex life of insects – are explained with imagination and enthusiasm.

A one-way road system circles the Valley floor and, to discourage pollution from cars, a free shuttle bus service – with gas-powered open-topped buses – operates from eight in the morning until ten at night. Unfortunately these buses are fitted with public address systems, and from a thousand feet above you can clearly hear 'The doors are closing, stand clear of the doors,' or 'Yosemite Falls, Yosemite Falls. The trail to your right will take you to the Falls in just ten minutes . . . Have a good day!' It is good to discourage petrol pollution, but these disembodied amplifications are a horrible intrusion and a different sort of pollution in this otherwise peaceful wilderness area.

We lived very basically at 'Sunnyside' campsite, the one favoured by our fellow climbers from all over the world. A blanket on the pine needles was our kitchen, dining and living room during the day, and the bedroom at night. The tent was too hot to live in and only used to store our things.

It was the hot season and I soon understood why most of the climbing areas were deserted. Dennis and I would get up just before first light, around 4 am, and, as the buses were not yet running, walk several miles to our chosen climbing area. It was always warm enough for just shorts and a tee-shirt. We would try to fit in a couple of routes before the first rays of the sun hit the rock around nine o'clock, for once it did, it was unbearable. The rock heated up very fast to the average daytime temperatures of around 100°F which burnt our fingertips and the soles of our feet, even through our boots. We would sweat profusely and after a couple of hours my feet felt as if they were immersed in bowls of hot water. When I took off my boots they looked like it too, shrivelled like prunes. My rubber-coated climbing boots smelt dreadful, and I could hardly bear to make a move which involved placing my foot anywhere near my nose.

We would eat and sleep the day away until three o'clock in the afternoon, when the opposite side of the Valley was again in the shade and we could continue our climbing until dark.

Once you get used to the heat and the enormous scale of the climbs, Yosemite is a paradise. The problem with most British routes is that they are never long enough. Two or three pitches is average. In Yosemite the climbs and pitches are long, and a climbing rope of 165 feet is really necessary. Often you can either abseil down from halfway up the cliff at the end of one climb or continue on up on another route. The abseils were mind-blowing. The rope often had to be put through a bunch of slings attached to a ¼-inch bolt. Climbing certainly requires a lot of faith, not just in your own ability but in the equipment to which you entrust your life. The fixed bolts which are left in permanently make you question your sanity most of all. Set in a drilled hole in the otherwise smooth granite, just about the depth of a thumb nail, these were our anchors as we slid down the rope one hundred and sixty feet at a time. Many of the bolts are rusty and I wondered what the electrical corrosive action of rain water was doing to the bit we could not see.

By the end of July the weather had become even hotter, and we decided to escape to the High Sierra of Tuolumne, the area above Yosemite Valley where the cooler air at 8,600 feet meant that one could climb right through the day and enjoy pleasantly cool nights.

Tuolumne is very different scenically from the Valley. It has verdant meadows with huge conical domes of grey rock scattered amongst them. Instead of abseiling to get back down these after a climb you walk on the least steep side. It is like walking down a smooth roof, and took quite a while until I felt confident enough to copy Dennis and run down, twisting and turning like a downhill skier to control the speed.

One climb that had been highly recommended to us was Cryin' Time, a 5.9 route on Lembert Dome. The first time we did not even get off the ground, there were several ropes waiting to do the climb. 'It seems to be a climb favoured by female climbers,' I observed, noticing that all the pairs climbing and waiting were couples. And we went off to try something different.

The second time we arrived early, and there was just one pair already climbing. We roped up and Dennis led off. When he arrived at the first belay point I waited for his 'Wuh' call to tell me to prepare to climb. Nothing happened. Fifteen, twenty minutes later I was still waiting but as I was tied on underneath a small overhang, I could not see what was amiss. 'You'd better come on up,' Dennis finally shouted down, and thankfully I was on the move again, up, over the projecting roof and on to the steep wall covered with delicate holds. I mantelshelfed onto the ledge to join Dennis and almost fell over the prone figure of a girl. She was lying with her sunhat covering her eyes, holding the rope for a young man who was obviously having a lot of trouble.

'Gee, will he never get up?' she grumbled.

'He's been stuck there for ages,' Dennis explained, 'says he can't get up or climb back down. Better make yourself comfortable; it looks as if we're in for a long wait.'

It was almost an hour before the unfortunate lad finally committed himself to the next move, and we all heaved sighs of relief. Patsy followed him up. 'Hold the rope tight,' we heard him order her as he set off on the next pitch, and felt a little nervous as he traversed rather unconfidently two hundred feet above our heads.

'Think I'll lead on up,' Dennis said. 'It looks as if Patsy could do with some help on the next section.' When he reached the small ledge, Dennis untied one of the double ropes which joined us together and linked it to Patsy's harness. Now her boyfriend could pull in the rope which joined them in front of her while Dennis gradually paid out his rope from behind. If she fell as she went across the traverse she would only drop down a little way instead of swinging in a long arc.

119

She certainly was a game girl. Three times she fell off and bounced on the springy nylon ropes. She was getting very tired. So were Dennis and I, from the waiting. After the fourth try, she gave up. 'Think I'll try to go straight up,' Dennis told me, 'might be easier for the girl too. I can give her a strong tug with the rope from above.'

It was delicate but interesting climbing on sharp rounded pockets eroded into the rock by dripping water, and Patsy obviously felt more secure following Dennis. Eight hours from the start of the climb we reached the top.

'I'll never climb with that idiot again,' swore Patsy, crying with exhaustion as she pulled up over the last ledge.

So that was it! I understood how the climb got its name. It was the favourite for young climbers eager to show off their skills to inexperienced girlfriends on the other end of the rope. It was way above the capabilities of many of the girls and, like Patsy, they ended up in tears. Yes, Cryin' Time was an appropriate name.

We had made friends with another couple, Pete and Lorraine, who were not only climbers but both teachers of Tai Chi. We bumped into them on our way back to our tent in the lupin wood.

'We're going to get married next week,' they announced. 'Would you come to the wedding?'

'Where will it be held and when?' I asked, picturing a wedding at the little chapel I had seen in the woods.

'We don't know yet. First we have to find a priest. We'll let you know,' Pete said. 'We still have to find a place we like too,' he added.

When we saw them again they looked pleased. 'We've got someone to marry us. A friend of mine joined the Church of America, for a laugh really. It cost her seven dollars, but she's allowed to marry and bury for that. The wedding's planned for Monday,' Lorraine told us happily.

'What time will you start?' Dennis asked.

'Whenever you like,' came the unexpected reply. They were really casual these Californians.

We looked at each other. 'We'd like to do a climb first,' Dennis said, jokingly. 'OK, you go off and do your climb, then we'll have the wedding,' came the reply.

On 17 August we managed two climbs, and excelled ourselves by climbing a holdless 5.11 route before heading back to the campsite. I put on my freshly washed shorts and tee-shirt and we walked over to our friends' tent.

'Go and collect yourself a wedding bouquet. We've had special dispensation from the rangers to pick the wild flowers,' Lorraine told us, and we spent a relaxing half hour selecting and making up the posy. When we returned we were introduced to Tip, the 'priest', the best man, Mike, and to Jo the bridesmaid. I felt very underdressed, even in the sylvan setting of the woods, as the girls were wearing pretty long dresses.

'Are we all ready?' asked Mike.

'OK, let's go and get these two lovely people married,' and we set off in a crocodile along the narrow path through the caravan site. Out across the lush green meadows we went until we reached the banks of a gently flowing river. There were three pine trees to give shade.

'We want to tell each one of you why we wanted you at our wedding,' Pete said as we stood in a semi-circle around the couple. I felt quite humble when he had finished. Then we individually told them our personal wishes for their future together. The vows followed: not in the restrictive set church form repeated in parrot fashion, but freely in their own words, spoken from the heart. Loving, heartfelt words which would be remembered in the good times and help them through the bad patches. It was the most sincere and beautiful wedding I have ever been to.

'I declare you man and wife!' the lady priest spoke for the first time, and after the kisses and photographs we all headed back for the reception.

The day after the wedding Dennis teamed up with an American friend Paul to do another harder multi-day route on Half-Dome. They would sleep on ledges on the face, tied firmly to the rock so that they would not roll over in their sleep and tumble into space. These routes are interesting to tackle, but the climbing is very different from the shorter climbs. Everything has to be carried up the rock face including drinking water, and you each need to drink at least five pints a day.

Since a pint of water weighs a pound and a quarter, for a three-day route for two people, you would have to haul 30 pints or almost 40 pounds of water up the rock face, as well as sleeping bags, cooking gear, food and a lot of heavy metal climbing equipment. To make things faster, the second climber often climbs up the rope using a prussiking clamp (a clogger or jumar) which slides up the rope but locks on a downward pull; so for him it is more a question of mechanics than climbing. To climb such a route is a slow, laborious task, fixing ropes and pulling up the heavy sacks of gear. I only had one week left before I had to go home, and there were still a lot of other climbs I wanted to do, so I decided to walk back down to the Valley twenty-four miles away and find another climbing partner.

One of the features of the area is the brown bears. Down in the Valley they are carefully controlled by the Rangers, and if they become a nuisance at a campsite they are trapped and flown in a special tube underneath a helicopter to an uninhabited area several miles away. If the same bear has to be trapped three times, it is declared a danger and shot. The visitors to the Park have to play their part; after all, the bears were there first, and it is Federal law that all food must be strung on ropes from the trees, ten feet from the ground, four feet away from the trunk of a tree, on a branch not more than two inches thick which could not carry a bear's weight. They are good tree climbers! It is once a bear has become addicted to human food that he becomes a nuisance and might attack to get his fix. Food can also be left in the boots of cars, but if anyone is silly enough to leave it in the passenger compartment, the bears will go to any lengths to get in. They may look like cuddly teddy bears, but these six-foot grizzlies are capable of causing a lot of damage. We saw several cars with windows smashed and the doors prised open as if they were made of tin.

I wanted to photograph a bear, but Dennis always discouraged me from trying to lure one close enough. The night before I descended to the Valley, I was alone and determined to try. I smeared some honey on a piece of wood and put it on a tree stump twenty yards from the tent. The bears are nocturnal animals, and we had heard several crashing through the under-growth during our stay at Tuolumne. I lay on top of my sleeping bag, camera at the ready, and waited. I had almost fallen asleep when there was the sound of breaking twigs nearby. I lay still for a few seconds and then quietly inched my way out of the tent. I had just got to an upright position when there was a terrifying hiss – not a growl as I would have expected – but a truly spine-chilling hiss. I could not see the bear, but the noise frightened me so much that I fled back into the tent, closed up the zip very tightly and hid myself deep in my sleeping bag. Some commercial pictures of bears would do for my lectures.

Back down at Sunnyside campsite, I was invited to tea by some British climbers and arranged to climb with one of them until Dennis returned. After doing a couple of routes on the Apron Slabs to see how we climbed together, Alan Church and I tackled a climb which I had always wanted to do – the Pillar of Frenzy. A series of 'strenuous' cracks is the key to this almost vertical pillar of granite, and my *bête noire* of climbing techniques, jamming, was really put to the test. I prefer delicate small holds to balance on, or climbs where you rely on friction to gain height. Wedging my fingers and toes into narrow gaps in the rock was painful. Sometimes only one or two fingers would fit, and then only to the depth of the first joint. It took a lot of confidence to entrust hanging my whole body weight on such a hold. By the time we reached the top, my feet were throbbing with pain from being squeezed into the narrow fissures; I had to soak them in the cold river to ease the agony. But it was an exciting climb, and I was thrilled to have achieved another of my ambitions.

High above Yosemite Valley is a startling needle of rock. When we were holidaying there with our children, Chris had kept staring up at it in fascination, especially when there were climbers on it. It had impressed him more than anything else in the Park. 'Will you climb the Lost Arrow?' he had asked me as I left home, and it seemed like a good idea . . . until I saw it again.

The base of the needle is over two thousand feet above the Valley floor, and massive erosion has caused this 800-foot phallic spire to stand dramatically alone. A gap of more than one hundred feet separates its summit from the main cliff face. To climb it you abseil down to the brêche where it is attached to the main cliff and then climb up the longest, most exposed side. To get back to the mainland the climber tows up the abseil rope, which has been attached to a tree at the top of the main cliff, and ties the free end to a bolt drilled into the rock on the tip of the pinnacle. Then, hanging over an awful lot of air, he pulls himself across the horizontal gap in a Tyrolean traverse.

'Gee, have you seen those guys up there? They sure must be crazy!' said a broad built American. It was a typical comment from neck-craning tourists as they peered through binoculars at a distant speck swinging high in the air across the clothesline rope of the traverse, and so far I had tended to agree with them.

'If we are going to climb Lost Arrow, we need one more person,' Alan's friends Dave and John said when we got back to the campsite. 'Are you interested, Julie?'

I thought about it for a moment. I had climbed well with Alan, and it would be a great finish to my trip. 'Yes,' I heard myself saying. 'I would love to come with you.'

Dennis came back from his epic on Half Dome that afternoon. He had just spent six hours walking down and, after the exertion of the long climb, was understandably very weary but said he would walk up with us and stay over to take photographs. I knew how tired he must have felt, as I had climbed Half Dome by an easier route earlier on my trip. It was another four and a half miles, and an uphill walk of three thousand feet to reach the camping place at the top of Yosemite Falls. We were going that evening so that we could make an early start next morning.

It was quite chilly at 6 am, and a white mist hung over the valley below. We fixed the 9mm diameter rope to the stout tree and watched it snake down the perpendicular cliff. We had to join two lengths of rope together with a knot to reach the rocky saddle 300 feet below from where we would start to climb. 'When you abseil down, if you keep well to the right, I'll be able to get some very dramatic photographs,' Dennis instructed. I put the rope through my figure of eight and attached it to my sit harness. At first I could hardly move. There was a lot of rope hanging below me and I had to lift its heavy weight and feed it through the friction-building circle of metal of the abseiling device every time I wanted to move. It was hard work, and I could only make slow progress. I came to where the ropes were tied together with the large knot and clipped on my clogger above the figure of eight to hold my weight while I detached this and replaced it below the obstruction which would not pass through the hole. Now the problems started. I realised I had no slings with me to step down into. On the usual route down there was in fact a large niche (far to my left) in which you could sit comfortably while you sorted out the knot, but I was unaware of this. For the sake of art and the camera, I had come down on the edge of a steep corner so that every time I made a movement I swung from one side to the other. I am sure it looked, as Dennis had suggested, dramatic. It felt it too! I looked at the rope on which my life depended. Stretched under my weight, it appeared as thin as the power cable from my vacuum cleaner. The figure of eight was back on my harness but its lower position made a foot of slack rope form a loop between it and the clogger. I needed to hold onto the rope with one hand to keep myself upright. If I removed the clogger with the other hand I would drop sharply onto the figure of eight and might not be able to control the speed of the rope passing through it. Now there was not so much rope below me, its weight would not pull it down, creating friction, and as it was a thinner rope than is ideal for abseiling, it would pass over the rounded metal much quicker. Once I was travelling downwards too fast, I would lose all control.

It felt very scary hanging in mid-air, swinging from side to side, and I tried to remember what the rope was running over at the top. Had Alan been awake enough at such an early hour to ensure that it would not be cut through by a sharp rock edge? My swinging must be causing quite a sawing action one hundred and fifty feet above my head. Lower your Centre, keep calm, I told myself, and took a deep, relaxing breath. Dennis and the others were getting worried and called anxiously down to me, but could suggest no solution to my dilemma.

I took another clogger and put it on the loop just above the knot and, after taking another deep breath, removed the top one. 'Ooh!' I fell with a jolt, and the elasticity of the rope, built in to help absorb the energy in the case of a fall, made me bounce up and down. I wrapped the lower rope round my foot and then held it in my hand as I took off the second clogger and dropped with a sharp jerk onto the figure of eight, and bounced again. At last I was able to slide on down. I had to hold the rope very tightly for the last twenty feet when it threatened to whip through very fast. I did not want to shoot right off the end and go flying down to the still sleeping Valley.

I crossed the little brêche and stood dwarfed by the enormous finger of rock. Alan wanted to lead the whole climb, and I was quite happy to let him. I am not a competitive or ambitious climber. I cannot climb often enough for that. I climb purely for pleasure, and although at times I want to have the fun of leading, deciding where the route goes and being on the more dangerous sharp end of the rope, I also enjoy the added possibilities that the security of the rope from above gives to try out more difficult moves and variations.

I rarely watch the leader, unless he is likely to fall off. I prefer to feel through the rope. It is amazing how much you can tell from its movement, even if the person attached to it is standing still. You can even feel the nervous trembles! I like to decide for myself how to tackle a move; after all everyone is built differently and does not have the same strengths and weaknesses.

Moving up the pillar was fantastic, getting higher and higher, feeling like Spiderman. On one side of the rock tower the thundering Yosemite Falls reflected rainbows as the wild river of water fell vertically through space for a couple of thousand feet. The view was stupendous, breath-taking, and I felt like letting out a loud yell as I made the last move onto the top. Instead I sat down quickly; the summit was not very big, about ten foot square, and the steep sides of the monolith made me feel as if I was floating in space, like sitting on a magic carpet.

Our two friends who were bringing up the abseil rope for the traverse were still quite a way below us. 'Don't like the look of the weather,' Alan observed. Black storm clouds were gathering and moving rapidly in our direction. By the time the others reached the top, we could hear the sound of distant thunder.

'Better hurry up,' Dave said, and John, his climbing partner, threaded the rope through the iron ring of the bolt and secured it with a knot. The first person to go across has the hardest crossing, as at this point only one rope bridges the gap. Dave opted to go first and started across, the free end of the rope attached to his harness. When he got to the other side we would untie the knot on the bolt and he would tie his end to the abseil tree so that the rope formed a loop from the tree, through the bolt, and back to the tree again. That way we would be able to retrieve our expensive rope by pulling it back once we were all safely across.

The rest of us watched rather nervously from our little tabletop perch as the storm closed in. We could feel the tension of the static electricity in the air; then it started to spit with rain.

'I don't care if it's ungentlemanly, but I'm going next!' Alan informed us. 'I'm not staying here a moment longer than I need to. It's bloody dangerous.' There was a lot of strain in his voice. Doesn't look too easy, I thought to myself as I watched first Dave and then Alan heave themselves strenuously across.

By the time I was halfway across, the thunderstorm really let rip. Thunder crashed explosively echoing off the steep walls of the cliffs, and I could feel the lightning tingling through me as I moved along the wet perlon rope. I was lying underneath the rope, with two cloggers attached to it from my harness to help me slide myself across. I also had a safety carabiner as an extra safeguard. Getting off the top of the pinnacle was easy: you simply dropped down onto the rope as for a conventional abseil, but as the top of the cliff was much higher than the summit of the pillar, at the bottom of the loose arc the rope started to go uphill. At first it was a gentle angle and not difficult to slide backwards along. I used one clogger for my hand, and the other one I had fixed to my foot with a tape sling so that I could push in a sort of upside down pumping action. It was the upward sloping section before it became vertical again that was such hard work and when I reached that the wind started. Hanging in space three thousand feet above the miniaturised trees of the valley forest, my threadlike lifeline began to pendulate, whipped by its force. To add to my discomfort, it started to hail. The hard, round stones of ice peppered me, stinging the many exposed areas of my bare flesh. I was only wearing shorts and a tee-shirt.

The hail coated the rope, making it impossible for me to slide the cloggers forward. I hung there helplessly, swinging violently, soaked to the skin, feeling desperately sorry for John who was still marooned on the pinnacle. No one could come to the aid of either of us. I glanced down and the to and fro movement of the rope made me feel sick. It seemed like an eternity before the hail eased and I could inch my way on across to the rock wall of the main cliff. I was totally exhausted by the effort, the nervous tension and cold.

'That was even worse than in Peru,' Dennis told me later. 'I was so frightened for you that I could not keep my hands still enough to take photographs.'

Climbers will chat happily about the epic adventures they have had, often embroidering them to add to the drama. But try to get them to admit that the sport is dangerous and they will, like me, think up many excuses to defend it. I always compare it to the uncertain hazards of driving a car. Some dangers you can avoid with your own skills, others are fate? luck? chance? all things over which you have absolutely no control, although your reaction at the time can have a strong bearing on the outcome.

At the beginning of September I flew back to San Francisco and home. What a marvellous six weeks I had climbed away. We had achieved forty-six classic Yosemite routes up to 5.11 grade which would live in my memory for ever, and better still were recorded on film so that I could in some way share my experiences with Terry and the children. At forty-one I finally learnt to use a camera!

Terry had tried on several occasions to interest me in photography, but as he was not just an amateur photographer and always had rather complex-looking cameras, I was not terribly interested. He took all the necessary pictures and, although I understood the basic principles of shutter speeds and f-stops, photography had an aura of technical mysticism about it which I found very off-putting. I also felt rather shy picking up a camera in the presence of such experts as Terry and Dennis.

It was the trip to Yosemite that motivated me. I wanted to be able to share my adventures with my family and friends. However,

I did not just want to take snapshots to put into an album, I had a great urge to put together an audio-visual story, as Dennis did so well, using two projectors. That was the challenge, not so much to take technically correct photographs, but to be more creative and take blending and linking pictures that would connect to tell the story of my trip. Perhaps it was being a little ambitious, but I suddenly felt a great need to be creative. I had spent many years sheltering under the ideas of others; now the children did not rely on me so much, I wanted to think my own thoughts and, even if they were not successful, try out my own ideas.

Terry was as supportive as ever and, as a going-away present, bought me a camera. It was love at first sight. The little Olympus XA was small enough to slip into my pocket, no heavy weight to hang around my neck and bounce uncomfortably against my, albeit small, bosom when I walked. I could use it with just one hand, which is very important when you are in the middle of a climb, and it was flexible enough for me to experiment with exposures and timings. Great! But perhaps Terry should be allowed to tell the story from his point of view (with a touch of lighthearted male chauvinism).

I opened the airmail envelope eagerly and crept back into bed to read it. Being without your wife (to remind you of the time) has some compensations. But as I read the letter through I felt the panic rising. It was just that one sentence which made me worry. 'Darling, I'll never complain ever again about the amount of film you buy!'

Two weeks previously I'd waved goodbye to Julie at Gatwick. I'd bought her a small camera because she'd always complained about the weight of mine. For once she seemed quite interested in photography. I'd given her two rolls of colour film, and really thought that was the end of it – a quick look through the slides when she got home and then file them in the ten slots I had spare in one projector magazine.

I waited for the next letter with bated breath. Nothing too alarming. She was having a great time and the climbing was superb. It was really too hot to climb except in the early morning and the cool of the evening. I looked outside at the dismal English summer and thought how lucky she was ... but then, right at the end of the letter, 'I've had five films developed locally already. They don't take three weeks to develop here, like yours do, and Dennis thinks they're good!' I knew Dennis was kind, but I didn't think he lied, especially about photography as he used to work as a lecturer for Kodak. He never said anything nice about my slides!

I put the letter down and worked it out. Five times thirty-six, that's one hundred and eighty! Well, I supposed there might be about fifty slides in that lot.

The letters kept coming, and the photography news got worse. The weather was fantastic, the climbs were getting harder and she was enjoying herself immensely. 'Oh, and by the way, I've had seven more films back and Dennis says they'll make a good audio-visual show.'

Oh my God, the thought of her taking over my projectors and, even worse, my darkroom, the only possible place in the house where I can take undisturbed refuge, made me break out in a cold sweat.

At last the six weeks were over, and I spent a day making the house habitable again. I drove to Heathrow to meet Julie.

She came through Customs, and I didn't really recognise her. Her hair was ten shades fairer, bleached by the sun, and she looked as if she'd spent ten weeks on the beach.

She was all enthusiasm. Fantastic, great, beautiful, stupendous, the superlatives rolled off her tongue as we drove home and she told me about the trip. Later that evening I could contain myself no longer. 'What about the slides? What are they like?'

'Oh,' she said casually, 'they're pretty good, but I've still got some more to come back, and a few more rolls to send off for development.'

Hells bells, I thought. I had given her two films, plus the five she had developed in California, then seven more, 'some' to come (that must mean more than two), and a few to go off, say three . . . She must have taken about twenty films, more than she'd taken before in the whole of her life!

We had dinner and I got the viewer out . . . the moment of truth. I had all my lines worked out. 'No, these are under-exposed, that's bad framing; oh dear, you got camera shake, etc.'

After the first box I felt about two feet tall. They were good . . . very good. We spent our spare time in the following weeks putting the slides into order and sorting out music to go with the mood of the pictures; then came the first showing.

'Are you nervous?' I asked her. My mind always goes round in circles before I start to lecture, checking projectors, plugs, cables and, most of all, hoping the slides are in the correct order.

'No . . . should I be?' she queried in all innocence, and sailed through the evening without a hitch.

For my next birthday present, Terry upgraded my camera to a proper SLR 35mm. Strangely I did not mind having to carry its extra weight and bulk, and the additional fun of being able to use interchangeable lenses made the extra effort more than worthwhile. I always carried it with me and made little audio-visual stories from every interesting trip I did.

In June 1980 I had agreed to make the necessary arrangements for Kurt to give a lecture tour in Britain the following January. He then went off to climb and film with an American expedition on the unclimbed East Face of Everest. I had learnt through the media of the deaths of two mountaineers on Everest and also knew that Kurt's expedition had not made the summit this time due to appalling weather, so it was with considerable relief that I heard a healthy-sounding Kurt on the end of the telephone from Copenhagen in November. He was already on the lecture circuit around Europe. After giving me the expedition news, he asked about his lectures here.

'Yes, they're all fixed,' I told him. 'I've arranged every one of them within forty miles of London. It can be hopeless trying to travel during a British January. The smallest amount of snow, ice or fog and everything grinds to a halt. I couldn't possibly guarantee that you would arrive, even on the appointed day, anywhere more remote.'

'Oh!' he sounded disappointed. 'But I wanted to go to Scotland. I have never been there.' I already knew that Kurt was a man who liked to make an adventure of everything, and should have realised that he would see the difficulties not as a reason but a challenge. Ten days later the tour was rescheduled and the venues for January 1981 ranged from Brighton in the south to the north of Scotland.

The first lecture is always the most nerve-racking for the organiser of any tour. As I was also promoting the first three, my anticipatory worries were doubled – but completely unfounded. Kurt arrived on time, gave excellent lectures, and the halls were full. It was interesting later to observe how other people who organised the individual lectures coped. There certainly is a lot to plan: tickets have to be printed and sold, advertising spread around, the hall and seating arranged, car parking organised, and it only takes bad weather, or a few good nights' viewing on television, to make the evening a financial disaster.

But the tour went well, and the audiences really appreciated Kurt's enthusiasm and humour as he related tales of his many fascinating adventures all over the world, beautifully illustrated by his superb colour slides.

However, even though it was an exceptionally mild January with no frost or fog, it was still the travelling which gave us the biggest problems. On 29 January, Kurt had a lecture in Kendal. Chris Bonington was in the audience and after the lecture he asked Kurt if he could borrow five slides to copy for inclusion in his new book. He returned them the following morning at Penrith Station when we caught the train to Edinburgh, but I wondered how many people would lend unique original slides from their lecture in the middle of a tour. I hate to let mine out of my possession at any time; even picture editors do not always treat them with care, and a scratch or a fingerprint can destroy a treasured memory or captured historic moment. Kurt says that his slides are like his children, and I tend to agree with this. Now during the journey he replaced the slides carefully into the gaps in the trays.

The train was to divide at Carstairs and we asked the guard how many carriages we had to move back to get into the Edinburgh half. 'Just one,' he told us.

Kurt had been amused that we had a 'guard' to look after us on the train. 'Ve are not prisoners!' he said when the 'this is your Captain speaking' type announcements came over the public address system.

As the corridors were crowded we decided to move our bulky luggage along the platform when the train stopped. 'Carstairs! Carstairs!' the loudspeaker announced and we leapt out with four of the six large pieces of our luggage and hurried along the platform to the rear of the long train. Just one carriage the guard had said, but where the train was to be divided there was a row of four first-class carriages, and the following two second-class compartments were already crowded. In the seventh carriage we found two seats and dumped the luggage down. Kurt rushed

132

back to collect the remainder of our bags but, just as he was about to enter the carriage, that half of the train moved slowly off and he was left staring at the ever widening gap as his suitcase with all his clothes and the expensive Leica projector disappeared towards Glasgow.

A loud hum from the other half of the train brought him to his senses and he only just managed to leap back into the carriage before that started to move too. Naturally I began to worry at that moment, sure that Kurt was still in the other half heading for Glasgow, and I racked my brains for some way of contacting him when we each arrived on either side of Scotland. It was ten minutes later when Kurt rejoined me and I could tell from his expression that he was not amused. The guard had been very off-hand. 'I don't understand how he could give all that information over the public address system on the way up, even on which side of the train the platform would be, and not make any announcement when half the train was leaving Carstairs. I now understand the British Rail logo,' he went on. 'It means that the same train can go in two different directions at once!'

It was while I was planning that lecture tour to Scotland that my filming career really began. I was just settling down in the gloom of another English winter, and was chatting with the children about the imminent Christmas holidays, when the great change in my life was heralded by the ring of the telephone. It was a murky Saturday afternoon on 28 November 1981.

Kurt was on the line. 'I'm in Paris,' he said, 'trying to arrange with the French to climb Nanga Parbat next year. If I can fix it, would you like to come as my assistant and sound recordist for the film?'

To give me time to talk it over with Terry Kurt said that he would call me back next day. He has a wonderful facility with languages and I always try to visualise in which country he is when he calls from his English accent at the time. Immediately he is involved with different people he picks up their national characteristics, idiosyncracies of speech – the louder excitable Italian, deeper more solid German, faster higher-pitched speech of the French, and so on.

133

'You're in Germany now,' I said next day. His accent had already changed.

'Yes, I'm in Kaiserslautern. Can you come to Nanga Parbat?'

'Yes, please, if you can really manage to arrange it.' I was hardly able to believe my luck.

'Good . . . Actually, I already have; the forms will be with you later this week. You will have to fill in your measurements for expedition clothing, and arrange a visa for Pakistan if you need one.'

And that was that. It was almost like arranging to have lunch: but in reality, in May, just six months away, I was going to climb a Himalayan mountain in distant Pakistan, at 8,126 metres the eighth highest in the world. I was so excited that I could not eat properly or concentrate on anything for several days.

Terry and the children were marvellous. Christopher, who had grown into a handsome young man, was nineteen and had just started work in a residential home for handicapped children. Previously he had been an instructor at an Outdoor Pursuits Centre and then had spent three months in America on the staff of a summer camp. He had been in charge of a group of rather spoilt seven-year-olds, all from very wealthy families, and taught archery and canoeing as well during the day. When he came home he announced that he wanted to work with handicapped children and his first job was at a somewhat depressing home for extremely handicapped young children, many with only a few years to live. I was very proud of him. It takes a special quality to care for such sad cases. However, Terry and I were a little concerned that he should not live too long in such an environment without a break. Young people need life to develop and maintain their own vitality and happiness. After almost a year Christopher arranged his own transfer to a very lively instructional and holiday unit for mentally and physically handicapped children of all ages, from birth to sixteen years, in Sevenoaks, twelve miles from Groombridge where he is still working. The children visit the centre for one week, or longer, several times a year.

Christopher and his colleagues not only look after the youngsters and teach them basic personal skills, but are free to develop their social education according to their individual needs. Trips

134

to the zoo, museums, the seaside or a restaurant can be arranged on the spur of the moment, when the mood is right. Chris says that his charges are the best behaved children around when he takes them out; sometimes he wishes that they would be more naughty and noisy.

Lindsay, now 18, was also settling down to a new life outside school. She wanted to learn hotel management, and was spending a year getting practical experience of the most menial tasks in hotel life before finally deciding to take a full training. Just now she was convalescing after breaking a leg in a bad motorbike accident.

Before going to Nanga Parbat I had to brush up my sound-recording skills. Dennis Kemp was my tutor and he not only had the knowledge (photography and sound had been his profession and remained his hobbies) but owned a Nagra identical to the one I would be using on the French expedition. The Nagra SN is a pocket-sized tape-recorder of superb quality and put together with typical Swiss precision. It is very lightweight – 2lbs – ideal for high altitude filming. A new Nagra SN would cost over £2,000. I had my first lesson in a mountain hut in North Wales during one of our climbing weekends. Dennis is such a good teacher that when I operate the Nagra in the mountains I often clearly recall his instructions word for word.

To learn how to be Kurt's film assistant was a far more complicated matter.

Terry and I had been involved with many film crews over the years, the various sandstone outcrops at Harrison's, High Rocks and Bowles provided excellent sets for many feature films, such as *Robin Hood*, for episodes in television series such as *Doctor Who* and for commercials ranging from Oxo to deodorants. We had been employed in a wide variety of roles from stand-ins to arranging access and safety ropes for actors and crew. We are always curious to learn as much as possible from asking and watching, and in the few months leading up to the expedition I latched on to any film crew that was down, assimilating as much knowledge as possible. Some of these crews had as many as twenty people; our crew on Nanga Parbat, in far more rigorous conditions, would be just two. So I had to study the jobs of several different people to find out what I needed to know.

One thing that I could not learn on the sets at the Rocks was how to change a film inside a 'black bag'. I was always very impressed when I watched the magician-like movements of the hands of the cameraman's assistant manipulating the film in and out of the camera magazine without being able to see what he was doing.

One cameraman suggested that I telephone Alex Culley, the chief technician at Samuelsons, the largest film hire company in Britain, and ask him to help. Alex kindly agreed and not only showed me how to load and unload the film magazines, but the same afternoon taught me all about the big Arriflex camera and lenses. This is a 16mm camera which runs so silently that you can record sound at the same time and my Nagra tape recorder has a small crystal generator, half the size of a matchbox, which synchronises it to run at exactly the same speed as the camera. The camera body alone is worth £10,000 and the film magazines have to be loaded and unloaded inside a black bag. It is a heavy piece of equipment, which is designed to sit on the cameraman's shoulder or a tripod. I also had to learn about the different kinds of 12-volt batteries from which it was powered. A battery belt, which felt like a weighted diver's belt, needed a generator to recharge the cells, as did the type which sat on the back of the camera itself. There was a mass of cables to understand, and we would have more for the 8-volt batteries which fitted the Arriflex standard, a smaller camera which is too noisy to use for sync sound but more versatile on the mountain. We would also have disposable lightweight batteries for them both.

Kurt had to go to China in March 1982 to do a reconnaissance and exploration film for the Italian K2 expedition the following year. He would join us in Pakistan. This meant that I would be thrown straight into the deep end of the film which we were making for French television and on which the expedition's finances would rely quite heavily. I would have to cope alone for the first two weeks of the expedition, organise collecting up and packing the filming and sound equipment by myself before we left for Pakistan, and then get it all safely to Base Camp. This heavy responsibility, coupled with travelling to a remote part of the world with a group of total strangers whose language was not my own, could have been fairly daunting – it was also my first Himalayan expedition – but thanks to the confidence that my martial arts training had given me, I could accept it all with eager anticipation. Early in 1981 I had been awarded my black belt, become a Shodan, which means taking the first step forward. Going to Nanga Parbat was taking a different kind of step forward – into international mountaineering and professional film-making.

9

French lessons – bewitched by Nanga Parbat

The 1982 expedition to Nanga Parbat was led by Pierre Mazeaud, an eminent politician and lawyer. He had been a Minister for Sport in France several years before. Pierre was a famous mountaineer, and Kurt had been with him to the summit of Everest in 1978. That was when he had made the first sync-sound film ever taken on the roof of the world. I had visited Paris to be vetted both as a person and medically. I was approved on both counts and as I left Pierre embraced me 'as a friend'. I was to be the only woman on the expedition with six French, two Germans, one Czechoslovakian, one French-Italian, one Austrian – Kurt – and two Pakistani climbers making up the team.

Three days before our departure from Paris, I had to travel to Munich to pick up the Arriflex SR16 sync-sound camera and other pieces of film equipment from the Arri-hire department.

The day before I had been walking across Tunbridge Wells common when suddenly, for no apparent reason, my knee started to hurt. In great agony I limped to the doctor, terrified that I would not be able to go to Nanga Parbat. I could not understand why it was so painful. I had even stopped practising martial arts in case a last minute injury might prevent me from going. The doctor looked puzzled. 'You've got an inflammation of the knee,' he told me as he handed me some pills, 'I hope these will help.'

On my way to Munich I had to stop off at Paris to deliver some metal film cases full of film stock and my kitbags of personal gear.

The baggage was to be delivered to Pierre's nephew Jeff Mazeaud, our expedition doctor. I must not let Jeff see that my knee is painful and stiff, I thought to myself, fearing that he

138

might stop me from going. It was a hard job trying to walk normally and not show how much I was suffering when he accompanied me down three flights of stairs. By the time I left him my knee was so swollen that it would no longer bend at all.

The next morning I flew on to Munich and carefully checked all the hire equipment that I collected against Kurt's comprehensive list of instructions. It all fitted into three metal boxes; only the big wooden tripod was separate. One case held the heavy Arriflex SR16 camera, zoom lens, my hired Nagra tape-recorder and other fragile bits. The second case contained all the lenses and rechargeable and disposable batteries for the cameras, together with the delicate tripod head and important papers. I already had the smaller Bell and Howell Autoload clockwork summit cameras at home, and Kurt would bring with him from China his Arriflex Standard and the other clockwork Bolex camera. The third case housed the film magazines and black bags. It was case number 2 that caused all the trouble at the security gate.

'Zeeze could well be restricted items,' the security guard pronounced. He fished out a battery and held it up in front of me.

Another man was called for. 'Vat are zey made of?' he asked me sternly, as if I had planned to sneak them on board.

'I don't know,' I said.

'Ve vill have to know before ve allow them onto the plane; they vill have to be tested.'

My heart sank. I would miss the plane and half my valuable film was already checked in and stowed aboard. It would arrive unattended at Heathrow and never be seen again. I racked my brains.

'I think they're made of something beginning with L,' I recalled in a flash of inspiration.

'Ah, lithium.' The word was long drawn out and had a worrying tone. He consulted his list.

'Zaire are two types of lithium batteries,' the official pronounced, 'and one is restricted as from this week by this airline. Are yours hermetically sealed?'

'I don't know; they are specially made for film cameras and

have already flown all over the world. This type was used on Everest: how do you think they got there?'

At last a third security official was called. This time it was a woman. She was quick and decisive.

'You can take the camera case onto the plane, but the batteries must go into the baggage hold.'

Before I could protest she seized the battery case and marched off.

My tired befuddled brain tried to sort out the mess and weigh up the situation. Could the batteries really be dangerous? Should I refuse to get on the plane and make my way home by boat and train? Apart from the time involved, it would be very hard with all the heavy cases. After all, they were the experts on dangerous items, and it was their decision to put the batteries into the baggage hold, and yet . . .

There was no time for further thought. I was hustled aboard the plane with my large camera case ahead of the other passengers. As my fellow travellers started to settle into their seats around me I worried more and more. Was I putting these innocent people at risk? It had been the airline's decision, but I had condoned it. Through the long minutes to take-off, I sat strapped in my seat, tense and very worried. Then we were moving. When would the pressure change affect the batteries most: during the rapid height gain to take-off, or was it a more gradual process, once we had arrived at our cruising height which the pilot had so cheerfully announced would be 31,000 feet? Could they explode? How much force would they have in the confined space of the baggage hold? There were not many passengers, so therefore not much baggage to cushion the blast. There was a lot of turbulence. 'Please stop shaking around,' I begged. I had visions of the baggage-hold doors being blasted off, the cabin floor with a gaping hole; oxygen masks descending from above; the panic of the passengers. Did the chemicals make you choke? At the very least, if they exploded with only a small bang, they could ruin everything around them. Was I insured? It was a wide-awake nightmare, which seemed to last a million years until we began our descent to Heathrow.

I had another brush with bureaucracy as I went through

Customs. As everything was in transit and would be leaving the country again in three days, I headed for the Green Channel.

'Stop,' I was ordered, and I hurriedly explained. 'Not good enough,' the serious official told me. 'We could impound all your goods if we felt inclined. You have entered this area with undeclared imported goods.'

I pushed my trolley to the Red Channel. This was empty and I had to call for someone to come. I explained my situation and asked what I should do.

'Nothing,' the man said. 'It's far too much hassle for me to fill out all those forms in triplicate; off you go.'

Heaven save me from the insanity of officials, I prayed as I headed for the automatic doors.

As soon as I got home I telephoned the company that made the batteries. 'Are yours hermetically-sealed and safe to fly?' I asked. 'Of course they are,' came the reassuring reply.

I had no such problems leaving England two days later. I met the rest of the expedition members at Pierre's flat in Paris the night before we left for Pakistan, and picked up the French atmosphere. The flight to Rawalpindi was uneventful too, probably because the Pakistan Airways plane observed Muslim rules and was 'dry'. Miraculously my knee had made a full recovery.

Pakistan was quite a culture shock. The heat as we left the airport hit me like an oven door opening, and the noise and bustle of Pindi made me retreat to the peace of my hotel room the first afternoon. We were staying at Mrs Davis's hotel, a long established dilapidated left-over from the days of the Empire. I had a mini-suite consisting of a sitting room, concrete-floored bedroom, and a bathroom that had not been cleaned for months. I know that the Muslims do not approve of western sanitary arrangements, but you could almost scrape the dirt off the bath and toilet pan. The Victorian dining room with its revolving fans and black and white tiled floor was the well-known meeting place for expeditions to the Karakoram mountains from all over the world, and the spacious garden and accommodation was full of cases and crates of camping and mountaineering equipment. This was the time I began to get to know the other members of my expedition and really try out my schoolgirl French on them.

When I did go out into the street I was surprised how many of the women still had their faces covered, and in crowded places I was jostled by the men who did not approve of a woman in public having bared arms and the line of her crutch uncovered (I was wearing jeans). Some of us went to cool down in the swimming pool of the tourist Hotel Intercontinental, and I noticed an advertisement for a martial arts club. The next day I went back to visit the class. The Pakistani instructor was very pleased to meet me and I was surprised to learn that they too practised budo, several disciplines together, like my club. 'Could you show us some sword-work?' the Sensei asked after we had compared techniques, and he produced the most rusty *katana* that I have ever seen. While we were chatting the students gathered on the spacious green lawn of the big hotel. They were all men, and I asked if any women came to practise. 'We do have just one. Do you think that you could teach her something? It is very difficult for me to do some of the techniques with her . . .' the Sensei said. He coughed, embarrassed, 'Some of them are a little indelicate for our social rules.' I was taken to meet the girl, who was hidden behind a hedge. She was small-boned and rather fragile, but with a keen desire to learn. However, after ten minutes she was worn out.

The Sensei looked at me. 'It's not usual here, but would you like to take the class?' he asked. It was one of the nicest but hardest classes I have ever taken. There were about fifty students, all young, fit and very supple, and very few spoke English. Martial arts soon break down even the most rigid barriers and it did not take long before the students could accept a woman touching them to correct their techniques and stances, and could attack and grab me with enthusiastic vigour.

The next evening we set off for the 600-kilometre drive along the dangerously twisty Karakoram highway which winds along the friable mountainsides above the broad brown Indus River to Bunar Bridge where we would start the walk-in to Base Camp. I was feeling very sad as I learnt of the deaths of Pete Boardman and Joe Tasker, two of Britain's best climbers, on Everest that afternoon. Nine of us and a lot of gear were tightly crammed into a mini-bus for the hot, dusty drive, and it was a relief to get to our destination twenty hours later. Two brightly painted lorries carried the rest of our equipment and the three members who had travelled with these had a far longer and more uncomfortable journey.

It was at the beginning of the walk-in that I began to realise that Pierre had no comprehension of my lonely job. The expedition had 300 porters. Scattered amongst these were eight I had to keep a special eye on, as they carried loads for the film team. The evening before we started the approach march, Pierre suddenly said, 'I want you to go ahead tomorrow and film the porters.' I explained that Kurt had told me that I did not need to film on the approach; he would film anything necessary on the way back, and I would only be wasting precious film stock. However, with Kurt absent, Pierre was the boss and although he had been told that I was a sound recordist and not able to operate the cameras, he insisted that I did so. Before we left Paris I had signed a lengthy contract, which stated clearly that unless I obeyed the orders of the leader I could be sent home, and I certainly did not want that to happen. So I reluctantly agreed. I told Pierre that I would need two porters to carry the camera and sound equipment, who would always stay with me, and in Kurt's absence one different member from the expedition to help me every day. It would be the ideal opportunity to get to know them, and decide how they could be involved in the film later on. Making expedition films is very different from making a standard documentary or feature film. There can be no pre-written script. Many different story-lines have to be followed simultaneously because nobody knows what is going to happen or how different mountaineers will behave in front of the cameras. Which are the most dramatic sequences will only become apparent later.

For the first day of the approach I asked for one of the three members of the expedition who knew the way already to accompany me, or one of our two Pakistani mountaineers who could converse with the porters.

'Non!' Pierre said firmly. 'I need them all with me, take Raymond.' This was not a very good choice for me as Raymond hardly spoke any English and I had not yet polished up my French enough to understand or explain anything at all complicated. He was rather wild-looking, too, with Marty Feldman eyes and a tangled growth of bushy beard. I was a bit nervous of him at first, but in fact soon discovered that he was not only harmless but a kind gentle-hearted person.

We hurried off along the narrow sandy track to get ahead of the main group. After four hours of walking, when we reached a green oasis in the dry brown foothills, tne two porters made gestures of eating and sleeping, put down their loads and scuttled away up the hill towards a village.

Raymond and I, both exhausted by the walking and the unaccustomed heat, lay in the grass by the river and slept. I was woken by something tickling my ear. Sleepily I brushed it away, but it returned and I heard a giggle. Opening my eyes I found that I was surrounded by a group of dark-skinned children who were examining my face with their very dirty fingers. I tried to amuse them by winking and pulling faces, but they kept pulling at my clothes and poking me and I soon had enough. 'Go away and let me sleep,' I told them firmly, but without success. They had not seen many European women and were very curious. When Raymond got up to fetch some water from the river – we were both dehydrated – the children and some women who had joined them pulled at me violently, indicating that I should run and get the water for him. Their fingers were no longer gentle and I was very tired. But there was no peace for me until our porters reappeared after three hours' absence and led us to another village.

Two hours later we discovered the remainder of our companions comfortably resting. 'How did you get here?' I asked Pierre's nephew Jeff. 'You didn't pass us.'

'No, we took a short cut across the river,' he explained.

'I told you to film the porters,' Pierre expostulated. 'Now it is too dark anyway.'

I tried to explain that our porters had taken us to the wrong village, and that I could not communicate with them, but he did not want to listen.

For the next three days of the approach march things got no

better. My only consolation was the sight of Nanga Parbat gradually rising higher and higher as we moved up the valley. Every morning Pierre insisted that I set off to film in the early morning well before the others. My plan to get some help from one of the other members each day did not work at all. When they arrived at the next camp they would lie down and sleep in the shade. Before he slept, Pierre would give me a list of things to be filmed, and I would spend what was left of the day setting up the tripod, filming, changing films and taking sound. At the third day's camp, he got very excited.

'Come on quickly, Julie, you must film an important event.' I had run out of film for the smaller camera that I had been using, and could not find the porter load with the spare film in it. I did not want to tell Pierre as he was very scathing about any inefficiency so I reluctantly got out the big Arriflex SR16. I had never used such a complicated and expensive camera and before he left for China Kurt had told me not to take it out of its sealed box in case the dust on the approach march damaged it.

I hurried over to where Pierre was gesticulating furiously. 'What do you want me to film?' I asked.

Here, here!' he said, and pointed at a goat which was about to have its throat cut. Although I filmed the gory scene as ordered, I knew that the television company would never show it.

'I don't have time to feel lonely,' I wrote home to Terry, 'but I'd like to be shown a little more . . . kindness perhaps. They just don't realise, I think, how much work I have done – maybe it's the Latin temperament.'

On the last day of the walk-in I set off at five-thirty in the morning with a thumping headache. We had climbed up to 13,000 feet (4,265 metres) in the past three days and as well as the effort of walking long distances in temperatures of 80° or 90°F the cumulative effect of working hard had exhausted me. The concentration of speaking and trying to understand French was also tiring. I asked Jeff for an aspirin.

'I haven't got one,' our doctor replied. 'They're all packed away!'

When I arrived at Base Camp at ten o'clock, Pierre, who had gone on ahead, was fast asleep. My head was bursting with headache and four days of mad activity and new experiences. The other members of the expedition seemed rather introverted, but I had made good friends with our Hunza high-altitude porters. They all spoke some English, and the cook, who was also a Hunza, spoilt me. He gave me some aspirin and quite soon I felt very much better.

Between filming the arrival at Base Camp I collected up my eight porter loads. When the 300 porters set off back to their villages things were likely to disappear, and it only needed one filter or cable to be stolen to render a camera completely useless. The sky started to cloud over and I asked François Hess, who was handing out stores, if I could put up a tent to protect my equipment in case it should snow.

No one offered to help me as I struggled to erect it, but I did not expect to be treated any differently. I had come on equal terms. When I had finished I ferried load after load and stowed them away inside.

Ten minutes later Pierre came rushing over. 'You'll have to move! We want to put the kitchen here.'

It started to snow as I took down the tent and put it up higher up the hill. Again I moved all my boxes, drums and bags.

This second site was also commandeered. Pierre announced that the tent was too large for one person. I must make do with a smaller one. And so I moved on again. I ended up, after having to shift my home and possessions twice more for various reasons, quite a way up the hill above the mess tent: there was no suitable flat spot left lower down. I lugged up my eight twenty-five-kilo loads and swore that, whatever happened, I would not be evicted again.

That night I slept well, but woke up feeling cold in the early hours of the morning and could not seem to get warm again no matter how many clothes I put on. I felt better when the sun came. All that day I worked to sort out the additional film tent which I had erected and establish some sort of order in our films and equipment. It was during the second night at Base Camp that I again got a headache and I lay awake a long time listening to the roaring sound of avalanches spilling down the high peaks. Several hours before dawn I felt really cold, and shivered till

146

daybreak, dozing intermittently. I could not find the willpower to get out of my sleeping bag and assumed that soon someone would come and see if I was all right or call me for breakfast. I was having trouble with my breathing and by ten-thirty felt really ill. I summoned up all my strength and called for help. Michel Berruex came to my tent.

'Please can you get Jeff, I feel pretty bad,' I gasped.

A message came back from the hospital tent. 'If Julie's feeling ill, she must come to see me!'

I felt totally alone and demoralised. 'I can't walk! Tell him that I can't even walk!' I told Michel. But it made no difference. Michel and Ludwig Kratochvil (nicknamed Krako), our Czechoslovakian member, had to carry me down to the doctor.

As soon as I got some care and attention I felt better. Part of the problem was that I had been storing up urine. On the approach march the three hundred porters made it virtually impossible for me to even spend a penny. If I strayed off the narrow mountain track they would follow me, curious to know where I was going. In any case, it was dangerous to do so as the slopes on which the path was built was very steep and loose. Often I had hung on for several hours, trying to find a suitable place, or simply been too busy filming to stop. Jeff's diuretic soon sorted me out, and a short burst of oxygen completed the treatment. I worked again for the rest of the day and that night slept like a baby.

At breakfast the following morning I discovered that one of the French, Michel Affasnasieff, had been very sick during the night and had a pulmonary oedema. Jeff had diagnosed the same thing for me the previous day, but Michel was definitely much more ill than I had been. His chest was bubbling and wheezing and he was coughing very badly.

Jeff decided that Michel and I should leave Base Camp and go down to the lower altitudes of the last villages until we had acclimatised properly, and in the full heat of the mid-day sun we set off. I had almost to run to keep up with Michel's long lanky legs. He is a typical rangy mountain guide, with a mobile face full of Gallic expression. We carried very heavy rucksacks as Michel felt that we should take lots of tinned food, and that day we walked for six hours. But when I checked my pulse the following morning it was down to 60 again, so perhaps the exercise had been good.

Later that day we walked back to a higher village that was full of goats and human kids. It was very primitive, with tiny one-roomed stone houses, and was inhabited only in the summer, when the people walked up with their animals and children from the Indus valley. The houses did not have windows, just earth floors and a central fireplace, with not even a hole in the roof to let out the smoke. The babies and young children ran around with bare bottoms, their clothes ragged. But the people were kind and helpful to us, even though we could not speak to them. We put up our tent on the green grass amongst the goats.

The following day, Michel and I went for a walk. He was still weak, and after twenty minutes decided to return. But by this time I felt very fit and climbed a mountain which was much higher than our Base Camp site and gave me a really good view of Nanga Parbat. I came down feeling even better. That night we bought and grilled a chicken over our charcoal fire; it tasted delicious.

We left the goat village at five-thirty the next morning. Michel was bored and wanted to get back to Base Camp, and I was happy to return. The rest away from all the pressures had done me good, and it was just possible that Kurt might arrive that day.

Before the expedition left Pindi we were given a reception by the Alpine Club, and its President, General Mirza, had mentioned that he might pay us a visit at Base Camp. When he added that he would arrive by helicopter, my ears pricked up, and I had a quiet word with him, suggesting that if Kurt had arrived in Pakistan in time General Mirza might give him a lift. I had mentioned it to Pierre who told me he would make the necessary arrangements for Kurt, but nevertheless I left my filming partner a note with the details of the possibility at Mrs Davis's hotel. That day, 10 June, was the date of the proposed visit.

Michel and I set off back up at quite a reasonable pace. As we got to the woods above the village on this lovely cool morning I looked around in surprise. In just four days spring had arrived and flowers were beginning to appear in profusion – irises, sedum,

tiny white star flowers, buttercups, primula and a taller deep
purple flower which I later learnt had special healing properties
stood in the shade of the trees. Between these and the sprouting
green bushes of willow were clumps of forget-me-nots spread out
like blue carpets.

It was a beautiful walk back to Base Camp, such a contrast to
the approach march when I had rushed through feeling so
miserable with a pounding head. I stopped to take some photographs as Michel went striding on ahead.

Then at eight o'clock I saw General Mirza's helicopter fly
overhead. I hoped and prayed that Kurt would be in it. At the
first set of meadows Michel had left me half a tin of pears and I
sat and ate my breakfast before having a good wash in the icy
river. I washed out my blouse and put on a sweater, hanging the
blouse on the back of my rucksack to dry as I walked up the
brown-green meadows which spring had not yet reached.

The last two miles to Base Camp were a delight and at ten-
thirty I dropped down across the last icy glacial river to Base
Camp. General Mirza and Pierre were standing by the helicopter
and, to my utter relief, next to them was Kurt. They greeted me
warmly, and asked if I was better. The final cure was simply
knowing that Kurt had arrived safely from the unexplored wilderness he had been filming, in one of the remotest parts of China.

That afternoon, as we sat by our tent, he told me how worried
he had been when, on his arrival, he had been told that I was
very sick. 'Where is Julie?' he had asked Pierre, and had become
very angry when he heard that Michel and I, two supposedly
seriously ill people, had been sent down to recover without
anyone to look after us, or even a radio to call for help if
necessary.

Life got much easier for me now, but time and again Pierre
behaved aggressively towards Kurt, who was very patient until he
was told how to make the film. 'I am the film director,' Kurt said
firmly, 'and I decide what should be filmed.'

'I don't know what's wrong with Pierre,' Kurt confided, looking
puzzled. 'He certainly wasn't like this on Everest.'

Making the film was extremely interesting. The setting was
superb. Our Base Camp sat in green meadows sprinkled with

hundreds of flowers. As the weeks passed new varieties grew in colourful patches and the mountains around changed colour too as the winter snows melted, exposing the many shades of brown below. The higher mountains framing the head of the valley, with Nanga Parbat sitting majestically in the centre, took on new shapes as rock ribs and buttresses emerged, cleared by the many rumbling, tumbling avalanches. The mixture of nationalities amongst the members gave our actors even more character and it was exciting gradually to develop ideas which would enable the pieces of the jigsaw which made up our film story fit together.

As I got to know my companions better, I particularly liked the gentle Czechoslovakian, Krako. Michel Berruex was a very likeable French mountain guide, who longed to climb an 8,000-metre peak. Walter Cecchinel was a sympathetic dark swarthy Italian who had been one of the best ice climbers in the Alps, until he had a fall and broke both his ankles. He had tremendous courage to undertake such an expedition as his ankles had healed in a fixed position and he suffered a lot of pain when walking and climbing. We built the main theme of the film around his story. The two Germans, Hans Engel and Hubert Hillmaier, who did not speak much French, had a calm world of their own, but they were very helpful to everyone. Our two Pakistani mountaineers, Karim Imabahad and Shah Jehan, were very competent and strong. They both spoke good English and told me many interesting stories about their country. I am sure that individually they were all nice people, but collectively the combination was unfortunate. At times it had the atmosphere of a boys' boarding school. I wrote about one rather silly incident in my diary:

> . . . this morning Jeff called me into the Mess Tent where a little group of them were sitting. They had obviously just been smoking 'strong cigarettes' with the cook, and were laughing raucously. 'Come in, Julie,' Jeff encouraged, Gelaal says he wants to f. . . you!' [Gelaal was our very corrupt Pakistani policeman guard, who also acted as a very incompetent mail runner. He would disappear for days and return with no letters. I do not think that he ever got as far as the Post Office.] 'Well, what do you say?' Jeff, our supposedly responsible doctor, giggled. 'I would say that it was

typical of you and your friends, you all seem to keep your brains in your balls,' I retorted and walked out.

These Latins are not easy. I think that British men accept women far more easily as equals and friends. I get the impression that the French are only initially interested in going to bed with women, it takes them a long time to become friends with them. Perhaps it is not considered a macho thing to do.

However, I have nice memories too. Kurt and I one day asked François Hess, who as a successful businessman was a natural choice to be our Expedition accountant, when we could film him. We were trying to put together a complicated humorous sequence which would introduce all the expedition members in the film by showing their reactions to somewhat regular stonefalls which came down quite close to our Base Camp from the slopes above. The two unruffled Germans had simply glanced up from their reading and calmly returned to their books; Kurt and I had rushed out from our tent clutching our cameras and sound equipment (as we had done several times during the night when we heard boulders rumbling down from above); Karim, the Pakistani climber, had stayed in his sleeping bag and put on his climbing helmet, muttering 'Inshallah'; we wanted Jeff to jump out of his tent, still inside his sleeping bag like a 'frog' (his nickname) and so on.

We asked François, who had a very expressive face, to be listening to his Walkman, so absorbed in Beethoven that he did not realise that the extended drum roll did not belong in the concert. It would take about ten minutes to film the scene.

'I'll have a think about it,' he said, and an hour later he called me over to his tent. 'Jeff and I have a bet on – there's a meal at the best restaurant in Paris at stake,' he explained with a serious tone in his voice. 'You see I have this torn pair of shorts that need sewing. He says that I will never get you to fix them. If you do, I will agree to be filmed!'

I took the shorts and went back to tell Kurt what had transpired. We had suffered so many obstacles in our filming, this seemed a minor one, but there could be complications. 'If I do mend Francois' shorts, then Jeff will be annoyed at losing the bet and be difficult about being filmed,' I explained. 'I think the solution is for you to sew them, then technically neither of them will have won. I will have got them fixed, but not done the work myself. They'll have to go "Dutch" on the meal!'

Kurt laughed. When he had arrived at base camp he needed a pair of trousers shortened. 'I dislike such sewing and had stuck them up with adhesive airline labels (on the inside). The others knew this and trying to get me to do a 'woman's job' was how the bet had arisen. Poor Francois was quite upset by our deviousness, but could not argue that I had not fulfilled his conditions and we got our film!

The mountaineers got on with the job of climbing the mountain. The weather was very changeable and they were constantly driven back down from Camp 1 and Camp 2. Nanga Parbat is a very impressive mountain; it gave me the feeling that it had a strong mind of its own. From Base Camp to summit it is one of the longest climbs on any mountain in the world. Thirteen thousand feet of steep mountaineering stood between us and the top. It is also the mountain that has claimed the most victims. More than fifty people have died trying to conquer it.

By the beginning of July the expedition was running out of time and, if the summit was to be reached, the attempt would have to be made very soon. Camp 3 had still not been established as every time the expedition had tried, deep fresh snow had impeded their progress. Three mountaineers, Hans Engel, Hubert Hillmaier and Michel Berruex, decided to make a concerted bid to reach the top as soon as the weather and conditions on the mountain looked better. On 11 July, together with some of the strong Hunza high-altitude porters, they left Base Camp. Hubert looked far from well as he set off; he had developed a bad tummy complaint during the night. Over the radio at Base Camp during the following days, we were relieved to hear they had finally reached Camp 3, and then Camp 4 at 7,200 metres (24,272 feet). That afternoon, 12 July, the porters came down, their job finished. After a night of strong storms Michel and Hubert both felt unwell and decided, very sensibly, to go down too. Hans Engel, who was always very placid and self-contained, stayed on alone to try to make a solo attempt for the top. The next day he moved his camp to 7,400 metres and nearer to the summit peak which rose up two thousand feet above the snow plateau.

Down at Base Camp we had lost radio contact with this brave German mountaineer the night before and the highly emotional drama of the mounting tension which built up during the hours of waiting we captured on film. Hubert's worry and concern for his friend's safety makes me cry with sympathy every time I see it. The following morning, appropriately for the French on 14 July, in very cloudy conditions, Hans reached the summit alone, just as Hermann Buhl had done on his epic first ascent of the mountain in 1953. It was an incredible feat, one that should go down in the annals of mountaineering history.

I had a hard apprenticeship into Himalayan mountaineering and filming on this, my first major expedition. I had really only been involved with the mountain through the film. Nanga Parbat looked so tantalisingly beautiful, but I was never allowed to go much above Base Camp. After patiently waiting to acclimatise properly I had gone with Kurt to 5,000 metres (16,500 feet) to film on the mountain. I felt very strong and well and when I returned the same day to Base Camp I told Jeff that I had no problems with fitness or altitude.

That evening Pierre stormed into the Mess Tent where everyone was gathered. 'Julie!' he roared, 'You are not well enough to go high on the mountain. You must never go above Camp 1!'

Kurt and I were shattered. How could we make a film with such restrictions?

Kurt tried to argue with Pierre, but it was no use; he was adamant. I got up from my stool and went outside. I walked for two hours, down the meadows which were now green and rippling with delicate grasses blowing in the wind. I was desperately disappointed and upset. Why did Pierre have to be so chauvinistic? I was no threat to his success on the mountain. I felt terribly sorry for Kurt. The film team already had a serious problem. When he was travelling in China Kurt had been bitten by a spider and this had affected a nerve in his right arm. At night he suffered terrible pain and could only get some respite if he slept sitting up, and during the day the recurring pain drove him crazy. None of the pills Jeff gave him seemed to help, and I was really worried about how he would cope on the fixed ropes, and filming alone.

I longed to explore the steep sides of Nanga Parbat. I had spent four weeks continually looking up at it while I waited to acclimatise. My dream was to reach the clouds so often lying in bands across its upper snowfields, to climb through them and come out the other side, to look down from its lofty heights and see the world spread out at my feet. I wanted to discover my strengths and weaknesses, how it felt to climb and live on such a giant mountain. I had watched the others coming down looking tired but they always wanted to go back up. What was the special magic of Nanga Parbat? It was awesome, but so inviting, how I longed ...

It was almost dark when I returned to Base Camp. I walked along the edge of the glacier beside the camp. I stopped to look along its broad ice pathway leading to the object of my dreams, which had so suddenly been shattered, and I felt very sad. I was about to turn to go when I glanced down. Thirty feet below was a round patch of flat sand. I felt drawn to it. I had to go down and explore it. Thank goodness I did for it turned out to be the solution to my problems. Two days later I sat down there and wrote a poem:

Martial Arts on Nanga Parbat

New experiences; new countries; new people;
different cultures and attitudes; languages; ways of life.
My practice was so involved in the everyday living.

Then, we started climbing.
The movement, balance, harmony with my companions,
and this difficult, dangerous mountain,
the joy of being was so much budo.
When the going became tougher and more arduous
the Centre, breathing and understanding of self
kept the happiness in my eyes.

For the filming my eyes and mind are open wide
and peaceful.

French lessons – bewitched by Nanga Parbat

Then . . .
>   the neurosis of human emotions tried to destroy everything!

But . . .
>   that evening I found my *dojo*.

It is just four minutes across the grassy meadow
a jump across a mountain stream from our Base Camp civilisation.

There are several entrances and exits, but I choose to boulder hop
   down the dry stream bed to reach its soft circular sandy alluvial
   floor.

The side of the glacier forms one wall, the deep solid ice covered in
   boulders of all sizes,
which give another dimension as they slide, now and then, into the
   unknown watery depths below
– the noise reminding one that a glacier is ever moving,
with a history of a million years.

I walk through a narrow gap between the ice and the grassy bank,
into the next 'sky-covered' room, where a stream flows musically
   down, and I can wash before I practise.

I sit in *zazen*, peacefully . . .
away from the noise of our little thirty-five-people multi-racial
   community with all their different social rules
– an infinitesimal speck in the beauty that surrounds me.
Nanga Parbat in its majesty towers above, in front of me;
this powerful mountain of many men's dreams and lives.
Behind me is the distant green valley,
and miles beyond the mountains of the Hindu Kush.
On either side snow-covered peaks and sharp rock pinnacles
rise steeply skywards.

Birds, marmots, wind, ever-melting water
make the orchestration for the nature music;
Stonefall and constant avalanches the full range of
percussion.
The sound of my own breathing, so difficult to control at this
   altitude, harder still when moving,
even gently in *kata*.

The flow of the *kata*, like the movement of a mountain stream,
   sometimes slow, quiet, gentle,
then suddenly stronger with force as it drops from stone to stone.

. . . I don't want to stop, but even here time rules everything.

One of the very special treasures of this *dojo* is another stream
    which starts high, high in the mountains above, but does not
    begin to flow until late in the afternoon.
By evening it starts to wander across the floor,
finding its way slowly up to a shapely boulder which decorates one
    corner and gradually encircles it
as in a Japanese garden.
Each night it washes the whole floor, compacting the fine grey
    dust,
making it smooth again in this uneven place.
I left by climbing up a gentle hill which is a
rock garden, full of little mountain flowers

. . . and I knew that there was nothing to restrict,
to take away – only from themselves . . .

I had everything . . . nothing!

The strength which I gained from my visits to my *dojo* helped me
give Kurt the support that he needed. I had plenty of time to
learn about filming – and there was a lot to assimilate – and to
take photographs of my wonderful surroundings, especially of
the flowers and the playful furry marmots which tumbled around
the campsite. I spent time talking to the Hunzas, learning more
about their society. The Hunza Valley used to be a separate
principality, ruled by the Aga Khan, the leader of the Islami
Muslim religion which is so different from the restrictive Muslim
religion practised in the rest of Pakistan. After the expedition
Kurt and I visited their village, high up in the mountains close to
the Chinese border. In Gulmit men and women lived as equals,
sharing the tasks of working in the fields and looking after the
children. The Hunza people are tall, often blue-eyed, descendants
of the armies of Alexander the Great. They are well educated;
every village has a school and dispensary. They live without a
great emphasis on money – most things are bartered – and we
found them a happy, contented people. I thought it the ideal
civilisation of open doors and open hearts. It was truly good to
be with these strong, reliable people on Nanga Parbat and
comforting to know that Kurt had their support on the mountain.
    My time spent on this expedition was by no means wasted. In
retrospect it was the best introduction I could have had to

expedition life and filming. I had time to stand and stare, to learn and absorb the many new skills and savour the pleasures of living so close to nature in such a beautiful place, to get used to the vast scale of things in this very different Himalayan world and be able to link it to my other joy, the martial arts.

There is one more story which should be told. The expedition had adopted a cockerel as a mascot. This colourful symbol of France had strutted around Base Camp crowing loudly, especially at a very uncivilised hour in the early morning, since we had arrived. In the last days of the expedition (only Hans reached the summit) some villagers brought another cock and a hen. They were mangy birds, particularly the cock, which had dirty white broken feathers and several angry red bald patches. The elegant chestnut brown and iridescent green-feathered French cock immediately chaperoned the new hen, but never tried to mate with her. Whenever the other bird came near, 'Le Coq' would attack it or place himself strategically between it and his female. I needed the sound of the cock squawking for the film and decided the only way to get him to make the right noise for my recording was to chase him.

'Shoo! Go on, run,' I ordered him, and chased him round the back of the Mess Tent. He made just the right noise when a great burst of laughter ruined everything.

'Que passe?' I asked as I rounded the corner.

Kurt had tears running down his cheeks. 'The cock.' He spoke between waves of laughter, 'The minute you chased the other one round the back of the tent, he was on to that hen so fast that she fell over with surprise.' The elegant cock was not pleased, nor was Pierre – he was furious. The honour of his mascot and of France had been defiled!

When I was home again it was the good, positive side of the expedition that stayed with me, until the publication of Pierre's book stirred up bad memories.

At the La Plagne Film Festival in France the following winter the book was entered in the Literary Competition. Terry and I happened to sit at a table for dinner with one of the book judges. I asked her what she thought about the Nanga Parbat book.

'Terrible!' she exclaimed. 'By the end of the first thirty pages Mazeaud had said so many bad things about so many people that I just could not read any more!'

The unfair thing was that his accusations were not even true. 'She played with the Nagra throughout the expedition and never did any work,' he wrote of me. Kurt and I had made six and a half kilometres of film and I had taken twenty hours of sound. The finished documentary has won three major prizes in France, Spain and Switzerland!

Then I noticed that Kurt had written on the frontispiece of the book:

> One has to overcome the past, and be ready for the future, thus the good of the past will live on . . . think of the ice cliffs and walls, the clouds, of the avalanches . . . think of the birds singing and the meadows full of flowers . . . they are still there.
>
> > Tassa – it was
> > Susa – don't worry
> > Imaka – perhaps

. . . these three words from Greenland belong too to Nanga Parbat.

He was right. We called the film *Diamir* [the name of the valley from which we approached the mountain] – *Les Envoûtés de Nanga Parbat* [the bewitched of Nanga Parbat]. We were certainly all affected by the mountain in different ways, and I was definitely under its spell. It was the foundation for all that was to follow. Past becomes present and present becomes future. It was only three years before I went back.

The correct exposure

During the 1982 Nanga Parbat expedition and the following year Kurt and I realised that we had both taken many colour slides which were virtually identical in style and composition. This was a wonderful discovery as it meant that in future we needed to carry only one main still camera and set of lenses between us and could trust each other to take the kind of pictures that we both wanted. Like moving from a Mini to a Rolls Royce I graduated to using the Leicas which Kurt has on permanent loan.

It is not always easy to switch your mind from filming to photography. When shooting movies each sequence must have a beginning, a middle and an end in order to have a meaning and to be able to join it onto the next scene. Continuity is very important. In many ways still photography is far simpler; you need a steady hand for only a fraction of a second, and each picture can stand by itself; but that photograph must, of course, be well composed and, even if it is a straight view, say what you want it to say. For a book illustration, or lecture purposes, each shot must give as much information as possible, or portray a feeling very strongly, very different from the 'this is me at so-and-so' snapshots for the family album.

Photographs tend to be as personal as handwriting in their composition. I can identify Terry's pictures easily from, say, those of Dennis, even though both are excellent technical photographers. So it is very unusual to find someone else who can take the same sort of photograph as you would yourself and, with the limited amount of time that we have for still photography when we are filming, this compatibility is a tremendous help. While Kurt is busy with the movie camera, I can take still shots, and while I am changing a film in the 'black bag', Kurt can take over. Of course we both have our strong points. Kurt's scenic views are superb. He can line up several shots of a mountain panorama, even without the help of a tripod, so that they can be joined together to show the whole mountain range. My forte is portraits. I love experimenting with the camera, and it is always exciting to see the results. We are both critical, but in a constructive way, and I learn a lot when we look through our slides together. We take, on average, four thousand pictures on each expedition adventure, and about eight thousand metres of movie film.

But sometimes photography can be surprisingly dangerous. When we had to cross and re-cross the wild turbulent waters of the mighty Shaksgam river in China on our way back from K2 in 1983, we often had to ride on our sure-footed camels as the waters were too strong for us to wade across or swim through. On one section I had taken the risk of carrying my camera around my neck in order to get some pictures. As I jumped down the seven feet from my rather insecure perch, the strap of my camera caught on the animal's saddle and my feet had already reached the stony bed of the river before the force of my jump released the weighty camera body and zoom lens in a catapult action. Crack! Three pounds of Japanese wizardry hit me on the forehead with such force that the camera ricochetted straight over my head and landed on the stones behind me. For a moment I was completely dazed, not realising what had hit me and, when I did, my first thoughts were for the camera and not my head which was badly cut and bleeding. Miraculously, despite a few dents, it was unharmed. Once Terry had dropped a brand new lens which he was examining while sitting on the toilet. The fall of just two feet onto a soft carpet had completely destroyed it.

It is a great pity that photography is so expensive. It would be so good if children could be taught creative photography in school, just as they learn art; after all they are more likely to take photographs than to paint later in life. Using a camera opened my eyes a little wider, and enabled me to see beauty in many odd corners and mundane objects. It is a confidence-builder too, as it takes quite a lot of courage at first to make yourself take close-up portraits of people. A lot of mumbo-jumbo is talked about the technicalities of photography, and I feel a little sad that it put me off taking pictures for more than half my life. Now it is something from which I get a great deal of pleasure, some of which I hope, through lectures, I can share with others.

Kurt and I are often very similar in our way of thinking and doing things. As with our still photography so it is with the filming, and this could have something to do with the fact that we were born on adjoining days, though the year of our birth was seven years apart. Like most people, I always read my horoscope but never take it very seriously. Perhaps it has nothing to do with it, but Kurt and I are both typical Pisceans.

I had found my introduction to filming fascinating. In Paris, helped by a very good and experienced editor, Annie Copens, Kurt had put together an excellent film about the Nanga Parbat Expedition. I went to the cutting rooms several times, to help and learn. This was the other half of making a film. With no script to follow, the storyline has to be fitted together like a jigsaw. The 6,500 metres of film correspond to ten hours of viewing time, which had to be condensed into a fifty-five-minute documentary. The sifting and selection of the material was the first job, building the plot at the same time. Then linking the scenes was a continuity problem, as they are not always filmed in an orderly sequence. Often we climb and film some sections of a mountain several times and occasionally need to use these scenes out of the original context. Sometimes a light difference makes this joining-up impossible, or the camera moves in the wrong direction to carry the action on.

When all this had been overcome, the film had to be pared down piece by piece to the right length, and the commentary written and recorded. When the difficult choice of music had been made and laid in the spaces where it was to go in the film, the dubbing of the commentary and any missing wild-track noises took place. This is when film and sound come together, an exciting moment. The final operation was for the finished rough copy of the film to go back to the laboratory where every frame had to be found on the original negative and re-graded if necessary to the correct exposure. The editing took two months' concentrated work. So much work for a fraction of an evening's viewing.

Working on a film in the cutting rooms is when the real creativity takes place, and the atmosphere is sometimes quite electric, especially if you are working with an editor and producer who care about what they are doing. Feelings get quite sensitive and tempers fray. Kurt says that fights over editing are good news; they show that people not only care but are thinking themselves and sparking off ideas in others. He and I find it extremely difficult to back down in the cutting room if we feel strongly about something, as by the time we have completed the filming, being so deeply involved in the struggle of the climb ourselves, it has become part of us. Handing over a film for editing is like handing over your child for someone else to bring up to maturity. Of course we have to be flexible. Ideas which we try to follow in our filming do not always work in the final story, or there may be no space for a scene which we would dearly love to include.

Our problems start months before the expedition sets off with hours spent travelling around trying to find a company willing to back the film and employ us to make it. After we had filmed together at 8,000 metres on K2, Kurt and I called ourselves 'The Highest Film Team in the World', and our mini-film team is becoming quite well known, but finding backers is still not easy. For the Everest expedition in 1985, we only finalised a contract with the BBC a few days before we left for China.

While we are travelling to the mountain we have to be constantly curious about the country and area we are visiting and about the local people. Documentary filming needs facts and makes you ask questions. It takes a lot of extra effort and often it is not easy to get the truth; people tend to spout theories with the authority of certain knowledge. But the quest sharpens the mind and is far more interesting than just passing through places with the only object getting to the mountain. We have to keep our eyes open to spot interesting or unusual things, places and events and often travel long distances to capture them on film. The aspiration is to do this precisely and clearly using the minimum amount of film and maximum sync-sound, but as many things happen unexpectedly and only once we don't always succeed as well as we would like. We are still perfecting the methods to make packing and unpacking the cameras and other gear faster during the journey, but to protect all the delicate equipment from bumps, dust and rough handling we need heavy bulky cases which take time to move around, and we have no minions to help us.

But being only two people has its good points. As we need to be ready for instant action, we have to be highly organised. In the chaos of a tent it is easy to forget where a filter is, and difficult to keep the down from our insulated clothing and dirt out of the cameras in particular. A speck of fluff or grit loaded with a film in the black bag can ruin many scenes. Luckily we are both very orderly and careful.

Although filming with Kurt is not always easy, as he is a perfectionist and will take the utmost trouble to get things right, I appreciate his dedication, which is always apparent in the finished film. Whatever the difficulties and limitations placed on us by filming, we both agree that it is worthwhile to be able to bring back the adventure to share with millions of people who will never be lucky enough to see or experience such wonders of our world for themselves.

Kurt has been making films for many years and I now have personal experience of many of the jobs involved. Using a camera, cutting the film, acting, writing the commentary script and then recording it, choosing the music and deciding where it should go to balance the sound side of the film, developing ideas for future projects. I even helped the graphics girl build the Pinnacles on the North East Ridge of Everest on the three-dimensional model at the Royal Geographical Society. When we went to film it and discovered they had been omitted, we created these important obstacles which bar the way up the last unclimbed ridge on the world's highest mountain with Blu-Tack; after a quick coat of paint they looked as if they were part of the original.

We wrote the script for the Assignment Adventure film for Channel 4 in 1984 in the same way as we worked on Kurt's second book in Salzburg. It was about a Swiss K2 expedion and called *K2 the Elusive Summit*. We had two days of the weekend to write the commentary and, watching the film on a video at home, pieced it together between us. The job was made more complex because Kurt and I were sharing the narration and although some things sounded better spoken by Kurt with his lovely Austrian accent, getting the two voices balanced throughout the film was quite difficult.

As neither of us had spoken a full commentary in English for a film before, the producer Chris Rallings suggested that we might feel more relaxed recording it at his house. 'I've got a very quiet room,' he assured us. On Monday morning it was decided that I would record my parts first. I settled down in a chair and read the first paragraph. 'Can we run the video while I read it?' I asked. 'It's impossible to know how slowly I should go without seeing the picture it has to fit.'

Chris turned on his television and we started again. It was much easier, until I had to repeat a phrase. While I was rehearsing, trying to get the right tone and emphasis, the 'hold' would jump off the video and a schools broadcast would blare out from the television. I found this very off-putting, especially when later in the day *Play School* would interrupt my concentration on *K2*.

We had another problem with the sound recordist's tape-recorder. His fast-return facility was playing up and if we wanted to hear how something had recorded, we could only go back at the normal speed, by which time the television would have played its game of switching back to the normal programmes.

None of this made the job easy, and was very time-consuming, but the thing that turned it into a 'horribility', as Kurt so aptly put it, was the noise of jets taking off from Heathrow Airport a few miles away from the house. Poor Chris, it seemed that they had changed runways that day, and with monotonous regularity they took off – one a minute! We pressed on, trying to work round them, but I felt myself and heard my voice becoming more and more tense as I was constantly interrupted by the roar of yet another aeroplane heading skywards. There was also a dog barking two blocks away, doors slamming somewhere and finally the noise of the cars revving up their engines at the traffic lights in the rush hour. By the end of the day Kurt and I felt nervous wrecks.

Although we managed somehow to complete the script, thankfully it was decided to record it all again the next day in a proper studio. I still had a tightness in my voice from the previous day's experiences, and almost freaked out when, even with headphones on, I could hear the sound of a tube train rumbling underneath the studio. I was assured that it could not be heard on the tape, but it was very distracting, especially as, due to lack of time, we had to record the whole thing without even seeing the picture first to help us get in the right mood.

But sometimes it is getting in the right mood to film in the first place that is more difficult. By undertaking to make expedition films we already set ourselves a very difficult task. I have not yet been on an expedition where we have had competent film porters to help us transport all the paraphernalia necessary to make a professional film. On Nanga Parbat we did have a good film porter, but I was not allowed on the mountain. For the Swiss K2 expedition, we had planned for two film porters but we had to send one home because he was so incompetent. He could not even put on his crampons properly. The other porter was very lazy and spent more time at Base Camp than on the climb. When he did go on the mountain he fell off – three times!

On K2 with the earlier Italian expedition, we were supposed to have two mountaineers to help us whenever we needed them but this did not work because of the vast distances involved. They were always busy carrying camping and climbing equipment and we did not have the heart to ask them to carry for the film as well. Almo Giambisi did offer to help us one day, and was very interested in the cameras.

'Could you bring me the Arriflex? I need to check in the black bag to see if there's a film in it,' Kurt asked his willing assistant.

'Oh, you don't have to bother,' Almo told him. 'I know there isn't.'

Kurt looked surprised. 'How?' he asked.

'I opened it up to show Giorgio how it worked,' Almo replied proudly. It was a wonder that Kurt did not hit him for such stupidity. If there had been a roll of film in the camera, our work would have been ruined.

It is because of several incidents like this that we carefully lock up all our film equipment and stock when we are not using it, but even this precaution does not guarantee that it is safe. On Everest someone, perhaps not thinking clearly because of the effects of altitude, wanted more space in the Mess Tent and moved out the drum containing all the exposed films. Luckily only two of the topmost films were ruined by the temperature variance between the hot sun during the day and the freezing cold of the night, but that was bad enough. Movie film is very costly and far more sensitive than still film to such treatment.

Approach and return marches are particularly traumatic for us. We constantly have to watch the porters carrying the film equipment to make sure that they do not drop their loads heavily to the ground when they take a rest, or when they are tired at the end of the day. Bent film cans can let in light and there is so much delicate film equipment. Not much else gets gentle treatment from porters – biscuits usually arrive as crumbs. With donkeys and yaks it is a constant battle to get the drivers to tie the loads on securely. Too often we have felt sick in the stomach as loads have tumbled down mountainsides, praying that they did not contain anything too fragile. Kurt always carries as much as he can himself, and I carry my sound equipment, but it is not possible to transport everything ourselves. The most perturbing experience we had was getting the films safely back from the Chinese K2 Base Camp to the road-head at Ileka. During the return march several camels floundered in the flood waters of the Shaksgam and loads were swept away.

When I saw the poor beasts struggling in the turbulent waters I felt sorry for the discomfort we had caused to one of them for the sake of the film. I had seen a camel driver giving a spoonful of cooking oil to a camel and suggested to him that we would like to film it. 'OK,' he agreed in Chinese, and went away. We set up the camera and sound but when he returned, instead of giving the animal another spoonful of the thick treacly substance that looked like tractor oil, he emptied a gallon container of it down its throat. Nobody wanted to walk behind that camel for the rest of the day!

When I returned to Britain, the popular children's programme *Blue Peter* showed the clip of the camel getting his oil. The programme goes out live and, during the interview one of the presenters, Janet, threw in a question which we had not had in the rehearsal: 'Why did they give that camel medicine?' she asked. I searched my brains for a quick answer. Interviews on *Blue Peter* are timed to the second. 'To keep him regular,' I blurted out in desperation, the picture of his loose motions marking the path for several kilometres still fresh in my mind.

Appearing on television is another new challenge that has evolved since I started my second life. Being on the other side of the camera is something that I enjoy immensely, even if sometimes things go slightly awry. One afternoon show that I did with Una Stubbs was such a case. I took along twelve slides to illustrate what I was going to talk about. Somehow in the busy confusion before the show went on the air I got the impression that I would be interviewed twice and that half the slides would be shown in each piece. The first interview was going well when, one by one, all twelve slides appeared on the monitor. I could not ask what was happening as the interview was being transmitted live, so I just carried on telling the stories connected with them all.

'What on earth are we going to talk about in the second half?' I asked Una when they switched to a recorded item.

'What do you mean?' she asked. 'There is no second half!'

It is particularly nice that over the past few years I have appeared regularly on some programmes and I feel as if I am visiting old friends when I go to the *Blue Peter* or *Pebble Mill* studios. Despite the pressure they constantly live under putting out several live shows each week, I always feel welcome and somehow they find time to listen to the story of my latest epic.

I personally find radio interviews more of a challenge than those on television. Everything has to be carefully described as there are no pictures to help create atmosphere or set the scene. But the main problem I have with both media is the lack of time available. Four months' adventures have to be condensed into eight or twelve minutes and you can never really do them justice in such a short time. At least we have a better chance to do this with the film we have made ourselves.

When our films are shown on television, we do not get much feedback on how the public like them, so a nice way to test public reaction is through film festivals. Many European countries run special mountaineering and adventure film festivals, and these are great social occasions as well as a chance to see what other film-makers in our field are producing. San Sebastian is my favourite. It is an informal festival, more like a family gathering, for people who make films, and mountaineers and adventurers from all over the world. Every mealtime is an excuse for a gourmet feast.

I am glad that San Sebastian was the first festival that the Nanga Parbat film competed in. It somehow made up for the Mazeaud hassle when we made it. I felt the audience had sympathy for all the films, and was completely delighted when the panel of international judges awarded ours the prize for 'Best Mountain Film'. Later this film won major prizes at two other film festivals, in France and Switzerland. While these were not quite as impressive as the 'Emmy' Kurt had won for his *East Face of Everest*, for the first film we made together it was very satisfying.

I always get a great reception in the San Sebastian film theatre, as they discovered that my father's home was near Bilbao and gave me a Basque flag to carry on my expeditions. However, as he was actually born in Catalonia, the people there have given me a Catalonian flag as well. Actually, I am lucky with my family background. Because of my mother's childhood, the Germans and Swiss readily accept me too. It makes it much easier for me to fit into international expeditions.

But perhaps the most enjoyable thing about film festivals is that they give Terry a chance to share the excitement and fun of a part of my life from which he is rather excluded.

The only disastrous film that Kurt and I have made was not in the difficult conditions of the Himalayas, but in Britain's Lake District. *Blue Peter* commissioned us to film Doug Scott and Peter Duncan climbing a frozen waterfall. They also wanted to film Kurt and me filming them.

It had started raining during the night and by the time we reached the footpath leading off the road the following morning we were soaked through. Kurt was suffering most as the water-proof jacket which I ordered from a manufacturer to be sent direct to the hotel had not arrived and he only had an Icelandic sweater to protect him from the elements.

By the time we were ready to start climbing and filming, the rain had washed away much of the ice at the foot of the climb and we had to scramble inelegantly up snow-covered boulders at the side of the waterfall. As we made our way up to the only climbable section near the top, the rain penetrated everything. We felt like sponges. Kurt's heavy sweater had become water-logged and stretched to double its original size, and water was flowing down my trouser legs into my boots. They felt like drainpipes.

One by one the cameras were drowned out of use, my micro-phone ceased to function and the radio mikes went silent. Only Kurt's Arriflex continued to work, but the eyepiece was so full of water that he could not tell whether he was filming in focus or not. It was dark when we squelched our way back to the car, and still raining.

'If today is anything to go by, I'm not surprised this place is full of Lakes!' Kurt commented.

11

Ciao to China – explorations in Sinkiang

Three days before Christmas 1982, I was wrapping up presents when the telephone rang. (It always seems to happen around Christmas!) 'Here is Kurt. Julie, how good is your Italian?'

'I don't speak a word,' I retorted, wondering what my Austrian friend might have in store for me this time.

'Well, Spanish then . . . you must speak Spanish, after all your father is a Spaniard.'

'No, I'm sorry, I don't. I did learn it for one year at school thirty years ago, but apart from a few words, I remember nothing! But why do you ask?'

'Well, it's OK anyway, you can learn, you have plenty of time,' he said, with his usual nonchalance. 'We have been invited to join the Italian K2 Expedition to film them attempting to climb the mountain from the Chinese side, but we don't leave until the end of April.'

The excitement welled up in me; what a Christmas present! A chance to climb the most beautiful of all the world's highest mountains, at 28,244 feet higher than all the other peaks except Everest . . . and by the 'route of routes', the magnificent North Ridge, which had only ever had one other ascent. For a moment I completely forgot about the phone until Kurt's insistent 'Julie, Julie, are you still there?' brought me back to reality. Of course I would learn Italian in four months . . . Chinese too, if it was necessary.

Next day I bought a *Teach Yourself Italian* book and tape. Whenever I went out in the car I would play the tape and talk back to it, and every night I would study one lesson in the book. I thought I was doing quite well, but did wonder how useful tourist Italian would be on the expedition. There would not be many chances to ask 'When is the next train to Milan?' or 'Have you got a single room with bath?'

When I had been learning for three weeks, Kurt came to England. 'How's the Italian going?' he asked. I said a few words so he could judge for himself. 'That's fine, but you know the best way to learn a language is to sing it, that way you pick up the music and rhythm of the speech.'

'Great,' I said, 'but I can't just stand and sing!'

'No, of course not, you accompany yourself . . . on a guitar.'

'But I don't play the guitar,' I protested.

'Well, you can learn that at the same time.'

So to go to K2 I learnt Italian, and how to play the guitar.

By the time I went to China I was quite proud of my progress, but on the expedition I got little chance to practise further as most of the mountaineers wanted to speak English. A year later, however, I reaped the benefits. I again met Walter Bonatti, this time at the Kendal Film Festival and as I was the only person in a crowded room who could speak Italian, got a unique opportunity to have a very special conversation with him.

The next months flew by. Terry was fantastic. It is not easy to cope with the idea that your wife will not be around for the whole of the summer. However many good friends you have it is lonely living for long periods by yourself after so many good years of companionship and love. Most husbands would have said that once was enough, and there can't be many who would allow their wives to go off to a far corner of China with twenty Italians, knowing also that they were going to tackle one of the most demanding routes in the world on such an enormous and dangerous mountain.

The whole idea had grown from a book in Kurt's library, *Blank on the Map* by Eric Shipton. Many times he had read and re-read the story of what must have been one of the most fantastic adventures in exploration of this century.

It was Kurt's dream to follow in the old pioneer's footsteps, to see for himself this remote corner of China which lies between Chinese Turkestan, Hunza and Kashmir.

In his book Shipton wrote, 'I was fascinated by the idea of

penetrating into the little-known region of the Karakoram. As I studied the maps, one thing about them captured my imagination. The ridges and valleys which led up from Baltistan became increasingly high and steep as they merged into the maze of peaks and glaciers of the Karakoram, and then suddenly ended in an empty blank space. Across this blank space was written one challenging word "Unexplored".'

In 1937, Shipton's small expedition of legendary explorers, himself and three friends, Tilman, Spencer and Auden, together with seven sherpas, came across the watershed from Pakistan into the uninhabited Chinese area north of K2, exploring and surveying – an incredible five months' enterprise of discovery. 'When you read this book you understand why the eyes of explorers shine when they speak of unknown valleys and mountains to discover, of passes to find and to cross – it's an adventure incomparably greater than climbing even a big mountain on an already well-known route,' Kurt had told me.

Now he had at last managed to persuade an expedition to visit this remote area, which no European had entered since Shipton's 1937 exploration. He went with the expedition leader to Peking to sort out the protocol permissions and regulations, and somehow persuaded the Chinese authorities to allow us not only to climb the north ridge of K2, but to send a small party of expedition members to explore the Gasherbrum Glacier, an enormous highway of ice pinnacles which leads to the foot of the Gasherbrum mountains and, at its head, the mighty Broad Peak. Although it was detailed on the map from satellite pictures and surveys taken from surrounding peaks, no man had ever penetrated this glacier. We were going to be the first, extremely privileged, people to enter a space on our world which still bore the stamp 'unexplored'.

I made first acquaintance with the other expedition members in Venice, the night before we left to fly via Moscow to Peking. Immediately I was in the atmosphere of a large happy family, easy to enter, uncomplicated to live with, and this ambience lasted for the whole of the four months we were together. The Italians are very much family people; many grandparents still live with their grown-up children, or at least very close by, and they spend a lot of time talking to one another, a pleasure that many people elsewhere have given up in favour of passively watching television.

I got to know them better on the long plane journey to Peking, and we had our first expedition problem in Moscow, where we had to change planes. The Russians decided that it was necessary to re-weigh all our luggage. As a concession to the expedition the Italian airline to Moscow had not charged any excess when we flew out of Venice. K2 is an important mountain to the Italians; they made the first ascent from the Pakistan side in 1954 and it was considered to be the 'Italian mountain', just as Nanga Parbat is thought of in connection with the Germans and Everest with the British. But we did have to put up with the inconvenience of having our drums and kitbags stacked up the centre aisle between the seats of the aircraft, as the baggage hold was full.

Augustino Da Polenza, our likeable mountaineering leader, whom Kurt nicknamed *La Scatella* (the box) because that was how he was built, came back from the check-in desk with a very long face. 'Aeroflot want an extra 14,728,000 lire (£7,000) for excess baggage, and say we can't go on until it's paid,' he told the anxiously waiting group. We did not have that sort of money with us and finally managed to persuade the Russians to send a telex to the main expedition leader who was still in Italy, asking him to forward the money. When they received his affirmative reply they let us get on to our connecting flight. On the way back, at the stop-over in Moscow, the same problem occurred, but of course we did not have so much extra luggage as the food had been eaten and many tents and much climbing equipment, like ropes and snow stakes, had been left on the mountain. Nevertheless, we were asked for £2,000 excess. When we explained that the expedition simply did not have enough funds to pay this, the airline officials added together all the small amounts we had individually written on our Customs declarations as cash in transit, and we all had to dig in our pockets to pay the bill. Many people arrived back in Venice penniless.

I was a little disappointed with Peking. I do not know what I really expected to see, but it certainly was not the grey city with many impersonal high-rise flats it turned out to be. Although

China was recovering from the Cultural Revolution, it was still only an embryonic capitalist society in 1983, with few outward signs of western individuality either in possessions or dress. I was overwhelmed by the number of people everywhere, especially during the bicycle 'rush hours', and it was a relief to be on our way again to the less populated areas. K2 was 5,000 kilometres away on the edge of the western side of this vast country.

We had two plane journeys: from Peking to the industrial town of Urumchi, and then on to Kashkar, a rural town that was far more interesting than Peking. The people were more colourful: the regulation blue and green of the state military-style dress was intermingled with more decorative home-woven clothes, and the market was a blaze of dazzling rolls of silks, multi-coloured fruits and characterful faces. Shipton had been in charge of the Consulate there. It was a disorderly town of nooks and crannies, alleyways to peer down, corners to explore – a place to make travellers happy. The Italians took up the relaxed mood in the evening, turning suppertime into a party.

There were nineteen mountaineers in the group. Francesco Santon, the non-climbing expedition leader, and Giuliano de Marchi, our altitude doctor, were following in a couple of weeks. Giuliano's wife was about to produce their first child, and obviously he wanted to be at home for the birth. Unfortunately even doctors cannot be precise about these things and he had to leave the day before his daughter was born. He heard of her arrival when he reached Peking. For the first few weeks of the expedition we also had a mixed group of Italian trekkers with us, which swelled our numbers to over forty. The idea was that they should act as porters to help ferry supplies to Advance Base Camp, a fifty-kilometre round trip up and down the ice hills of the K2 glacier from Base Camp. This plan did not work too well as at first they were not well enough acclimatised, and then in the short time left they understandably wanted to carry their own camping and photographic equipment to see and record as much as possible of the spectacular scenery. They ended up eating almost as much as they carried for the main expedition, but they were a happy bunch, enthusiastic for our success, and helped to take the mountaineers through the difficult period before they truly got involved with the mountain.

When such a committing dream suddenly starts to become a reality, many climbers go through a period of self-doubt and start to question their motives for becoming involved in a situation which could put their lives in jeopardy.

Many of these Italian mountaineers had already had Himalayan experience, but when we were shown the film made by the Japanese, the only other expedition to attempt our North Ridge route, the year previously, everyone was very quiet. The Japanese expedition had reached the summit but two men had died and it looked a formidable undertaking. Our trekker/porters kept the mood light.

As well as being contagiously happy people, they loved to sing, and I spent a lot of time recording their spontaneous choral efforts. One song seemed to be their favourite and, thinking that it might make a good theme tune for the film, I often taped it, being sung solo and with many variations of harmonisation, at which they were so good. It started off robustly, 'with vigour', and slowed down in the middle to a poignancy that stirred the feelings, even though I could not understand a word of what they were singing about. It was about some men and a girlfriend, my friends told me casually with a smile. When we were on our way home, in the full throes of a very boozy farewell party with our Chinese hosts, our liaison officer asked for a translation of the song. I was called over to explain in English to our Chinese interpreter, who did not speak Italian.

'E mi e ti e Toni . . .' the first line was easy. 'And me and you and Tony,' 'Andrem dalla tetone,' 'Will go to visit the woman with the big . . . tits . . .' At that point I realised what I had been recording! The next line was impossible to translate to the Chinese: 'E palperem la mona.' It was more explicit than any rugby or climbing song I had ever heard, positively pornographic! No wonder they had sung it with such enthusiasm. I hurriedly backed out of the explanations with a feeble excuse. But what about my tapes, what on earth would the television company think? I sat down and drank another beer. Well, even the expedition leader had encouraged me to record the song. I would simply add after one version that I did not understand the words but thought it might make a good theme song for the expedition, and let the joke be on them.

I think the Italians are a very open-minded race anyway. As my vocabulary increased I picked up the mountaineer's favourite swearword '*cazzo*'.

'What does it mean?' I asked Kurt when he swore violently after a lens cover slipped from his hand into the dust.

'Hmm ... Well, the literal translation is "penis", but it's a little like you in England use the word "balls".' *Chacun à son goût!* ... So every country has something different to swear about.

It is a word that I could have found useful earlier. When the expedition leader Francesco Santon caught up with us two weeks after we had arrived at Base Camp, he foolishly fell asleep in the sun and got badly burnt. Poor Francesco, he could hardly move with the pain. Only Kurt and I were there with him. 'Can you help me please, Julie. I cannot reach all the places I need to put on the cream that the doctor has recommended.'

He lay on his tummy in his tent. He was as red as a lobster. 'Ow! Ow!' he screamed with pain as I started to spread the supposedly soothing anaesthetic cream onto his shoulders. It took about ten seconds for the cream to take effect; rubbing it on made the skin smart and some of the pain was caused by my expedition-roughened fingertips. The only thing I could do to help was to blow hard on each area as I administered the cream to speed up the evaporation process on the skin. It was a strange way to get to know somebody. And I got to know him fairly intimately that day, for during his sunbath he had only been wearing the briefest of trunks. By the time I reached his delicate places he was rendered totally helpless by the constant pain, and I was exhausted from the effort of trying to be as gentle as possible, and from blowing. Base Camp was already at over 13,000 feet, which made everything an exertion.

The more sensitive area around his crutch was even more tender, and I blew even more furiously after applying the cream. Realising that I wanted to spread it on the other side of his genitals, he rearranged himself underneath the towel which covered his private parts. 'Stop!' I shouted as he pushed everything towards the newly bedaubed side. '*Attenzione! Tuo* . . .??' and not knowing the Italian word for penis, desperately filled in with '*balles!*' Anyway, he got my meaning and winced at the thought of what the stinging cream might have done.

Later on the expedition we had a panic radio call one night from Almo Giambisi, a solid, stoic mountaineer. 'Get the doctor, quickly, I am in agony!' he wailed. At Camp 2 in the confusion of a dark tent he had picked up the wrong tube of ointment and rubbed a heat-inducing rheumatic cream onto his piles. The actual climbing is often not the only dangerous part of an expedition.

After the convivial evening at Kashkar we continued our journey to Base Camp. First we spent three dusty days driving across the strange 'mountains of the moon' of the Kwen Lun range which borders the higher peaks of the Karakoram, until we arrived at the end of the road.

On the stony bed of an almost dry river we met our next form of transport. We had already travelled for thousands of kilometres by plane; now we were to get the 'boats' and 'trains' of the well-known song all in one go. One hundred and twenty two-humped camels were waiting to transport us and all our equipment to Base Camp. It was quite a sight. I soon understood why they are called 'ships of the desert'. To ride on a camel is like sitting in a bouncing, wave-tossed dinghy: they have no easy rhythm like a horse. They are animals of a thousand voices, and can grumble and swear like a trooper, and, if they take a dislike to you they will spit slimy green half-digested cud at you which has a foul smell.

We had to carry all their hay with us, as there was almost no grazing in the dry mountain desert area we had to traverse. It was very expensive, the equivalent of camel caviar, costing the expedition £6,000.

While we were there I had another glimpse into the very human side of my Italian companions. We were preparing to set off on the next long five-day section of our journey to Base Camp when one of our donkeys gave birth to a foal. The baby animal lay helplessly on the lumpy bed of river stones and the whole expedition circled it, encouraging it to take its first steps. For three hours it struggled to control its sprawling lanky legs, and the audience waited, enthralled, putting off all the mundane chores until this little creature finally made it. A beautiful scene, which happened at the perfect moment, just as we were leaving behind the last easy communication with the outside world and entering the true world of nature.

On the second day of the walk-in we filmed the camel train moving above a spectacular river gorge. I stayed on on the lower side of the steep mountain path with Joshka Rakoncaj, a Czechoslovakian mountaineer who was with us, to film them going up while Kurt went on ahead to film them coming down once they got through. Joshka and I had just finished and packed up the camera and sound equipment as the last twenty-five animals started to zig-zag their way up the narrow track above the rocky gorge. I hurried to catch up with Kurt and was in the middle of the lowest traverse when one of the camels on the highest track stumbled, lost its balance and fell. The camels were joined together in lines of three connected by strings of woven camel hair attached to pegs through their noses. Luckily this string broke, or many more would have become entangled and pulled off their feet. But to see even only one great beast somersaulting, falling, completely out of control, loaded with a hundred and seventy kilos down a steep slope made of delicately balanced dust, straight for me, was terrifying. I could not move. To my right was a close-to-vertical unstable slope of stone-encrusted dry mud, and if I tried to move left out of the way I would most likely panic the other camels next to me who were still not used to the colours and smells of the Europeans. I held my breath. Between me and the falling camel stood the short lines of the other twenty camels and four donkeys. It was likely that they would be skittled off their feet and fall over the gorge two hundred feet to the churning river below. My chances were not good either. I could only risk trying to move swiftly to safety when I really knew what would be falling and where it might land. It looked as if the expedition was about to have a horrible disaster. No one could help me or the camels. It all happened so quietly, no noise from either humans or animals, just a thumping and scuffling as the camel bounced and slithered in the dust. It was as if we were all too scared to cry out. Even when the top camel finally landed just ten feet away from me, pinned on his back by his heavy load, there was total silence. Nobody dared to move in case they scared the animals.

Slowly two of the camel drivers went down, moving carefully between the dazed beasts to sort out the mess. Loads had been dislodged and balanced precariously on the steep slope. Two of the donkeys had also tumbled down to the bottom path where I was standing. One had ended up between the legs of a camel but seemed unharmed.

It took a long time to get the camels reloaded. They had almost finished when suddenly, for no reason, the donkey standing beneath the belly of the camel by me took two steps forward and fell over the cliff of the gorge. It fell endlessly before landing with a heavy thump on to the rocks by the river. I wanted to cry. The tension of the near catastrophe and the relief that nothing had been seriously hurt had drained me. Why did the donkey have to fall? There was no reason to make it go forward.

The Chinese camel drivers rushed down to the river, and to my relief, even above the roar of the turbulent water, I could hear their shouts of joy when they discovered that the donkey was still alive. Two hundred feet is a long way to fall onto rocks. Miraculously it had landed on its soft load of blankets and hay. It even managed to walk on for a further five hours to the next camp. I recorded the story and my feelings on my tape recorder at the time – it still sends shivers up my spine.

The day after the donkey incident, we crossed the famous Aghil Pass. It is a high saddle, 15,800 feet above sea level. From the top we got our first glimpse of the Gasherbrum Glacier, a tiny white speck in the distance. The road leading to it was the broad dry bed of the Shaksgam river discovered by the British explorer Sir Francis Younghusband in 1887.

It was hard to believe that in less than a month there would be so much water rushing down from the glaciers of the surrounding mountains that it would be a mass of interconnecting rivers, all raging torrents. Impassable! Our expedition would be cut off from the outside world by these waters for two months. That was why Giuliano could wait no longer for his baby and our Italian porters had to go back so soon.

When we finally did return at the end of August the volume of water was still a problem. It was not possible to walk along one bank continuously as the wild deep waters quite often swept the sides of the vertical rock and mud cliffs. We had to cross and re-cross the deep icy channels, island hopping, along the broad river bed.

It was impossible to wade or swim through many of the waters, the current was too strong, and we were ferried across on the swaying backs of our camels. Even these sure-footed creatures were knocked off their feet by the force of the flood. We had many heart-stopping moments as they were swept away downstream. Camels cannot swim and they could only wait until they were washed into a shallower, less turbulent section. If their loads had not already fallen off they would immediately make every effort to throw them off, terrified by the frightening experience. These poor animals had never been in such a situation before; normally they were used to carry coal and grain along the roads. As most of our expedition equipment was packed in waterproof plastic drums, the next problem was to try to catch these as they floated rapidly away. We lost six of our drums. Marco Pretti lost all his personal mountaineering equipment and all his precious exposed films. Our food for the return journey was also swept away, and we had to walk for eight to ten hours for four days with only a bowl of watery soup for breakfast and supper. There was nothing to replace it in this wild inhospitable area.

On the way in at the foot of the Aghil Pass our small exploration party of five split off from the main body of the expedition. Apart from Kurt, myself and Joshka there were Gianni Scarpellini (a second cameraman) and Pierre Angelo Zanga, who was super strong and had a wild appearance but was gentle in character. Gianni was a lovely gnome-like man in his fifties who reminded me of Dennis Kemp; he had the same twinkling eyes and energy for life. We turned left along the Shaksgam towards the Gasherbrum Glacier, and the others went to the right for another three days, until they reached the place of our Base Camp.

We spent our first very cold night at a tiny oasis in this vast mountain desert. Durbin Jangal got its name because Francis Younghusband lost his binoculars (or Durbin) there. Jangal means a green place. In the early morning I took my first bath for ten hot dusty days under the falling waters of a thermal spring. It was a strange experience to be warmly encased while all around me snow was falling and the temperature was below zero. It did take courage to take off my clothes at the start, but it was well worth it.

Three camels helped us transport our film and camping equipment to the foot of the Gasherbrum Glacier and then returned to the pleasant grazing at Durbin Jangal to wait for five days while we did our exploration.

It was a forty-kilometre day's walk – the length of a marathon – to our camp at the glacier. From the top of the Aghil Pass the river bed had looked like a smooth grey road, but once we started to walk along it we realised just how deceptive that view had been. The millions of stones, of all shapes and sizes, colours and textures, were very hot to walk on, baked by the sun which shone relentlessly down on us during the day, surrounding us in a temperature of 90°F, so that even without loads to carry we were soaked in sweat. The channels caused by the floodwaters of the previous year were bordered by ridges of stones, and we had to cross hundreds of these undulations, many only five to six feet deep but some as big as a two-storey house. The odd patch of sand did not offer much relief either, for then it was like sinking into soft snow. We learnt a lot from the camels and found it much easier to adopt their soft, flat-footed way of walking. The most surprising thing was that in this enormous river bed there was almost no water to be found, and we often went for two or three hours with no chance of having a much-needed drink.

The Gasherbrum Glacier was a fairy-tale world. Ice-tower pyramids stood like an army of white hooded Ku Klux Klan. Their beauty was bewitching, and I found it difficult to tear myself away from sitting and staring at their crisp whiteness and the razor-sharp outline of their shape. The position of the sun would change their colour, through turquoise to brilliant blue, shimmering silver and sparkling gold. All around them were the mountains I had read and dreamt about; the lofty Gasherbrum peaks, Kurt's Broad Peak and, just a summit tip in the distance, K2.

As we explored our way up the stony side moraine which followed along the side of the ice towers I felt like a child at Christmas, the excited anticipation and then the thrilling pleasure of actually discovering what was hidden by the wrapping paper. This exploration was certainly a great gift of nature. I had a wonderful feeling of being alone with the world; it needed nothing more complicated than just being there to discover treasures of creation far more valuable than the most precious of gems.

On the second day we walked among the magical ice, weaving a way through to the easier terrain of the central stone-covered moraine. Between the pyramids were fantasy ice formations, arches of ice like graceful Japanese bridges, spires glinting in the sun; some were like castles, or other mountains of the Alps, or had intriguing holes; one was like an open-sided two-floored house. That night we slept in our bivouac bags on the ice under the stars. Pierre Angelo was an excellent cook even on a camping stove and we had dined well on a tasty, imaginative, spaghetti.

The next morning we awoke to see the sunrise light up the summit tip of K2 and soon set off to try to find a way through the maze of ice towers to the foot of Gasherbrum II. It was not easy; the side glacier leading to our objective was tightly packed with these mini-ice mountains standing shoulder to shoulder, and we spent many hours climbing up and down their steep sides trying to find a safe way through. It was Kurt who finally discovered it. The others had given up in despair; every way they had tried had ended in a sheer drop, a high wall of unclimbable ice or a lake, and the effort of such strenuous climbing at 15,000 feet before we were fully acclimatised was exhausting. 'It's no good.' Even the strong Pierre Angelo had given up. Only Kurt would not accept it. He went off in yet another direction and fifteen minutes later gave an excited yell. 'It's OK, come on. I've found a way through!'

It was eight o'clock when we stood beneath the high snowy

flanks of Gasherbrum II. Sadly, only Kurt and I had the energy left to go so far; our friends had tried but turned back when they realised that they could not be fast enough to make it before nightfall. I looked at my footprints in the snow, the first steps anyone had made in this place, and I was glad that they would disappear with the thawing sun the next day.

'Do you want to build a cairn?' Kurt asked.

'No,' I replied, 'let's not spoil it. Who does it matter to, apart from us, that we have been here?'

Kurt smiled. 'I'm glad you feel that way.'

A week later we rejoined the rest of the expedition at Base Camp. Suget Jangal was a green oasis on the bank of the Sarpo Largo river. It looked very green to our vegetation-starved eyes; in early June just a few hairs of grass sprouted through the dusty sand like an adolescent's beard, but there were large clumps of bushes with delicate fernlike leaves, which later produced sweet honey-smelling pink flowers. The whole place had a holiday atmosphere with its sandy beaches and our big-top, circus-type Mess Tent. Many times during the expedition we would retreat from our Advance Base Camp at the foot of K2, twenty-five kilometres away up the glacier, to recover our strength and rest our eyes from the harsh glare of the snow on the comforting, restful greenery.

We made it as comfortable as possible. After all, it was to be our home base for three months. Kurt and I made a little garden by our tent, a tiny four-foot patch in which we planted sunflower seeds. I had brought a packet of special soil improver with me and mixed it with the infertile sand. We asked the Chinese for the seeds, which they had carried to roast and eat. When we counted them we found there were thirteen and all but one grew into solid plants and gave us a great deal of pleasure. We had to protect our garden from being eaten by sheep, for we had walked in with us a flock of fifty as a fresh meat supply. Unfortunately there was a wolf in the area who also fancied our mutton. He raided our mobile larder several times; on one occasion he killed eight animals at a single go. He must have been either very big or

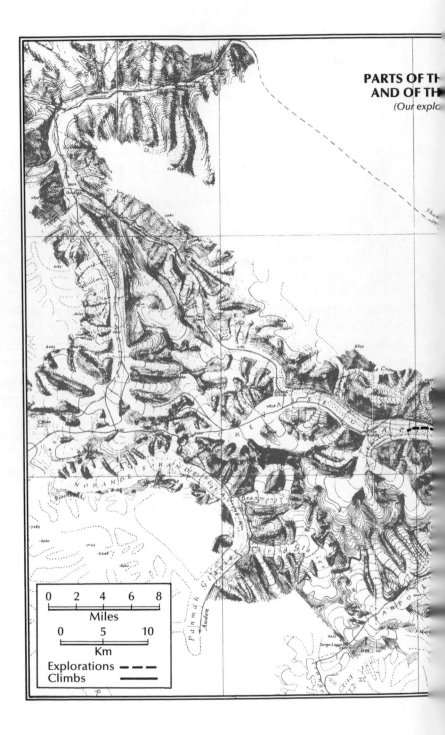

PARTS OF TH
AND OF TH
(Our explo

0 2 4 6 8
Miles
0 5 10
Km
Explorations — — —
Climbs ————

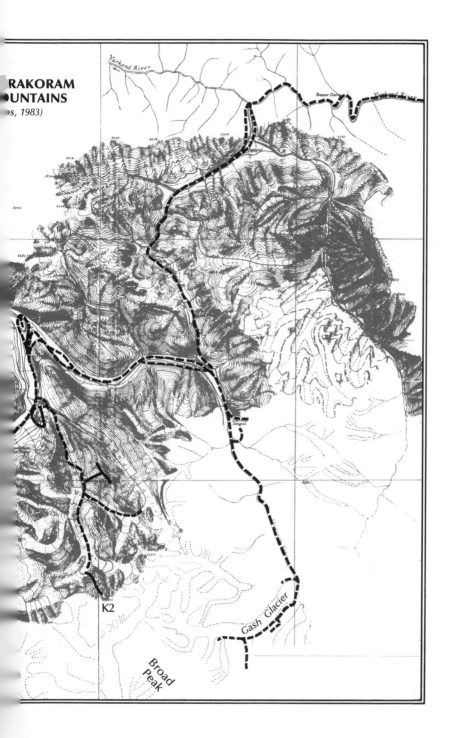

KARAKORAM MOUNTAINS
(...os, 1983)

Yarkand River

Bazar Dara

Yarkand River

K2

Gash Glacier

Broad
Peak

extremely hungry, and although we were always on the look-out for him we never saw him.

The route from Base Camp up the K2 glacier to our Advance Base Camp was not easy, and it was very long, 25 kilometres of hard slog. As there are no indigenous people living in the mountains in this whole area, and, in any case, the people of Sinkiang rarely carry things on their backs, preferring to use donkeys, camels or even goats to transport the loads, there are no Chinese high-altitude porters, and we had to carry everything up to this camp at 16,500 feet.

The first section of the route led up from our oasis 'Campo Casa' along the wild glacial river flowing down from the K2 and Skyang Kangri icefalls. One place was impassable because of the strong current, and the Italians had fixed a rope traverse along the rocks above the churning waters. However, there was always some ice-cold paddling involved along the way which became more dangerous as the summer progressed and all the rivers got bigger and more forceful with the glacial melt. After four hours of getting wet and walking over river stones and dried mud slopes the ice cliffs at the end of the glacier formed a solid wall. The path up the bordering stony moraine covering the ice of the slopes at the side of the glacier was steep and hard work with a heavy pack, and we certainly did carry a lot all the time. It was Hobson's choice: you could either transport as much as possible in one load or make several journeys. Kurt and I preferred to do the former as it left us more time for explorations, but it meant constantly being weighed down by loads of up to 45 kilos for Kurt and 30 kilos for me. Often I could not lift and put on my rucksack by myself and someone would have to help me. But once it was in place, in balance on my back, I could carry a lot. However I did not like it as the pain from the strained, tired muscles in my neck, back and legs would send me inside myself and shut out my awareness of the beauty of my surroundings. In such mountaineering you have to work hard for the pleasures!

Several deep waves of moraine led to Glacier Camp 1, and there were many things to make you smile on the way, which always seemed to lighten the burden of carrying on that first section to the mountain. Tiny flowers would unexpectedly appear, nestling between the endless stones, and occasionally a wild hamster would sit immobile with curiosity: no reason to be afraid for he had probably never seen a human being before. The whole area had been closed to foreigners from Shipton's time up to the 1982 Japanese expedition.

Sometimes an eagle would soar overhead, and we always felt impelled to stop and watch his powerful, graceful flight. How swiftly and effortlessly he covered the distance which took us hours to walk. Flocks of snow geese would taunt us with their trilling coo-ing, but were so well camouflaged that they were almost impossible to spot among the rocky scree on which they sat. We did see herds of bahril, Marco Polo sheep with large curling horns. Life abounded even in these stark, seemingly barren surroundings.

Above Glacier Camp 1, we had to completely cross the glacier, climbing up and down over slippery hills of stone-covered ice. It took about six hours to the next camp by the side of a fast-flowing river. There a family of tame mice would visit us in the kitchen tent at night. We fed them on spaghetti and watched them grow fatter and fatter as they chewed their way up the pasta strings.

Moving on from this camp was a problem once the night ice on the small river which bisected the glacier had thawed, but the last stretch to Advance Base Camp was very interesting: a long but gentle climb up through avenues of ice pinnacles and then what we called the central highway . . . a broad strip of moraine about a mile long with K2 standing like a tantalising prize at the end.

The medial moraine was fascinating. There were so many treasures to be found among the ordinary stones. In certain lights it was easy as the pyrite sparkled in the sunlight, the multi-faceted crystals of gold, silver and the deep red glow of garnets reflected the sun's rays. At other times, even though we could not see them, we knew they were there and would walk with our eyes down, concentrating on finding them. It certainly took the boredom and fatigue out of the last long straight section to Advance Base Camp. Life at this Camp was comfortable enough for we had carried up a large Mess Tent and plenty of food. We even had fresh meat, from our Base Camp sheep, which we kept deep-frozen in a hole in an ice tower. Our camp was set up on the central moraine between two long rows of these white pinnacles – above us always towered the enormous, spectacular triangular shape of K2.

The Italians worked in teams of four to lay siege to the mountain. One team would push out the route, supplied with ropes for fixing and the snow stakes and metal spike pitons necessary to attach them to the mountainside, by a second group. At certain intervals camps would be established and stocked with tents, sleeping bags, cookers and food. While two teams worked the other two would be resting, awaiting their turn. They worked efficiently, but constant fresh snowfall prevented them from reaching Camp 2 at 22,300 feet. When they did eventually establish it at the end of June, another storm drove them back down again and avalanches destroyed half the camp. Just after this one of the younger mountaineers, Luca Argentero, a tall athletic twenty-six-year-old from Courmayeur had a nasty accident. He had been cooking at the small stores camp below the mountain. The lack of oxygen affected our Gaz stoves badly and it took an age even to make a cup of tea. Often to speed things up we would put two stoves under the pot. Luca must have been tired and not thinking properly when he put the two stoves inside a discarded biscuit tin to shelter them from the wind. Suddenly, when they had been burning for several minutes, he realised what he had done and hurriedly lifted the pot to switch them off. Too late; one had overheated the other. Just as he was bending over the biscuit tin there was an explosion and fragments of torn metal flew up into his face. Only Alberto Soncini was with him, and he was horrified at the sight of poor Luca's lacerations. His nose had been pushed completely out of position to one side and he was covered in blood. Fortunately he had been wearing snow goggles which, although shattered by the blast, had protected his eyes.

Helped by Alberto he managed to stagger back down the two-hour way to Advance Base Camp. Our Mess Tent was turned into a hospital as our three doctors operated to remove bits of metal and repair his breathing passages, so important to a mountaineer, and reset his nose.

Luca was very brave, he could hardly speak or eat for several days and had the worst black eyes I have ever seen. It was decided to let him recuperate at Advance Base Camp. Even if the altitude would slow down the healing process, at least the atmosphere was sterile. At Campo Casa, down by the river, there was so much dust blowing about and there were also mosquitoes and flies. Three weeks later the great day arrived for the bandages to be removed, and the poignant moment when Dr Simini asked Luca if he could manage to breathe through his repaired nose. At first he was scared to try, but gradually he managed it, and the smile on his face told us that he had succeeded. What rejoicing there was, for it meant that he could go back on the mountain. We had missed our friend's quiet cheerful company. Luca eventually went to Camp 3 at 7,600 metres (25,000 feet), a tribute to his courage and the skill of the doctors.

Before the expedition was able to get above Camp 2, Kurt and I had filmed all we could on the mountain and were able to pursue our great urge to explore the amazing mountain world that surrounded us. Unfortunately, our Chinese Liaison Officer, who sat at Campo Casa, was worried that we would go off peak-bagging and tried to restrict us by insisting that we did not stay out overnight. The Chinese have thousands of unclimbed peaks in the six to seven thousand metre range, but they guard them jealously and charge a high fee for the privilege of a first ascent. We did however climb up to five very good 'film viewpoints'!

But Kurt and I were really more interested in following the footsteps of the old explorers. It was the glaciers which fascinated us, but to get to them we always had to travel for several kilometres along wet and dry river beds. We were both fit, and luckily moved at the same pace. We developed a very fast walk for going as far as possible in the restricted time and travelled very lightweight for additional speed. I often had to smile when I thought of the safety rules I drummed into my students in the British mountains. Here I was in the middle of the world's highest mountains, traversing glaciers for hours on end at sixteen thousand feet, in nothing more than a pair of shorts, T-shirt and training shoes. I would not dare to be so casual in the mountains of Wales or Scotland, even in summer.

It would take a separate book to describe all our exploration adventures – they were all fantastic. Climbing on K2 was great, but the feeling of being alone with our wild surroundings, going into the unknown on our exploration wanderings, was truly special.

On our way to Glacier Camp 1, we passed the junction where the K2 glacier river was joined by another torrent coming down from the Skiang Kangri Glacier. We had seen it many times and were always intrigued by the glimpse we got of a rock gorge at the limit of our view. It became a 'must' on our long list of places to investigate.

We had to fit in our excursions between filming the progress of the mountaineers and the weather, and on 15 July we were not able to get away until 1.30 in the afternoon because we waited to film the butchering of meat to be carried up to Advance Base Camp. Even so we still had about eight hours of daylight for clocks all over China are set to the time of Peking. Just the other side of the Karakoram range, much closer in Pakistan, it was only half past ten.

We set off very lightweight, wearing training shoes. We had planned to carry our boots, but decided it would be quicker if we didn't, and we took only a small camera, a torch and a little bit of bread and cheese and a small tin of tuna fish. At 3 o'clock we crossed the K2 river with difficulty; it was already flowing strongly in the hot sunshine of the afternoon.

The beginning of the gorge looked steep and narrow and I felt awed as I entered its confines. The walls were worn smooth by the passage of water up to twenty feet above my head. It must take an incredible volume and power of water to erode this solid rock to such an extent. But this afternoon it was flowing fast but at a low level.

At first we tried to keep our feet dry, jumping from boulder to boulder, but soon realised this would not be possible for long, as with the afternoon thaw where the gorge narrowed most boulders disappeared underneath the water. Now we had to keep crossing the twenty-five-foot Skiang Kangri river for the best route and it was necessary to be very careful where we stepped for the water was waist-deep in places and the strong current could easily sweep us over. The secret was to feel with our feet and step from boulder to boulder under the water.

The canyon became still closer and narrower. It was beautiful because it twisted and turned, you could never see what was round the next bend, and we were gaining height very rapidly. It was really exciting. We hurried on as fast as possible for two hours, always expecting the next corner to reveal daylight and the glacier. In places, big sheets of old ice spanned the river, forming wide flat bridges that we had to crawl underneath or climb up to cross over.

Just after the ice bridges we got stuck. An enormous boulder blocked our way and on the top of it balanced a big sheet of thick ice at an angle of about 50°. It was all sloping towards a cascade which fell in a rushing white curtain of water down for sixty feet. For the first foothold to get onto the boulder we had to find a small rock to form a step and then, with a couple of delicate moves, reach the ice slab. We had no climbing equipment with us, so Kurt cut steps in the slab with a stone and his ski stick, and I watched him anxiously as he moved carefully from hold to hold on the slippery, semi-transparent, shiny blue surface. We had no rope with us either, and I was very aware, as I went up, how easy it would be to slip sideways and fall down the waterfall.

We were both so intrigued that after that obstacle the pace did not slacken at all. The gorge widened. We were hopping again from boulder to boulder, crossing and re-crossing the river. Higher up the walls of the gorge were made of dried mud with stones set in like currants in a cake. Any rainfall would flush these out on top of us and we hoped that the weather outside stayed fine. We crossed several new slopes of scree, which comprised very loose stones; they acted like a pile of large ball bearings when we stepped on to them and we had to run across before we were carried down.

Eventually we could see the opening at the end of the tunnel. The gorge had widened a bit more but we still could not see around the next bend. The river kept curving to the right and

191

was frozen across with sheets of ice, which soon became larger and more numerous, indicating, we hoped, that the glacier was near.

At half past five we got our first glimpse of the ice towers of the Skiang Kangri Glacier. It was a great moment to see the bottom ice moraine and the white pinnacles above, but it was still at least a mile away, and time was getting on. We were a little worried as we knew that during the day the sun would heat the glaciers, and the melt-waters would turn the already fast-flowing rivers into raging torrents. As we had been enclosed in our tunnel it was difficult to assess how long the sun had been shining on this glacier or whether the surrounding high mountains had shadowed it. On the smooth sheets of ice we could almost run, but had to be careful not to break through because there was water flowing underneath. The idea of getting close to the glacier was of paramount importance in both our minds, and our feet flew along despite the altitude of seventeen thousand feet. We reached the bottom of the moraine at a quarter to six, and by six o'clock we were sitting on a large rock buttress just below the glacier.

We had made it. But, of course, explorers are never satisfied, they always want to go on, and how we wished that we had bivouac equipment so that we could stay the night and complete the circuit which Tilman had made in 1937. He had explored the loop the other way round, coming down from the K2 glacier via a side glacier. From the map we have seen of Tilman's trip, he came down the lower section on the slopes above the gorge, so we most likely are the first people ever to manage to pass right through the long canyon.

We sat and ate our piece of bread, tuna and small hunk of cheese. We chewed it slowly, making it last. While we were moving we had not noticed the hunger pangs, but now we were starving. Soon we would have to hurry back. We didn't fancy crossing the K2 river in the dark. It had taken us from one-thirty to six o'clock to get there and the return would have to be much faster even with all the obstacles of the river to negotiate.

We ran down the ice sheets, and our boulder-hopping experience on the way up helped our speed on the way back. As we were going with the flow of the stream, we did not always bother to take the most sensible route but often plunged straight ahead through the freezing water. My feet went numb and it took a lot of rubbing to restore the circulation when we re-emerged at the end of the gorge. Going down I counted the number of times that we crossed the river or waded in it up to our thighs or higher, but at a count of eighty I gave up. It was great fun and we felt happy to be so extremely fit. Later on we worked out from the map that we had covered thirty kilometres that afternoon.

But we were not yet back in Base Camp. Although our side river had not become too much stronger the K2 river was quite swollen. As dusk was falling we tried to cross in one or two places and found it impossible, it was also colder than the Skiang Kangri waters. Kurt finally found a possible passage through it and started going across. I followed him and at one point had each foot on a big stone under the rushing waters about a foot and a half apart, but as I transferred my weight to step forward, one boulder toppled over and trapped my foot underneath it. With the pressure of the heavy stone and the water I could not move. It was a nasty moment, especially as Kurt could not hear my shouts for help above the noise of the churning torrent. I was trapped in the middle, and must have looked a strange figure in the gathering gloom, frantically waving my arms at him standing on the bank twenty yards away. By the time Kurt came to my rescue and prised the boulder away with his ski stick, my legs had lost their feeling, and I jogged back along the river bank to try to restore the circulation. We reached Base Camp by torchlight at ten o'clock!

After our river gorge excursion we were determined to have a look at the main part of the Skiang Kangri Glacier to see for ourselves how complicated it might be to complete the circuit to the K2 Glacier. We decided to do this by climbing a side glacier just below our Glacier Camp 2 which we had already previously explored. On that occasion we had reached a col after an eight-hour haul up loose scree, large boulder blocks and a never-ending but easy-angled snowfield. This valley had also been entered by the Japanese the previous year, as was evident from the precisely built cairns that we found, but they finished halfway up. For extra speed, as it had to be an afternoon excursion due to bad weather in the morning, I had decided to wear my rather well worn ten-year-old bendy boots, which were so much lighter than my double boots. When we arrived at the col we looked longingly at a high point above, which would have given us a view, but as it was already 5.30 there was no chance to try.

However just over the border in Pakistan it was still three hours earlier, only early afternoon. We decided to borrow some Pakistani time to climb a slightly lower protrusion on the other side of the col to get a good filming point down to the Shaksgam Valley. My boots with their worn-through toes were not really suitable for mountaineering at 19,000 feet, but the snow conditions were good and the view from the top of our 'Afternoon Peak' was outstanding.

For some reason the other high point haunted us and we made another abortive effort to get closer to it. On this occasion a bad snowstorm put an end to our endeavours before we even reached the col. So three days after the gorge exploration we made another try. We established a camp halfway up the side glacier, just below the snowfield, and the next morning we were making very slow progress up what had seemed from a distance very easy snow slopes. I quote from my diary:

> About halfway up there was a stretch below a wide serac, maybe thirty feet in length, the snow got incredibly deep. Kurt was on the point of giving up at this time because we were just becoming completely exhausted and seemed to be getting nowhere. I felt that if only we could get above the ice cliff we would reach more solid ground. I took over the lead and managed to reach the seracs, then Kurt went in front again. Between the seracs was even worse and he ended up literally burrowing his way through the passage he cleared with his ice axe. His tunnel was the height of his shoulders. When I followed the steps were still soft and unstable and I struggled, floundered and swore as I fought my way up. Above the snow only came to knee height again until we reached the next serac which was about forty-five feet high. Getting over this was harder than the first one, but we did not want to give up. When we climbed out above it we were completely exhausted.

Shipton, too, I discovered later, had climbed this peak to get a view of K2, and his experiences were mirrored by our own.

'Higher up, in spite of an intensely cold night, the snow was very bad . . . we began to sink in up to our hips. It was surprising to find such bad conditions . . . We began to wonder if in these parts the snow ever consolidates in the normal way,' he commented in *Blank on the Map*.

It seemed absolutely hopeless to go on as it was already five o'clock and because of the angle of the slope we could not see how far above the summit was. After a short rest, just when we were on the point of going down, I decided to have one last try to traverse to the east side of the mountain hoping to get a glimpse of the Skiang Kangri Glacier, the object of our climb. I made a diagonal ascent and after ploughing on through the soft snow for another twenty-five feet suddenly saw the top, but more importantly a little separate peak which would give us the viewpoint we needed. All tiredness seemed irrelevant and neither the horrible powder snow of the little plateau below nor the slippery rock ridge leading to the top discouraged us from reaching our goal.

I had the privilege of going first and at six o'clock we stood on the top of 'Julie Peak'. We had to go on for another forty yards before we could look down to the fantastic sight of the Skiang Kangri Glacier. We were well rewarded for our struggles. We could see almost to the point we had reached on the glacier, the ice peaks of the glacier ribbon and its top end below the broad base of Skiang Kangri where the snow was smooth and flat. We had a view of hundreds of mountains, most of them unclimbed, and could see as far as Tirich Mir and the Ogre. Julie Peak was only about 6,000 metres high but was in the most superb situation for panoramic shots; our time and efforts were justified and we felt very content.

A very different exploration was one that we dreamed about for several weeks, but could not think how to achieve. We wanted to visit the Mustagh Pass, over which Sir Francis Younghusband had travelled in 1887 on his great journey from Peking to India. The problem was that this was said to be three and a half days' walk from our Base Camp at Suget Jangal and our Liaison Officer was adamant that we could only have a Day Pass. We must be back by nightfall.

Kurt had a brainwave and went to see Mr Liu. 'We want to go to the bottom of the Sarpo Largo Glacier today, so that we can film the sunrise tomorrow morning,' he told him, 'and tomorrow we want to film several things around that area, so we might return the following day. We are not taking any climbing equipment with us,' he added quickly. Our astute Liaison Officer was not to be fooled. 'You may go this evening, but you must return by twelve noon tomorrow,' our interpreter translated.

'Well, we can explore some of the way, which will make it quicker if we do get another chance later on,' Kurt said philosophically, as we set off at six o'clock. This time I was carrying quite a heavy rucksack containing two sleeping bags, two down jackets, Kurt's overtrousers, the Leica R4 and lenses and some food. Kurt had a heavier load with the filming gear. In our determination to get as far as possible before it was totally dark, we went for three and three-quarter hours to the foot of the glacier without a stop. Below the ice cliffs we got out the stove and made some tea and had a snack of bread and sardines. At 10.15 pm we moved on by moonlight, climbing up the stony moraine hills. There were lots of big hills to go over. Sometimes the mud of the moraine was soft and we sank uncomfortably in, or the stones were loose on their bed of ice and we slipped awkwardly, unable to see properly where we should place our feet.

At almost midnight we came down to a wide glacial bed of soft sand like a mini-desert. An enormous rock seemed the perfect bivouac place. It had a large overhang under which we could cook, and abutting it was the perfect rock bed, a large boulder with a flat top; it even had a rock pillow in exactly the right place. We organised our camp and tucked our sleeping bags into a sheet of plastic as we had no tent with us. We cooked our supper of baked beans by torchlight and then lay in our sleeping bags gazing at the stars. It was a beautifully clear night, and we were very relieved after the unsettled weather of the past few days. I soon dozed off.

I was woken by wet snowflakes. I looked at my watch: 2.30 am. I tugged at the plastic sheet and pulled it up over our heads and went back to sleep. When Kurt woke me at 4.30 the snow had stopped, but something was wrong. When I pulled up the plastic to cover our heads I had unwrapped our feet and my sleeping bag was soaking wet.

It was still not light when we set off at five o'clock, after a breakfast of tea and sauerkraut, but we had investigated the difficult climb up the next riverbed the previous night without our packs and sorted out a possible route. We were able to move more quickly as we left most of our things at our bivi camp, and with the help of a torch made good progress over the difficult glacier terrain.

Above the river a side glacier came down and we had to cross a switchback of stony humps as it fanned out before merging with the ice. We tried to keep to the side of the main glacier, which was an impossible jungle of ice mountains and deep lakes, but even that was complicated terrain. After several tricky traverses in the half light of dawn, the going got a little easier and we pressed on until 8.30. This was the absolute deadline if we were to get back to Base Camp by noon and, tempted though we were to carry on, we knew that returning late would mean the end of any future explorations. At the time it was very frustrating; we had got within two hours of the entrance to the glacier leading to the Mustagh Pass and would not have the reward of looking into it. Later I read a revealing quotation in Eric Shipton's book *Upon that Mountain*: 'Travel in unexplored country is a curious mixture of freedom and cramping self-discipline, of careless abandon and rigid time schedule. Free from all the tiresome restraints of normal life, encircled by a boundless horizon, one is all the more a slave to the elementary considerations of time and distance, food and warmth, weather and season. The simple life is simple only in that it deals with direct fundamental things.'

We climbed partway up the slope bordering the glacier and from this elevated point fixed the view in our minds, then regretfully turned around and hurried back. We reached Base Camp at half past one and went straight to our tent to sleep.

Whenever we were at Base Camp we made an excursion somewhere every other day, and covered enormous distances of this fascinating area. When I added together the kilometres of the walk-in and our many journeys up the K2 Glacier, the Gasher-brum exploration and all our side trips, I discovered that we walked over one thousand kilometres during the four months we were there. It was on this expedition that I took full advantage of the European alliance to help me cope with the enormous scale of things. When walking I ticked off the long distances in kilometres; when climbing it was more satisfying to measure height in feet.

12

K2: the mountain of mountains

Christina Smiderle had been part of the porter group, but had stayed on unexpectedly when they left. Her boyfriend Marco Corte Colo was planning to ski down the extremely steep flank of K2 from 7,000 metres, just above Camp 2. As Christina was a doctor, and a very attractive one, it seemed a good idea that she should stay around to give him moral support. It was the last week of July and, after ten weeks of the expedition, she and I were alone in the two-tent camp at the foot of the mountain used mainly to store supplies for the mountain camps, and where Luca had his accident with the Gaz stove. It was the first time that she and I were together and had a chance to talk and find out more about each other. Christina was the only other woman in our very cut-off world.

Poor Marco had a very difficult time. He had to wait so long before Camp 2 was established – the gods had not been kind and the expedition had been driven down time and again by bad weather. Then he had to wait for the right snow conditions, essential for skiing on such a very steep mountain. Over the waiting weeks the mountaineers began to worry more and more about the dangers of his daring descent. I am afraid that Kurt and I did not help his psychological confidence. To protect ourselves, we had to ask him to sign a declaration that it was his own idea to ski down, that he and the expedition leader had asked us to film him; and we had not suggested he should do such a risky stunt for the sake of the film.

At last, on 24 July, he had gone to Camp 2 with his skis, and Kurt went to Camp 1 with the big Arriflex SR16 movie camera. I was waiting below the mountain with the smaller Arriflex. We were ready to film the following morning.

The day passed slowly, but Christina and I found each other interesting company and were very much in sympathy with each other's lives. She was not an experienced mountaineer, but had done a little climbing since she had known Marco. However she loved skiing and being in the mountains.

'Deposito to Campo Due, Deposito to Campo Due', we radioed, trying to rouse the sleepy climbers at our highest established camp at that point. The weather was fine for skiing and filming and we needed to know when Marco intended to start on his descent.

Fausto de Stefani answered. 'We're going higher today but Marco just wants to sleep a little longer,' came the reply. 'Call him again at 10 am.'

At the 10 am radio call we were again told that Marco just wanted to sleep. At 12 noon, the same story, but also that he did not feel well enough to ski that day.

Christina became worried. 'Julie, he is sick,' she told me. But she could not persuade the mountaineers at Camp 2 of her worst fears – that he was suffering from altitude sickness.

Altitude sickness can strike anyone at any time, even experienced mountaineers who have tried to acclimatise carefully; and the time from its first symptoms to death can be very rapid. I spent the day worrying with Christina.

At 7.30 that evening there was panic on the mountain. Oxygen was rushed as speedily as possible up the long and difficult section from Camp 1 to Camp 2. Thank heavens the weather was good. By 10.30 it was dark and very cold, and Marco was fighting for breath . . . and his life. We kept the radio connection open so that we could follow the drama on the mountain. Christina was very brave. Finally, half an hour after midnight, the oxygen reached Camp 2 and by 2.30 Marco was breathing more easily again. But one bottle of oxygen would not last long and to prevent brain damage the mountaineers would have to abandon the push up the mountain and get him down to a safer height as soon as possible.

'We must go up to Camp 1,' Christina kept insisting. 'I must be with Marco, to help him.' There was desperation in her voice. But in the dark of the night that was impossible.

I was in no way prepared to go onto the mountain at this point. As I have already said, this was not an easy expedition logistically, and I had not carried up sufficient gear to make a serious assault on the mountain. In order to film Marco's descent Kurt and I had concentrated on carrying up to the foot of the mountain just what we needed to survive and make the film. Even my 35mm SLR camera and personal diary tape recorder had been discarded at the Glacier Camp before Advanced Base in order to keep my loads within my carrying limits.

'All right, we will go up first thing tomorrow morning,' I promised, in an effort to console poor Christina. She took some sleeping tablets and tried to get some sleep.

Hell! The ropes were so heavy to pull out from under the fresh snow that had fallen since Kurt had gone up two days before.

The section to Camp 1 was steep and at the beginning very dangerous, with big broken seracs hanging directly over the route, threatening to fall at any moment. We had made an early start to get past this section before the sun reached the precarious blocks of house-sized ice and began to melt them making them even more unstable. We also hoped to reach Camp 1 before the cruel heat of the mid-day sun was upon us on the long, shadeless haul up the fixed ropes to make us even more fatigued with dehydration.

Our progress was slow as I had to keep a careful eye on Christina. Not only was she inexperienced in big mountains, but with the mental stress she had suffered recently, she would be below par both mentally and physically. Also I had to carry up all my sound equipment, plus some spare cine films, together with my sleeping bag, small tent, down jacket and spare food as we would be unexpected guests at the camp which nestled in a crevasse at 19,000 ft (5,800m). When we arrived there was not even room for another tent, so Kurt and I dug a snow hole to sleep in.

'Oxygen! Oxygen! Send up oxygen, urgently!' The frantic call came from high above us as the mountaineers struggled to carry

Marco down to Camp 1. They had tied his legs together and, trussed like a chicken, controlling him with the ropes, they slid him along the fixed ropes. It was an exhausting task.

Several interminable hours later Kurt and I filmed their arrival with their semi-delirious patient. More drugs, oxygen and the drop in altitude were essential to ensure a complete recovery. At this point, Christina was highly concerned as it was not certain whether he had suffered any brain damage as a result of his illness.

The following morning thankfully there was a marked improvement in his condition and the mountaineers and a more relaxed Christina helped him on down to Base Camp and safety.

Meanwhile, Kurt and I examined our situation. When you take a conscious decision to make a summit bid, you begin to prepare yourself mentally. We wanted to take advantage of having the sync-sound Arriflex camera on the mountain to film at Camp 2, at 6,800 metres and above, but was our limited personal equipment sufficient to cope with such high altitude? I only had my second, eight-year-old, well-used single sleeping bag; the warm inner bag was still at Base Camp. Neither of us had spare inners for our double boots. We risked frost-bite if the snow got into them and wet the felt and leather inner boots. To add to my problems I only had ordinary snow gaiters and not the thicker insulated overboots normally used at high altitudes; in fact the only spare clothing I had with me was one pair of socks! We also knew that we would again have to carry heavy rucksacks, not only with the film gear, but also our tent, sleeping bags, cooker, billies, food, etc., enough to make us completely self-sufficient at the next camp in case it was already full of climbers. In the end, we felt that we could risk going on up with our limited equipment, but that we should leave the final decision to the weather.

'Sorry, I'll have to stop again . . .' I was hanging on the fixed rope almost a thousand feet above Camp 1. The rope stretched out in a long traverse across the steep face.

'Why did it have to happen today?' I had been woken up the next morning by my stomach, grumbling and churning, and then . . . every mountaineer's dread, diarrhoea!

202

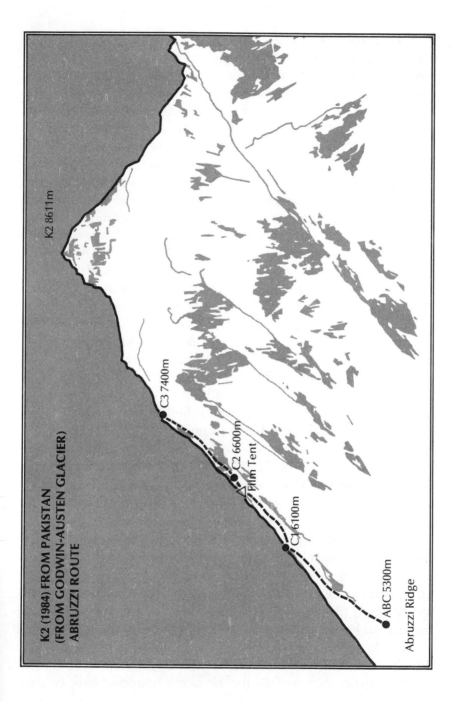

K2 (1984) FROM PAKISTAN
(FROM GODWIN-AUSTEN GLACIER)
ABRUZZI ROUTE

K2 8611m

C3 7400m

C2 6600m
Film Tent

C1 6100m

ABC 5300m

Abruzzi Ridge

We had been the last to leave the camp and head up the 60° snow slopes at the start of the long and very tiring section on the mountain. During the past couple of weeks we had been watching through the binoculars from the glacier as tiny dots moved slowly up and across the mighty face – like flies on a giant white pyramid. Why did they move so slowly, stop so often, and, in several cases, return to Camp 1 before they were even halfway? From some five thousand feet below and around three miles away it didn't look so bad. But we already knew the reason. Just once before we had actually been on the mountain to film and had ourselves turned back enervated before reaching Camp 2.

This time I not only had the hard work of climbing with a full pack but the additional problem of freeing myself of clothing whilst hanging on the fixed ropes, and later the debilitation brought about by the diarrhoea. Hour after long hour we toiled slowly upwards. Three more times I had to manage difficult manoeuvres with my double trousers. Kurt hung on the rope next to me holding my gloves and ice axe; this was no time for embarrassed modesty. Worse, we had run out of toilet paper and although using snow is effective, it is not very pleasant and can lead to uncomfortable chapping and piles.

We moved on up in fits and starts. Suddenly from high above me there was a whirrrrrr. I looked up, startled, to see what was causing the unusual noise. A rock the shape of a flying saucer had become detached from an overhang directly above and was zipping down the almost vertical snow slope, heading straight for us. I shouted to Kurt below me and he buried his face in the snow. The rock shot past me making a noise like an out-of-control noisy sewing machine and I held my breath, my body rigid with fear, as it kept its line directly for Kurt some eighty feet below. I could see a patch of his neck exposed below his crash helmet and knew that if the discus-shaped block hit him there, he would surely be decapitated. Without a pause the missile reached the level of his left shoulder and, although it was almost touching him, looked as if it would travel on just to the side of his body. But at that point it must have hit a rock lying under the snow, for it suddenly shot up into the air like a bouncing ball, cleared his shoulders complete with rucksack, and landed on his right-hand side to continue on down, down, down. For a moment I could not speak or move. Visions of what might have happened had it hit him flashed before my eyes and, as with many near disasters, I felt myself trembling, the reaction of over-tensed muscles and fear.

After nine tiring hours we were on the tiny snowshelf that had been cut out of the mountainside to make a space for the three small tents which formed Camp 2. I took off my crampons slowly and with great effort. Mercifully there was an unoccupied tent so that we did not have to dig out an extra space for ours, and I collapsed inside in my sleeping-bag and soon dozed off.

I awoke with a start. My stomach felt as if a dozen mini-gnomes had been holding a party in it and were now trying to punch their way out. I groped around in the dark tent for my boots and put them on, taking care to do up the laces. To trip over them while negotiating the tiny foot-wide ledge which ran along in front of the tents and formed the path to the 'loo' could result in a straight fall of six thousand feet to the foot of the mountain. But at that moment speed too was essential.

It was a dark cold night and the snow on the narrow path had refrozen after being melted by the hot daytime sun. It was lethally slippery. Kurt followed me out and grabbed my arm and steadied me as I was still a little drunk with sleep. I reached the tiny platform on which you could squat with your bottom hanging out over the long airy drop, and was relieved to see that some thoughtful person had left a snow-shovel, just its handle protruding from the snow, in the perfect position to hold on to.

My already cold fingers fumbled with the under-crutch zips which I had prudently had fitted to my trousers. I was wearing two pairs; Italian fibre-pile longjohns underneath French Gortex and Thinsulate overtrousers, but the problem was that the zips opened in two different directions – the French from front to back, and the Italian from back to front and, with cold, already numb fingers and a sleep-befuddled brain, this took some working out. Anyone who has ever had a fly-zip stuck when they have been in a desperate hurry to relieve themselves will sympathise with my predicament!

Ploosh ... in the still, dark night it sounded like an explosion to me, and then I realised the worst had happened. The 'thin shits', as Kurt so charmingly called them, had splattered everywhere, down my legs, right into my boots, covering my socks, between the two pairs of trousers. So there I was, at 11.30 on a dark, very cold night, 6,800 metres up the world's second highest mountain with only one spare pair of socks and not a drop of water to help me clean up. At that height there is only snow and the temperature that night was −25°C.

Kurt came rushing over. 'Julie,' he said very sternly, not realising my situation, 'put on these gloves at once! You are very lucky if you have not already got frostbite from holding that cold shovel with bare hands.'

I couldn't explain just then. I needed a few quiet moments to think, but I obediently pulled on the gloves, grateful for his thoughtful concern. It was obvious that I would have to sit there for a while yet.

At last it felt safe to stand up ... but what to do? I couldn't go back into the sleeping-bag in that state – the smell alone was disgusting. It was not just that I really did not know what to do next, but that I did know that, sensibly, I would have to go back down all the hundreds of arduous feet up which we had laboured so hard that day without even helping Kurt to shoot one metre of film. I had failed.

Self-pity welled up and tears began to roll down my cheeks. I didn't even care if they froze. I heard Kurt coming back over to me and my sobs grew louder – a typical woman's reaction when in need of sympathy! How could I explain to him? I thought of Bonington and his similar situation once, when he shat down the arm of his one-piece suit.

I stuttered out my problem, in English, through chattering teeth, and his calm, reassuring response already made me feel better. He took my hand and led me to the safer small area between two of the tents and hooked me onto a carabiner attached to an ice screw. Pierre Angelo and Fausto looked out of their tent as I stumbled by.

From our tent Kurt brought out the thin foam mat which we used as insulation between our sleeping bags and the ice below.

'Take off your trousers and clean yourself up just a little with snow. Then I have found these . . .' He handed me two tiny tinfoil wrapped tissues, the kind given away with in-flight meals. I did my best, grateful to have something constructive to do. The feel of the mat beneath my bare feet made my mind slip back to the *dojo* at home. This mat was a thinner version of the shock-absorbing mats we use for practising aikido and its feel gave me comfort and strength.

Wearing Kurt's overtrousers, back in the snug warmth of my sleeping bag with him snoring gently beside me, things no longer seemed so bad . . .

The next morning I felt better and decided for the moment not to go down to Base Camp. I tried to wash my trousers with snow, which was not very successful as the mess had penetrated deep into the fibres. There was no spare Gaz at the camp to melt snow for washing water.

Although I felt a little tired I enjoyed a short sortie that we made in the evening up to a filming point to fix some ropes. These were our safety ropes to tie onto the next day while we filmed the mountaineers. It was the first chance I had quietly to enjoy the view. K2 is a very steep mountain and from 23,000 feet we were able to look out over many of our exploration routes. Getting to Camp 1 with Christina and then to Camp 2 with the 'thin shits' had been struggles with no time to appreciate the panorama. Sometimes you can miss the point of being in such a situation; the problems can take you over.

On 1 August, when we returned from our filming on the ridge, Giuliano De Marchi, our mountain doctor, and Alberto had come up from Camp 1. We heard over the radio that Augostino and Joshka the Czechoslovakian had reached the summit the previous day. By coincidence they arrived on top on the same day and at almost the same time as the first Italian conquerors of this majestic mountain, Lino Lacedelli and Achille Compagnoni, on 31 July in 1954. Between 1892 when the first mountaineers had attempted to climb K2 and 1980, only four people had stood on its summit. Even by 1985, only eight expeditions, that's one in every seven, have been successful and less than twenty very lucky people have reached the top. (Over a hundred people have stood on top of Everest.)

We were delighted and hugged one another furiously. There was a little concern about the climbers' physical condition as they had been caught out by the night just below the summit and had to sleep without sleeping bags at 27,900 feet. They had also run out of food and had almost nothing to drink for two days. But they reassured us that they had no serious frostbite and were feeling tired but well, and would be coming down from Camp 4 the next morning. That evening we packed up our things in readiness to go to meet them and film their triumphant descent.

It was an emotional reunion and we shot some good film, and when they had gone on down to Base Camp Kurt and I again discussed our situation. Now the summit had been reached, Francesco the leader would probably end the expedition as soon as everyone on the mountain had made their try for the top. We did not have too much choice; despite our lack of proper equipment, if we were going to try it had to be now or never.

The way to Camp 3 was long and it was a very hot day. The snow was disgustingly soft, and we arrived dead tired. Unfortunately both the tents were occupied and Kurt had the unenviable task of digging a platform in the snow of the steep slope for our refuge. It was really perched on the side of the mountain and we had to clip into a safety line if we went outside the tent. I was weary when I arrived at the camp, but when I tried to sleep it was impossible and I tossed and turned. Bad nights are one of the problems of living at altitude, and many mountaineers resort to sleeping tablets. Generally I sleep well at any height, and fight shy of taking tablets. Some medication can have strange effects on the body at altitude.

I was very relieved when morning came although I felt pretty bad after my terrible night as we started up the snow slope above the camp. Another mountaineer, Giorgio Peretti, had also had a sleepless night, and he decided to stay at the camp and rest. Luca was not feeling well and decided to go down, the wisest thing after his accident, especially as he felt that his legs were not working properly. I was not sure how far up I would go, but as we gained height I felt better and just kept going.

We heard that the only tent at Camp 4 was full, so we found a lovely campsite an hour below, at 25,700 feet. It had an incredible view and our tent nestled in a sun-warmed rock corner. As I sat in the evening sunshine looking out over the thousands of golden peaks stretching as far as I could see, I felt so deeply happy and contented. I climb mountains for moments like this, not only to reach the summit – that is an extra bonus, a special gift. Gazing out from my elevated viewpoint over Shipton's 'unexplored country', I felt completely in harmony with my surroundings. It was like looking at, and at the same time being part of, a great work of art. It had an even greater satisfaction because I was no passive observer; mountains offer the ultimate human experience – to be involved physically, mentally and spiritually. During the past few weeks I had been down there wandering among the peaks in the picture that I was now contemplating and here I was sitting high up on the mountain that had filled my dreams and been the centre of my attention from below. It was as if I were seeing things from two sides of a mirror. The joy of being in such a situation was overwhelming.

As we moved on up the following morning, two more mountaineers, Fausto and Sergio Martini, came down from the summit and the weather began to change. Fast-moving clouds were heading towards us as the wind increased. An hour later, when we reached Camp 4, from which we would make our summit attack, the arrival of the storm was imminent. We moved as quickly as we could manage at 26,240 feet (8,000 metres) to put up our tent. At the time it does not feel that you are so slow; I just felt tired, but later when I saw myself on film I looked like a spaceman moving on the moon.

We were on a tiny platform, eight feet wide by twenty-four feet long, a small step on the ridge itself: not the best place to ride out a storm in a tent. It started to snow heavily, and while I sorted out the inside of our little tent Kurt finished anchoring it as best he could. He had really exerted himself, moving the biggest boulders he could find to secure the guylines. We were thankful later on that he had gone to so much trouble.

The intensity of the storm increased, and we worried about two of our friends, the only other people still on the mountain, who had set off for the summit that morning. Giuliano was a strong, competent mountaineer. He had been with Kurt on the Italian Everest expedition in 1980 and had spent seven days on the South Col at 8,000 metres riding out bad weather. His partner was young Alberto, who at 27 years old was on his first Himalayan climb. As they had not retreated to Camp 4, we guessed that they had set up a bivouac inside a crevasse on the exposed snowfield below the summit, but if the heavy snow continued they would be in serious trouble.

That night we got no sleep. Wind whistled and howled around us, funnelling up from the steep ten-thousand-foot drop on one side of the ridge and catching us in its full blast as it reached the top. It tugged and tore at the thin Gortex material of our tunnel-shaped tent, and we wondered how long it would be before the guylines broke or the fabric ripped. We had seen another tent here that had been torn to shreds by the weather. At first I got really nervous. Then I came to terms with the fact that there was nothing I could do about our situation; and worrying would only burn up the physical energy that we would doubtless need, whatever happened, if we were going to have any chance of survival. Kurt too was fatalistic, and we spent the long hours of darkness telling each other more about our lives. It was surprising how little we really knew about each other. Time spent together on expeditions was always busy with the film, and if we did have time to relax we were usually writing home, or sleeping. When walking or climbing I do not talk much. It is an extra effort and the person in front or behind cannot hear what you are saying unless you almost shout.

When daylight came the storm continued. We were getting cramped from continually lying in such squashed conditions. I needed to relieve myself, but soon discovered that it was not possible to stand up outside the tent. The wind took my breath away, its force was tremendous and I dropped to my knees clutching tightly on to the tent. 'It's hopeless,' I told Kurt as I hurriedly retreated back inside and zipped up the door. I tried to mop up the puddles from melting snow that I had collected on my clothing during my three-second foray. 'But I must go,' I said. 'I'm bursting!'

I searched around for a suitable potty – it is so much easier for men, they can manage with a pee-bottle. I found a polythene bag, and blew into it to check that it had no holes. Spending a penny is not an easy manoeuvre in a tent two foot high and three foot wide at its largest end, which is full of sleeping bags, rucksacks and all the necessary clutter for mountaineering at high altitudes, and Kurt. Then I needed to free myself from the restrictions of my clothing. You can't afford to have inhibitions in such situations. K2 had already taught me that at Camp 1. I hoped that the polybag would not split, and that it would be large enough. I thought of Terry after his operation. I had been storing it up, hanging on for a couple of hours already. But all was well, and I successfully slid the bulging bag out through a gap in the door.

On previous occasions when we have been trapped in the tent in hours of need, we have resorted to using empty tins, and even our billie cans and mugs. Urine is said to be sterile. For a more solid call of nature polythene bags are the only answer, and the worst experience I heard about was a mountaineer who had 'the runs'. He had settled down in his sleeping bag and was nicely asleep when he sneezed. The force of the 'atishoo' caused his bowels to open, and he was left lying in a very uncomfortable state. There are always worse situations to be in.

While I was digging around I discovered that we had a stowaway with us. As I left home Lindsay had pressed a miniature koala bear into my hand. 'To look after you,' she said. When we arrived at Base Camp and I unpacked, Kurt spotted my mascot.

'Where . . . I mean how did you get that?' he asked extremely puzzled.

'Lindsay gave it to me.'

'What an amazing coincidence,' he exclaimed. 'When I was in Vienna I was about to get on a bus when I saw an identical bear lying in the gutter. Normally I would have left it there, but something made me pick it up. I was going to bring it with me, but in the end I left it at home. Mine is identical, only his nose has fallen off. Next time I'll bring him.'

We named the bears 'K2' and 'K (for Koala) too'. It was a little strange to find my bear at Camp 4. I was convinced that I had left him at Base Camp, trying to save all weight possible.

We started to cook to pass the time. Getting snow was difficult. Every time we opened the door sufficiently to be able to scrape chunks from the wall of new snow that had built up in front of the tent, a deluge of the still falling flakes was blown into every nook and cranny inside. We had little solid food, a few biscuits and a small piece of cheese, but in any case it was liquid that we wanted and needed. Living and moving at high altitudes you dehydrate rapidly, and with more red corpuscles to thicken the blood, which could cause thrombosis, doctors recommend that mountaineers drink six litres of liquid a day. This is not always possible to achieve, as a lot of snow makes a small quantity of water (ice is much better but not always available), and the melting process takes a lot of time and fuel.

At twelve noon on 5 August, the storm calmed down enough for us to go outside. We had been trapped in our tent for twenty hours. We looked anxiously for our friends and, with relief, saw them coming back along the traverse towards the camp.

There was no question of trying for the summit; the weather had only improved temporarily. Giuliano and Alberto were weak from their ordeal; our doctor being violently sick from the stress and effort. We packed up our tent and rucksacks, glancing longingly up at the summit that was so near and yet still so far. Two thousand feet by itself is quite a long way, but not in relation to a mountain of 28,250 feet.

The enforced retreat was particularly sad for Kurt and me, as we had planned to continue our explorations on K2 itself. We had worked out a more direct route to the summit than traversing the snowfield; now we would most likely never know whether it was possible. Not many future expeditions would be able to afford to visit this side of the mountain. Climbing in China is terribly expensive and such finance is only easy to get for a new or rarely climbed route.

For the next two days we put aside our disappointment and concentrated on staying alive. We had been going down for three-quarters of an hour when Alberto started to act very strangely. He stared vacantly into space and did not move. When Kurt tried to help him, it was obvious he had no idea what he was doing.

What a descent! Alberto had to have his figure of eight

212

descendeur put onto each fixed rope and be told precisely which foot or hand to move, and when to stop. Kurt saved his life, helping him down, rope length after rope length, with infinite patience. There were so many hazards to be overcome, knots to be negotiated, muddled ropes to be sorted out. Three times, anchors pulled out of the snow, twice when Alberto was descending and Kurt had to hold him on the safety line, and once when Kurt himself was going down a rocky section. He fell, tumbling over, for thirty feet. The anchor pulled out when Alberto slipped on the fixed ropes below him.

We were all exhausted that night and slept deeply at Camp 2, thankful to be at a safer altitude. Alberto had made a rapid recovery as soon as he got lower down the mountain, and seemed to have suffered no lasting ill-effects.

I was rudely awakened the next morning by Kurt. Through my dreams I heard the panic in his voice. He was shouting to everyone to get up quickly and get going. 'Just *leave* everything and go down.' I soon learnt the reason for his concern. There was an incredible wind and fresh snow was falling heavily. 'It must have snowed a lot during the night too,' Kurt told me. 'I'm very worried about avalanches, especially on the long traverses. Hurry up, we must leave at once.'

I struggled out into the snowstorm, glad that I had stayed a few moments more to put on all my warm clothing. We ploughed a trough through the deep soft snow. It was horrible and very tiring, especially having to fight the wind. Down the steep section we went and over the rocks leading to the traverses. When we reached them Kurt was in front and had the strenuous task of pulling the ropes out from underneath a foot of snow.

It is so much slower to go across a traverse then straight down as the fixed rope is never taut and falls in an arc. The built-in stretch of the rope on a long run-out makes it very elastic and difficult to keep your balance if you try to hurry. The slabs which we had to cross had become sheets of hard ice, and I had constantly to watch my crampons as the bindings kept slipping. I had tied them on with pieces of string but they were still not safe enough for these conditions. To lose a crampon here would be disastrous – with boots slipping on the ice it would be impossible to pull myself across such a distance using only my arms. Kurt was also worried and kept reminding me to check my crampons every time I caught up with him. A few times small avalanches did funnel down from above us. One almost drowned me as it cascaded from a gully fifty feet higher up. My feet were swept away and my legs buried and I had to pedal furiously to keep on top of the mounting pile of snow that covered me.

We were all relieved to reach the sheltering crevasse of Camp 1 and have a welcome rest and lots of food. This camp had been well stocked and there were still plenty of tins of fish, meat and fruit to choose from. On the way back down to the foot of the mountain I fell into a crevasse and was saved by my rucksack, which caught on the lip of the fissure and prevented me from sliding right in.

Back in Advance Base Camp, after carrying enormously heavy loads of personal and film equipment down from the Deposito camp, I was so tired that I slept and slept. Whenever I was awake my head felt as if it were made of wood; my face too had been badly sunburnt. For several days I felt like a zombie. De-altitude sickness, I think!

Although the expedition had been highly successful, the mountaineers had not escaped entirely unscathed. Several suffered minor frostbite; but two, Fausto and Gigo, had ghastly black fingers and toes. Frostbite is like snow blindness; you are not always aware that it has happened at the time. Fausto had noticed that his fingers were cold, but it was not until later when he took off his gloves that he saw the extent of the damage. It must be a moment of absolute horror. There is no instant cure. Today amputation is only resorted to if an infection sets in; normally you must wait for up to six months to see whether the frozen parts will self-amputate or regenerate. This waiting period is a terribly painful time either way, and it was heartbreaking to see these brave mountaineers in tears with their suffering.

This expedition had more than made up for all the frustrations on Nanga Parbat the previous year. I had reached the magic 8,000 metres on the mountain of my dreams, the first woman in the world to do so. Best of all, I had remained fit and well, and had no problems at all with the altitude.

K2: *the mountain of mountains*

On K2 I had learnt the real pleasures of high altitude mountaineering and was totally captivated by the character of this beautiful 'mountain of mountains'. Even if I had reached the summit, I would have wanted to discover more about it, explore its other sides. As it was, I knew I would have to go back to K2. Of all the mountains, this one was the most special to me.

☄13☄

Why?

People are always asking why I climb. There is no short easy answer. It is a love, a great desire, a passion to be with the mountains, like a sailor feels for the sea. Mountains are all individual, like people. Each one has its own character, shape, composition of terrain, vegetation, animal life, type of rock, steepness and mood. Every side of a mountain is different as well, and again like people their moods can vary, particularly with the weather.

There are many comparisons to be made between mountains and the human race. You can love them but you do not always have to like them, and I often have a love/hate relationship, particularly when struggling for survival. There are times when you are sad to leave them, but others when you are relieved, glad to be away from the inevitable sheer hard work of achieving the closeness necessary to get to know them. But in a short while you long to be back and start dreaming, hoping, planning, scheming to make it possible.

It is not easy. International Himalayan mountaineering is expensive and time-consuming, for me now a full-time job, and although the general public are interested to learn more about mountains and mountaineers they do not attract the same publicity, and therefore the same personal sponsorship, as less dangerous sports such as football or cricket. Perhaps I should take up professional snooker or darts to finance my expeditions. It would not be good to have everything paid for by sponsorship; some of the best trips Terry and I had were those we had to work hard to save for. We made sure the fruit of our labours bought the best time possible. But financial sacrifice when I go on expeditions is not mine alone, as is evident from our simple cottage and battered motor car.

Ian Simpson who originally lent us the Bothy when we left the shop and later sold it to us tried to help. He is a generous man who spends a lot of his time doing things for other people. At eighty-one he makes daily visits to an old lady of ninety to ensure that she is all right. When he retired from his office in the City and most of his directorships he was looking for a new hobby.

'We could make scale models of old houses together, copies of Elizabethan and Tudor timbered houses as they were originally, and sell them to collectors to get you some funds,' he suggested.

The idea appealed to me as I enjoy working with my hands, and both Ian and Terry had a lot of knowledge about timbered houses.

We built our first house out of old oak floorboards. The white plaster between the beams was made of Polyfilla and paint. Ian was already an experienced carpenter. I acquired many new skills, using woodworking tools, and learnt more about electricity and soldering as we had concealed lighting in our models. This knowledge has been invaluable in my sound-recording career. Our second house was more ambitious with a minstrel's gallery in the solar. That one was on show at Liberty's as part of their Christmas display. We got commissions to make two more houses, replicas of the owners' present dwellings as they originally were. We were enthusiastic builders but useless salespeople, and still have three unordered models sitting at home. One I am particularly loath to part with is a copy of a Queen Anne building. The roof has ten thousand small tiles, and in the clock tower there is a bell, with a crystal from Mont Blanc to make it ring.

It is filming that has enabled me to be fairly self-financing. The first two films, about Nanga Parbat and the Italian K2 expedition while I was serving my apprenticeship, paid only my expenses. Now that I am a recognised member of a film union I can charge a proper fee: but documentary filming of this type seems to be a rather poor relation in the world of television; far more money is available for soap operas and pop stars than to enable people to share the real world through this medium. Our dedication and responsibility to the filming means too that Kurt and I have had to sacrifice the chance to get to several summits. But when one thing is balanced with another – without the films I would not be able to go at all – I know that I am extremely lucky.

As Kurt and I are freelance international mountaineers, we have to find different national expeditions prepared to allow us to film, and so far I have been very fortunate and had an expedition every year since I started this second Himalayan life. In 1982 I went to Nanga Parbat, at 26,629 feet the world's eighth highest mountain, with the French to make a film for French television. In 1983 the expedition was to K2 (28,250 feet) from the Chinese side with an Italian expedition. The film this time was for Italian television. In 1984 it was back to K2 and Broad Peak (26,400 feet), this time from the Pakistan side with the Swiss, but the film was for British television for Channel 4; and in 1985 we again filmed for British television, for both ITN and the BBC, on Everest (29,028 feet). Immediately after this expedition we returned again to Nanga Parbat and this we recorded for Austrian television. The whole of 1986 is, at the present moment, a horrible blank . . .

But I cannot allow the mountains to become a dominating passion. Even though Terry is the most understanding husband I could have, every time I go away we have problems with our relationship. After twenty-five years of living very closely together my travels have caused us to live very different lives for at least three months at a time. It is harder perhaps for my husband as I walk back into his everyday routine, feeling a little resentful that I am immediately plunged back into the routine of a housewife. The initial difficulty is that I do need time alone to come back from one world to another, which appears very anti-social when I have been away for so long. And of course any activity which takes one away for a long period and attracts a lot of publicity is bound to place a severe strain on a marriage. However, friendship has always been a strong part of our relationship and I am sure that will survive.

We both know that a sacrificial end to my mountaineering and filming is not the answer. Life must go forward. After all, if it had been Terry's vocation that took him away from home there would be less of a problem. It has always been socially acceptable for husbands to go off on business trips – or to climb mountains – while the wife sits patiently waiting at home. It is genuinely far more difficult for a woman, however modern-thinking and sympathetic the husband may be.

Unfortunately my situation is far from unique. It seems that many men in their late forties and fifties have reached a time in their lives when they want to sit back and relax; the career struggle is over and a quiet settled home life is important. Women of the same age, on the other hand, have just become free from the responsibility and ties of caring for children and are ready to take up the challenge of life again, to spread their wings. Sadly life and relationships are never properly balanced.

I said that mountaineering is a passion, and it is very akin to love. There are times of intense pleasure and satisfaction and others of utter frustration and hurt. But after all, an experience which ran at a level somewhere between the two would not have the same attraction or fulfilment. I know many people who try to live uncomplicated lives by passing on problems, making them the responsibility of others, shying away from anything out of routine that may crop up and who then complain that life is boring or has passed them by.

I have been accused of being self-indulgent, even though I limit my climbing to expeditions. All sports at professional level need time and I hope that through the films which Kurt and I bring back I can justify that by sharing our experiences with the vast number of people who are restricted to armchair adventures and dreaming.

Life is made of dreams. If it were not there would be nothing to live for. Everyone has some ambition, to gain someone's love, own something special, reach the top of a career or even just have enough to eat. And when one wish is fulfilled another replaces it. So it is with mountaineering, and just as in all desires the conception of the idea, the hopes, the plans, the small steps of success, especially after failure, are just as thrilling as when the dream actually comes true. Reaching the summit is not everything. Whatever results something is gained from simply trying to make it happen.

In my personal experience mountaineering is far more than a sport: it has a deeper meaning, trying to achieve a harmony with nature. I am often asked about my religious beliefs. The truth is that I cannot come to terms with orthodox organised religions. Most display their incredible wealth in their mausoleums of worship while all around is poverty and suffering, and I cannot believe that any God would delight in such an imbalance.

I find the parrot-fashion repetition of formal church services insincere and nonsensical. In Pakistan our porters insisted on praying, sometimes five times a day. They followed an elaborate ritual, even on the approach marches. They would either wash their clothes or turn their trousers inside out before starting, and always wash their feet. 'You have to be clean to pray,' they explained. On a flat spot facing Mecca they would start to chant, making various precise gestures with their hands, holding them behind their ears, then clasping them in front of their stomachs and genuflecting constantly. Only the men were allowed to pray in public. I was impressed; they must all be devout believers, perhaps the Muslim religion offered true comfort and guidance to its followers. Later I learnt that the people have no real choice. Those who do not conform are ostracised; male children who rebel and do not learn their prayers are thrown out of their homes at thirteen.

I asked our Liaison Officer what they said in their lengthy prayer sessions. 'It's very difficult,' he said; 'the prayers are all repeated in Arabic and these people simply memorise them. Most of them will never know the meaning of what they are saying.'

I remembered the enforced religion in my own childhood and my utter confusion with the language used in prayers and hymns.

I enjoy visiting cathedrals and find them awesome. They have the grandeur of mountains, and the smallest, simplest older churches have an aura of peace, but I cannot sympathise with the doctrine. Generally it is the priests who are the Church's worst enemies. I hated the hurried gabbling of the vicar at our wedding. There was no sincerity in his voice. And when he discovered that the hymn we had chosen after making the marriage vows was longer than his 'pep talk' about bringing up our future offspring to respect the Church and believe in God, which he made while the congregation were singing, he simply repeated the whole spiel again, like a recorded tape.

When Christopher was at the village school, the local bishop visited his class. 'Put up your hands if you have not been christened,' he told the class of eight-year-olds. Only Christopher's hand went up. Both Terry and I were appalled by the wording of the christening ceremony and refused to ask any of our friends to undertake the promises that it demands. We had chosen substitute parents with whom we had reciprocal arrangements to care for the children should we die, who would give them a stable loving home.

That afternoon Chris came home in tears. 'He was horrible to me, and now the others all tease me,' he sobbed.

'Listen, Chris,' Terry said as he cuddled him tightly, 'tomorrow, when you go to school, you do a survey of all the children in your class. There are just two questions to ask them: One. How often do they see their godparents? Two. Have they ever had any religious teaching or direction from them?' The results of the survey were quite an eye-opener. Baptism is far more a social matter than a religious one.

Another question I am often asked is whether I have had any great religious revelation while mountaineering, particularly in the moments when things have gone wrong and the line between life and death has been thinner than usual. 'If you are on the summit of a mountain, you are closer to heaven than most people get,' one reporter suggested and, in some ways, he is right. Although I cannot accept the principle of subordination to a single supreme being, I am filled with wonder by our world and its beauty and overwhelmed with awe at the forces of nature. Ueshiba Morihei, who founded aikido, once said, 'The Way of budo is to make the heart of the Universe one's own heart.' I would like that to be my philosophy too.

To live by 'Christian' principles is important to me, taking the definition of Christian as a decent, kindly, charitably-minded person regardless of religion. We need to care about one another, and to feel love for our fellow human beings. The only inevitable thing in life after birth is death, and the bit in the middle is terribly short. There is no time to be wasted. Basically, if you are

221

happy, you can share your happiness and help others, and I can understand the security of religion giving a base, a reason for happiness. Unfortunately, most faiths unbalance this with threats of hell-fire and damnation.

What concerns me very much is that the increased amount of leisure time we have gained through automation should be used to improve the quality of our lives. Somehow the technological advances hurry us through life faster and faster and the more affluent our society becomes the longer everything takes. We are over-protected with safety rules and regulations to the point where we hardly have to think for ourselves. There are not many opportunities to take decisions which can mean life or death; driving a car is the closest most people get. I feel very strongly that we need to take responsibility for ourselves and those about us in order to care about our environment, and we need physical and creative challenge in our lives, at whatever level, to be fulfilled.

Mountaineering provides that challenge for me, but the challenge is to myself not the mountain. Sport is about finding out whether you can run faster, jump higher, work in better harmony as a team to score more goals. Most sports use competition as the challenge to push up personal standards and at the ultimate level to break records. There is not this incentive of competition in either climbing or martial arts: no goals are scored or points won. You have to learn to push yourself through a desire to want to know more.

And this is what draws me back to the mountains time after time. Even though I know that the odds of injury and survival must be shortening, I have to go back. One in twelve Himalayan mountaineers die for their ruling passion. But life is short and there has to be a reason to live beyond purely surviving, an extension of that force of nature of which my body and spirit are a part, just as a river has to flow and broaden or it will stagnate.

I believe that fate has a strong hand in our destiny, but always leaves us with a choice whether to accept or refuse the challenge. There are many occasions when to say 'yes' or 'no' makes a great difference in the future of our lives. I am afraid that, rightly or wrongly, I have too much curiosity often to say 'no'.

☙14☙

Both sides of the avalanche –
K2 and a summit

Fate was certainly kind to me. Just nine months after I had returned from the Italian K2 expedition, I was packing my rucksack again to go back to my dream mountain, this time from its other side in Pakistan.

Kurt and I had been commissioned by John Gau Productions to make a film for their Channel 4 television series called *Assignment Adventure*, and were joining a Swiss expedition to the Abruzzi Ridge of K2. As an additional challenge we not only had to make the film by ourselves but also tell my story as a mountaineer, sound recordist and film assistant, and how practising traditional martial arts had changed my life.

The countryside was a soft fresh green, the daffodils were dancing in the sun and gentle spring breezes when I got ready to leave our pretty Sussex home in mid-April 1984. It is never easy leaving family and friends – not to mention the comforts of a modern home – for the restrictions and rigours of an expedition. But this time it had a special drama of its own.

Kurt was to fly from his home in Bologna to England on 14 April, and we were to leave for Pakistan with all our equipment from Heathrow at noon on the 15th. At 2.15 that afternoon the phone rang.

'Julie, I am afraid that I have missed the plane!'

I couldn't believe it. We had planned to spend the evening doing the final packing together and sorting out last-minute problems. It was important that on the approach march we both knew where things were if they were needed . . . and why had he been late today of all days? In the fourteen years that I had known Kurt he had never failed to catch a flight. In all the remote and unlikely places that we had made appointments to meet around the world, he had always arrived more or less on time.

He had left home in plenty of time but had forgotten that this day was a public holiday in Italy, and it seemed that everyone had taken to the roads. Kurt and his Teresa had finally arrived at Milan Airport ten minutes before the aeroplane took off, but as he had so much extra luggage, with the film cameras and expedition equipment, they refused to allow him to board.

'Don't worry,' he said reassuringly. 'If I drive to Venice I can get a flight this evening which will arrive at eight o'clock at Heathrow. But I'll have to hurry . . . I'll call you later!'

Driving to the local supermarket to do the final family shopping, I calmed down. If necessary we could get up very early the next morning and finish the packing.

It was a strange feeling wandering along the supermarket aisles, knowing that this would be the last time for three months that I would be performing this repetitive housewife's task. However, I knew that the euphoric feeling would not last long. As the months passed, I would crave the luxury of having such a choice, especially for certain simple things like apples, radishes, bananas, fresh potatoes, eggs, milk and cheese.

At home I went on with the packing. Why did we always have to take so much *stuff*? I hate packing, or even putting the clean washing away in drawers. Now I had to squash mounds of clothing, food, film equipment and climbing gear into plastic drums, weigh them on a spring balance and manhandle each twenty-five to thirty kilo load out of the house into the garage. This year we had to organise all our own equipment, as well as clothing, tents, sleeping bags and cooking equipment for our two Pakistani high-altitude film porters. The sheer volume of things needed for four people to survive for three months in a remote place with no mod-cons or shops is a mini-mountain in itself. A total of 450 kilos had to be tightly packed into the minimum number of future porter-loads, in watertight, thief-proof drums. How I wished that Kurt was there to help me.

Terry was marvellous. He had accepted the disruption of the house and garage as the equipment accumulated without complaint, realising that as the pile grew so our departure date was growing nearer. Now waiting for Kurt to telephone from the airport took my thoughts to Terry's worst moments when I am away on expeditions . . . waiting interminably for news. I try so hard to keep him up-to-date, but even if the mail runners get the letters and messages out of the mountain areas, back to so-called civilisation, there is no guarantee that they will ever reach their destination. So when poor Terry is inundated with calls from the Press and friends wanting to know if all is well, despite all my efforts, he often has the frustration of having to say, 'I don't know!'

Finally, the phone rang.

'At last,' I began my pent-up frustration getting the better of me.

'Julie, there has been a bomb explosion here at Heathrow, people have been hurt.' My stomach went cold. 'Are you all right?' I managed to stutter.

'Yes, luckily my plane was delayed by fifteen minutes from Venice, otherwise I would have arrived at precisely the time that the bomb went off!'

Relief and anger flooded through me. What sort of person could do such a thing, purposely set out to kill and maim innocent people? How could cold-blooded cruelty and total disregard for fellow human beings further any cause?

'I can't talk for very long, the police are trying to clear this terminal too. They have stopped all public transport coming into the airport, and I can't even get any English money. The police say I must go now, I will call you later,' and the phone went dead.

I switched on the television news and watched with horror the devastation caused by the terrorists' bomb. Thank God Kurt's flight had been delayed. But he still had a difficult night ahead.

Because there were no buses or taxis, he had, first of all, to push his heavily laden baggage trolley all the way along the narrow walkway through the Heathrow road tunnel. Whenever he met a passenger pushing a trolley towards the airport he had to unload his five heavy and bulky pieces of luggage, lift the trolley over the oncoming one and reload the other side – this happened about six times in the mile-long tunnel and it took him about an hour to get through. He then had to push the unwieldy beast a further mile until he finally found a taxi which would drive him to London. As he could find no hotel to accept his German Marks in return for a room after midnight, he had, in desperation, persuaded the taxi driver to drive him a further forty miles to our house in the wilds of Sussex, six miles outside Tunbridge Wells.

He had kept the taxi driver happy and awake during the long drive by telling him stories of his many fascinating adventures over the years, saving the most entertaining and exciting ones for when they reached the small country lanes. When they drew up outside the door of the Bothy at 2 am, the kind driver was so enthralled that he still wanted to know more about his seemingly crazy passenger and the strange woman who climbed mountains, so he stayed and had some tea.

He finally wished us well for the expedition and drove off into the night – an exceptionally kind man. Somehow his long drive into the depths of unknown countryside helped to restore our faith after the senseless cruel actions of the terrorists. I shall always be grateful to him.

The invitation to join the Swiss expedition had come from the leader, Stefan Woerner, whom Kurt and I had met during the French expedition to Nanga Parbat in 1982. We had liked this very affable Swiss, who with his shaggy blond mane of hair looked like a wild Icelandic pony. Stefan had been running a separate expedition to this mountain, which had been highly successful as two members reached the summit. Sadly, though, one man had died from a cerebral oedema at Camp 3 and another had to be evacuated from the mountain and rescued by helicopter. But such are the risks which you take when you tackle a high peak in the Himalayas and you have to learn to live with them.

Our expedition to K2 was made up of twelve members including Peter Habeler. He and Rheinhold Messner had been the first climbers to reach the summit of Everest without using oxygen. The others came from Germany, Austria and Switzerland, and once again, for the third year running, I was the only female and British mountaineer in the party. However, a small group of four

Polish women – Wanda Rutkiewicz, Krystyna Palmowska, Anna Czerwinska and 'Mrufka' Dobroslawa, had attached themselves to our enterprise. They had their own tents and food and called themselves a 'women's' expedition, but shared our base camp and camps on the mountain. The four girls got on well together and were very strong and extremely determined in their climbing, but I could never see myself as part of a 'feminist' expedition.

Besides K2 as the main objective, we also had permission for Broad Peak (26,400 feet), which was just half a day's walk away on the opposite side of the broad Godwin Austen Glacier. For any peak over 6,000 metres you have to arrange permissions to climb with the Ministry of Tourism in Islamabad at least six months ahead and pay a peak fee, which for K2 is £2,000.

Kurt and I met the rest of the members for the first time in Rawalpindi. I had seen everyone's curriculum vitae and tried to guess who each one was as they gradually drifted into the dining room of Mrs Davis's hotel for breakfast. Kurt and I had travelled to Pakistan three days ahead of the rest to get the filming in the town out of the way. We had already recovered from our jet lag and made the transition from the colder climes of organised Europe to the hot, noisy chaos of this Asian city. Our new friends had been jettisoned into this new world at two in the morning and were still trying to surface.

No group of mountaineers dressed in a reasonably civilised way ever looks as if it is capable of tackling a mountain. Our expedition consisted of males of a wide variety of sizes and shapes, their ages ranging between twenty-five and forty. Kurt, at fifty-three, and I were the oldest. In mountaineering circles you constantly meet a lot of new people, but the common bond makes new acquaintances easier. By lunchtime we had found out quite a lot about one another, and I knew I was going to like them all. Stefan was a very organised leader; he enjoys life and his happy attitude spread to the others. He did not make hard work of the many jobs that needed to be done, and everyone willingly did their share to get the boxes and sacks of food and communal camping and climbing equipment ready and loaded into the two beautifully painted, chrome-decorated lorries which would transport it, via the Karakoram Highway, to Skardu, 600 kilometres away. Unfortunately their mechanical condition did not match their handsome appearance, as Rheine and Urs, who travelled with the lorries, discovered to their cost. Rheine, a schoolteacher taking a couple of years' break from his profession to broaden his horizons, and Urs, our super doctor, were both of a similar short, slim build with very much the same energetic temperament. Although they did not know each other before, they seemed destined to become climbing partners, which they did for a while until they found that they were climbing for different reasons. Urs had tremendous drive, and wanted to get to the top. Rheine discovered on this, his first Himalayan climb, that he wanted to gently and peacefully enjoy the mountains, not to challenge himself through them, and so their partnership split up. I admired Rheine's honesty; it would have been easier not to admit his true feelings when everyone else was so dedicated to climbing the mountain. There are often situations in life from which we would like to withdraw but do not have the courage.

The general language was German, with Swiss dialects thrown in, but there was one French-speaking member. Stefan Schaffter was tall with a relaxed manner, the sort of mountain guide/ski instructor female students are happy and relieved to get, and usually fall in love with. He had a great sense of humour, and a heart of gold. He, like Peter Habeler, was kind and considerate to everyone. They became our lead climbers on K2.

The rest of us flew to Skardu in a small plane, which finds its way through the mountain valleys of the Karakoram foothills by groundsight. We almost had to turn back when large clouds built up, but we passed through the thick curtain going over the plains and the other side was clear. The pilot invited us into the cockpit to film Nanga Parbat and even made a special diversion to give us a better view of this magnificent mountain which has played such an important part in my life. Before landing he put the plane in a tight circle so that Kurt could film a spectacular panaroma. In the cabin we had no warning that he was going to do this, and several people had trouble keeping their lunch in their stomachs.

In the small Balti town of Skardu – one main road lined with rows of single-roomed shops – I got a local watchmender to help me re-solder a faulty microphone cable. He sat in the centre of a jumble of dusty watch and clock parts which looked as if they had been in the same place for ten years. Everything in his small shop was within arms' reach and in this unlikely setting we rectified the incorrect connections wired by a sophisticated company in London who even with all their electronic gadgetry had failed to get it right. What annoyed me was that they had not bothered to test it, and as it had been delivered to the airport as I left England I had no opportunity to check it myself. I could have been in a very bad situation through someone's inefficiency.

We all spent a day unpacking the lorries and sorting everything into twenty-five-kilo porter loads in the simple square-built adobe house of Gulam Rasul, our Balti Sirdar. Then we loaded the whole lot into trailers and with chugging, jerky tractors pulling them, set off across desert sand dunes and along the beautiful Shigar Valley to the village of Dassu where the road finished.

It took half a day to employ and sort out the three hundred porters from the local Balti villages. Gulam Rasul was our very experienced controller, or Sirdar. He had eight sons and a strong loud voice and his charges respected him greatly. For the walk-in along the Baltoro Glacier, one of the most difficult and dangerous approach march routes, the porters are paid £2 a day to carry twenty-five to thirty kilos on their backs for eight to ten hours. They also get a pair of rubber boots (which they don't always choose to wear), a pair of woollen socks, a sheet of plastic to cover themselves and the loads if it rains or snows, and two packets of cigarettes, appropriately with the brand name K2.

There are unstable slopes and slippery rock slabs to climb, wild rivers to cross and, for the last three days, glacier hills of stone-covered ice, and then snow with small hidden and deep open wide crevasses to negotiate. On the eighth day of the journey, as we started along the forty-four-mile-long Baltoro Glacier, it started to snow heavily, and we were worried about the safety and well-being of the porters. Some had wrapped their bare feet in dried grass and rags, and few had suitable warm clothing. Their thin cotton suits of wide-topped baggy trousers and knee-length shirts soon got wet. A few had well-worn sweaters or jackets acquired from previous expeditions, but most just wrapped themselves in their homespun blankets.

The nights on the glacier were extremely cold and they built themselves shelters out of the expedition boxes covered with tarpaulins. Sitting in these simple cramped makeshift houses, huddled together in small groups, they sang to keep warm. Their strength and resourcefulness gave us mountaineers, well protected in our down jackets and tents, a standard to live up to. Getting to the mountain was a great adventure in itself.

Three weeks after arriving in Base Camp, which we established on the still snow-covered moraine in the middle of the Godwin Austen Glacier, we were joined by an additional ten members who were only to tackle Broad Peak. These mountaineers had a much more light-hearted approach, and seemed almost like a bunch of holidaymakers in contrast to the K2 climbers, but then K2 has a very serious atmosphere. Most of our new companions had chosen to try Broad Peak because they thought it would be a safer, easier undertaking, possibly thinking also, as I used to, that some big mountains are mainly long snow plods. Broad Peak is certainly not that and this particular year their rather misguided optimism was totally wrong, as the steep sides of the mountain were covered in hard ice and the weather generally was awful.

The other reason for their relaxed mood was the presence of three young Colombian climbers in the group. It was their first trip out of their country and they were, with true South American enthusiasm, determined to enjoy every moment. Together with the Polish girls they organised a disco, which went on until the early hours of the morning whenever they were at Base Camp. The dance floor, in a corner of the Mess Tent, was made of a mosaic of sombrero-sized flattish slabs. Once you chose your stone you had to perform all the gyrations on its limited space, taking care not to fall off the edge. This dancing was a true test of balance and altitude fitness.

Our very international group had many lively evenings in the world's highest disco, or, in another part of the Mess Tent, singing mountain songs to the accompaniment of guitars, taking a deep breath after every line. It sounded very strange from outside with shouts of 'Olé!' and 'Viva! Viva!' coming from one side of the large tent and yodels echoing from the other.

During the two months we spent sharing life at five thousand metres and above, everyone got on very well, and we tried to make our Base Camp home as comfortable as possible. Hans, who had been a baker before becoming a mountain guide, made us fresh baked bread. I had a garden, but had to grow it inside a tent, which I called 'The Hot House', as outside it was too cold for cultivation. Kurt and I also made thirty-five litres of home-brewed beer in an expedition drum. We left the mixture to mature in the Mess Tent for three weeks, and although the yeast often got too cold to work properly, at the end of the recommended period it seemed to have fermented.

Then we transferred it into a pressurized barrel, which took us four hours because the air pressure was so low. With great devotion to duty Kurt sat patiently outside our tent holding the syphoning tube, even when it got dark and started to snow. To our surprise, at the bottom of the fermenting drum we found an odd collection of plates, cutlery, pencils, and even a toothbrush which had fallen in when the lid had been used as a spare table in the Mess Tent. The finished product did not look much like beer, but luckily had a good head of froth which disguised what was hidden underneath in our tin and plastic mugs. As everyone had been starved of alcohol for so long, the party we gave for our friends just before they went home was a great success.

The climb on the mountain had been a real struggle. The weather had thwarted every foray we made onto the wind-swept Abruzzi Ridge of K2. Storm after storm drove us back down to the safety of Base Camp. Kurt and I had been up on this steep exposed ridge eight times climbing and filming before giving up. K2 did not welcome us this year. Time and again the gale force winds and icy storms had prevented the expedition from getting any distance above Camp 3 at 25,000 feet, just two days of climbing from the summit. I recorded my feelings on tape for the film. 'Going up and down, up and down. Sometimes you don't even get as far as you did the time before. You come to hate the boring, repetitive, arduous climb up, and hate even more having to come back down. But something draws you back . . . somehow it's part of the fascination!' Of course there were many good moments on the climb, but towards the end they got lost in the cloud of disappointment.

On 15 July the expedition was due to go home. The closer the date came, the more often Kurt and and I discussed what we should do. We could leave with everyone else. We were longing to see our families again and return to the green and growing world after living with stones, ice and snow for three months. Summer had passed us by. But what about the film? The 23,000 feet of material we had already shot were good, but the dramatic events on the mountain had no conclusion. Our expensive cameras and film equipment were also still scattered about various camps high on K2, unrescuable at this time because of deep, dangerous new snow left by the last storm on the mountain.

The only satisfactory answer was to stay on by ourselves, with a couple of porters to look after our tents in Base Camp, and immediately try for the summit of Broad Peak. This was not such an isolated mountain as K2 and, therefore, although only four miles away, attracted a totally different weather pattern. This is what we eventually decided to do.

We talked to our expedition leader. Luckily Stefan was a very practical Swiss, and Fakkar, our Liaison Officer, a likeable, sensible, young officer from the Pakistani Air Force. It was Fakkar's first expedition, and he understandably wanted no complications if we got into difficulties by ourselves that might jeopardise his chances of going on future trips. The authorities in Islamabad have very strict rules governing the movements of expedition members, which they understandably do not like bent. The wild area around the Himalayas is a dangerous place and they need to know where people are, and that they are safe. Fakkar tried hard to dissuade Kurt and me from staying on by ourselves, but finally, after we had written and signed several statements saying that it was our own decision and that we took full responsibility for our actions and safety, he agreed and wished us luck.

We felt very alone when our friends had gone. We were well aware that if either of us had an accident or became sick we would be in serious trouble. We had felt well protected with a

K2 8611m

K2 (1983)
**NORTH-EAST RIDGE
(FROM CHINA)**

C4 8000m
△ Film Tent 7900m

C3 7600m

△ Film Tent 7000m

C2 6800m

C1 5800m

Depot Camp 5200m

ABC 5000m

group of thirty other mountaineers including a doctor around us, but now our isolation also made us feel closer to our surroundings, which was after all the reason why we were there.

The expedition's departure day was, ironically, beautiful: hardly a cloud in the sky. Could it mark the change in the weather at last? The monsoon is not supposed to affect this Karakoram area, but the weather we had been battling with over the past few weeks was typical of the monsoon syndrome, with fresh storms coming in almost daily. How frustrating for the others, who were already feeling very disappointed, having to walk away from the mountains, if the weather really was going to improve again.

Finally, at two o'clock, we were able to leave the now lonely-looking K2 Base Camp. Our three weather-beaten faded tents looked tiny and forlorn without the company of the other expedition tents as we looked back towards the soaring majesty of K2, its summit still hiding in the clouds.

The moraine in the direction of Concordia had changed during the months of May, June and July. The previously snow-covered humps of the central corridor of the Godwin Austen Glacier had become stone-covered ice mini-hills; gaping crevasses cutting across the previously simple direct route made long detours necessary.

We finally turned off to the left, into the broad band of ice pinnacles which still separated us from from the foot of Broad Peak. I began to feel apprehensive . . . would we have a chance to reach the top? I paused to look at our objective; its huge sprawling mass was beautiful in the late afternoon sunshine but it made me feel infinitesimally small.

'Come on, Julie,' Kurt's voice broke into my musings. 'We have to reach Camp 1 tonight to have any chance at all.'

It was a complicated route though the ice pinnacles. We had to climb up and down over the maze of broken ice cliffs and skirt the icy lakes nestling in the hollows between the ice towers. The cold world was silent apart from the grating of our crampons against the ice, and it required concentration to find the safest and most direct way through to our objective on the other side. It had taken us three and a half hours, but finally we were plodding up the steep snow slope towards Camp 1. It was amazing to think that after twenty-seven years Kurt was once again climbing on Broad Peak. It was certainly in a better condition than K2, but this year many of its steep slopes were covered in ice instead of the normal snow, which would make the climbing more technical.

We had not gone far before we began to regret the sun-caused melting process. The lower snow slope was like sticky porridge which built up thick platforms on our crampons and as the snow covering some small stones melted they began zipping down around us. We knew that it was more dangerous to be moving on such terrain in the late afternoon after a warm, sunny day, but we had no choice. It was only ten more days before our porters would arrive to help carry our gear back to civilisation. It was already dark when I pulled up the last fixed rope into Camp 1, perched on a tiny rib like an eagle's eyrie. Several other expeditions were trying to climb Broad Peak this year. Over a hundred people had tried to reach the top, but so far only five had succeeded. Four tents were perched on the tiny platform, but luckily for us only three were occupied, and we thankfully retreated into the empty one and started to melt snow for a brew.

We were starving. In our hurry to get away we had not eaten much and that little was eight hours before. For three hours we cooked – tea, soup and powdered potato, which we mixed with sardines; and then more tea, biscuits and chocolate. It was after midnight when we finally snuggled into our warm down sleeping bags. We had been up since four in the morning helping our expedition get ready to leave, so it was not surprising that we soon dropped into a deep contented sleep.

At six we were awoken by the occupants of the other tents moving around. They were not too polite to us when we emerged rubbing the sleep from our eyes.

'What the hell were you doing last night?' demanded an angry Frenchman, who had obviously had his precious sleep disturbed by our nocturnal picnic.

Had we really been so noisy? The thin tent walls have no noise insulation properties, but we had really tried to be as quiet as possible. Perhaps he was suffering from the common problem of not sleeping well at altitude? We apologised profusely in our best French, but when, during breakfast, they discovered who Kurt was their their mood changed and they became very friendly. They had only recently arrived and were still acclimatising their bodies and minds to the arduous high mountain life with its thin oxygen-depleted air. We followed in their tracks towards Camp 2, delighted that they were breaking the trail through the fresh snow as we would need all our energy that day.

We would have to 'front point' up the icy sections, some of which had no fixed ropes, using only the two front prongs of our crampons, which stick out like a beetle's antennae, kicking these in to spear the ice and attach us to the mountain. As the whole base of the foot hangs over space, this technique places a lot of strain on the ankles and calves. We had planned not to stop at Camp 2 but carry straight on to Camp 3 3,000 feet higher. Not only were we short of time, but the fine weather might not last for long. In fact, halfway to Camp 2, the clouds began to gather around the mountain. By the time we arrived there all the mountaineers from the German, French and Italian expeditions were hurriedly packing their rucksacks and retreating to the safety of Base Camp. Our friends from Camp 1 also went back down. It was not only the approaching bad weather that drove them down; some of them had already been living on the mountain for several days and were too exhausted to continue. Sadly, two were suffering from badly frost-bitten feet.

However, Kurt and I were both committed to going on. We knew all too well how fickle the weather could be. It could just as easily change again for the better and already this year we had plenty of experience of living with fierce Himalayan storms. It is as much a mental endurance test as a physical one, even if you are simply lying in a tent. Many of our friends on K2 could not stand the constant noisy flapping of the tent fabric in the high winds for hour after hour, especially at night. It is a strange form of torture for some people and certainly the imagination runs riot during the long hours of darkness as gale force winds batter the thin material shield protecting you from the elements. One sleepless night plays havoc with the energy level and your perform-ance the following day; you feel totally drained.

We crossed the featureless snow plateau below the snow cliff leading to the next exposed ridge. Once past Camp 2 we found renewed energy. We had made a drink there, had something to eat and left a depot of everything we felt we could manage without. It wasn't a lot: my little Canon Sureshot camera, some of our spare batteries, an extra pair of gloves – we would use our spare socks as gloves if necessary – and other odd bits and bobs of food. It was more psychological than anything, but our rucksacks felt lighter and we felt better, the climbing was going well and we were gaining height.

At the top of a short snow slope Kurt stopped and looked down at a tiny stone platform. 'This is where we put our Camp 3 in 1957,' he explained. We sat down and idly looked at the debris left by other expeditions who had during the intervening years also used this place for a camp site. Suddenly Kurt's keen eyes spotted something, and he dug in the frozen stones. 'Look,' he exclaimed, 'a piton which Hermann Buhl used to anchor our tent, all those years ago.' I looked at the heavy nine-inch metal spike with the two-inch ring through the top and began to understand where Kurt's incredible mountaineering strength, endurance and tenacity had begun. To survive at these altitudes with the very basic and terribly heavy equipment they had to carry and use then was a training that would last a lifetime.

The next section was interminable. We were getting extremely tired with the effects of altitude, as well as over seven hours' extreme exertion. Our loads were heavy for climbing at over 23,000 feet as we were not sure about the tents of the other expeditions on the mountain, whether they would be already occupied or destroyed by storms. Consequently we were completely self-sufficient carrying our own tiny bivouac tent, sleeping bags, foam mattresses, stove and gas cylinders, pots, food, still camera and films, spare batteries, head torches and a few bits of spare clothing, rope and ice axes, etc. When you think that a modern rucksack weighs over four pounds when it is empty and that your high altitude clothing, boots and crampons when they are snow free add a good few more pounds, we must have been carrying at least 40 lbs altogether. It would be quite an effort to

237

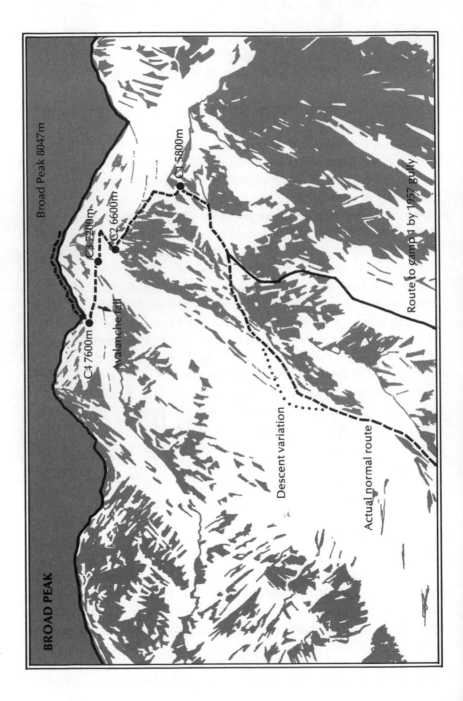

BROAD PEAK

Broad Peak 8047m

C4 7600m

Avalanche fall

C3 7200m

C2 6600m

C1 5800m

Descent variation

Actual normal route

Route to camp 1 by 1957 gully

carry this total weight around for eight hours at sea level, without going continuously steeply uphill.

Just after six o'clock we got a first glimpse of the tiny tent that was Camp 3. It was sitting high on a steep snow slope sheltered by a large ice cliff. I longed to lie in its protective depths and rest my weary limbs. Kurt took over the lead. Slowly we started to zig-zag up the last obstacle between us and a desperately needed rest. The last light began to fade and it started to snow lightly. My legs ached, and my arms, neck and back . . . Would we never reach that damned tent? It is strange how suddenly the will to go on can leave you. If only Kurt would stop for a moment! But I knew that he could not. We had to keep going, it was getting so cold.

When it was completely dark, Kurt took out his head-torch. We decided to use only one, saving mine for an emergency. I stepped into each of his footsteps as his foot was leaving it, on, on, on. But we never seemed to reach the tent. We hit a particularly bad patch of snow and sank into it up to our waists. Hell! It was like being in a bog. After struggling out it took time-consuming careful probing with a ski stick to find a safer way in the now total dark.

Suddenly we were there! Nine hard hours after leaving Camp 1 we had made it. We were now at the same height as we had reached on K2.

After the first hot drink we felt revived – bad memories soon fade. But it was a sombre thought that poor Dr Peter Thexton had died suddenly of a heart attack at this very camp the previous year when he was climbing with Doug Scott's expedition. The next day we moved on and established our little bivouac tent at 24,200 feet on a shelf Kurt dug on the lip of a crevasse which had opened up on the steep side of the mountain.

The following morning we had to wait for the weather to improve before we could move. It was ten o'clock before the visibility cleared and we could get going.

We struggled, so slowly, up the last four hundred feet leading to the col. Why did the snow have to be so soft and deep? I took a deep breath and swung my foot with a strong kicking motion into the steep snow slope, but as soon as I transferred my weight onto it, it sank down through the surface of the step I had just made as if it were made of expanded polystyrene granules.

Hell! One step up and two steps down! My top foot ended up just above my lower one, buried beneath the wet snow up to my thigh. I was already feeling tired and fed-up, and we had only been going for two hours. But we had to reach the col.

I set myself a landmark, a tiny rock sticking out of the snow, and made a rough estimate of how many steps it would take to reach it. Two hundred and forty, I guessed. 'No cheating,' I warned myself, and set off. Kick, step up . . . 'one', breath . . . kick, step up . . . 'two' . . . Every ten steps I stopped to rest and re-control my erratic breathing. It was a long exhausting way. Above me I could just see some fixed ropes below a chimney, and, higher, the heavy grey stormclouds hung menacingly overhead.

'Concentrate,' I commanded myself. 'Don't start to feel sorry for yourself. Just think how lucky you are to be here!' I looked down at Kurt solidly plodding up the slope below me and tried to regain my rhythm.

It was just after twelve noon as we topped the col. The wind almost threw us off our feet back down the slope up which we had just come, and it was bitterly cold. The wind-driven snow stung the tiny exposed areas of our faces not protected by climbing helmets and big snow goggles. We looked around desperately to find some shelter to protect us from its stinging bite rather than re-tracing our steps back down the exit chimney on which we had just expended so much energy. 25,600 feet! Just 800 feet, but still well over a mile, from the top.

We found a snow alcove and huddled together, our backs to the fierce wind. We tried to light our little Gaz stove, but the lighter kept blowing out. We took it in turns to try again, as we could not leave off our gloves for long before our fingers became numb with cold. At last the stove worked and we set to melting snow to make a much-needed warming drink. We couldn't see much through the swirling snow flakes, but knew that on one side of us the mountain dropped steeply down nine thousand feet to the Godwin Austen Glacier far below; and on the other there was an even more severe drop – over ten thousand feet, into China.

As soon as we had finished one drink, we started to melt the snow for the next. It was a slow process, as each quarter pint took nearly twenty minutes to reach the reduced boiling point of around 80°C, due to the altitude. We both were very aware how important it is to drink as much as possible at such a height, when the body is required to work at maximum effort and the oxygen level is reduced by two-thirds.

Three brews later and we were still feeling cold and cramped.

'My feet are very cold', Kurt told me. 'If they don't get better soon we'll have to go back down.' I felt an overwhelming disappointment, but knew that with such weather our chances of reaching the summit were very slim anyway.

Kurt stood up and started to stamp his feet and exercise his legs. 'Please, please let them get warm again,' I silently prayed to myself. It was not just the constant frustration of the past three months, continually driven down from K2 by fearsome storms. I wanted this summit for many reasons. I had looked up at Broad Peak, on the opposite side of the glacier from our K2 base camp, so often and had wondered what it would feel like to be up there, so high that you could look over all the surrounding giants of the Karakoram range, except of course K2.

I wanted it for my husband, who for the past three summers had so unselfishly encouraged my mountaineering adventures . . . for my children . . . for the film . . . for Kurt who had put in so much effort, and because this was his special mountain. But most of all, I wanted to reach the top . . . to stand with my own feet on the summit!

'Let's try moving round on the ridge to get out of this wind. I just can't get warm here.' Kurt's voice broke into my thoughts. 'We can wait for another half an hour, but if it doesn't improve we'll have to go down,' he added, and I knew in my heart that would be the logical course of action.

We picked up our rucksacks and moved slowly on, looking for a more protective spot. Neither of us noticed when the wind actually stopped, we were so involved in trying to reach the other side of a narrow steep-sided rocky ridge. Although it had some rather old fixed ropes to hold on to in places it still involved a delicate and airy rock traverse.

241

'I thought you said that the summit ridge was broad enough to walk along?' I said accusingly.

'Julie, in 1957 it was! It must have eroded over the years.' Kurt was also taken by surprise.

We moved steadily on up. After another hour and a half I looked ahead and my heart leapt. The summit was there, at the end of the next curve of the ridge. I moved on with renewed energy, up a steep icy snow slope. Nearly there. Almost at the top . . . Keep going. Step up . . . breathe . . . step up . . . breathe. I felt myself holding my breath as I took the last step. We had made it . . .

What my eyes saw my brain failed to register for a moment. The summit was still far away, about half a mile or another long hour of concentrated effort. The summit ridge curved round still farther, but this had been hidden by the false summit we had just climbed. It was getting late in the day, already after five o'clock. On the Chinese side of the ridge the weather was almost cloudless, but on the Pakistani side clouds were closing in. I didn't tell Kurt that I thought we had reached the summit, keeping my disappointment to myself. Please don't stop because it's getting late, or because the weather looks bad, I silently begged him as despite my disappointment I felt well, and as if he had heard my plea Kurt moved on with measured steps along the ridge.

About half an hour from the summit, the effect of going for several hours in the so-called 'death zone' at above 26,000 feet hit me; my legs would not carry me for more than twenty steps.

Kurt was very helpful and set me targets to reach. 'Try to get to those next rocks, then you can rest again,' he encouraged, and so we went on in short bursts until, suddenly, almost unexpectedly for me, we arrived at the foot of the summit snow slope. It was only the previous year that the first woman had stood on top of Broad Peak, and I wondered what her feelings had been.

Slowly we climbed the last twenty feet.

There were none of the immediate emotions I had expected to feel, overwhelming joy, relief, a feeling of conquest. Instead it all felt rather unreal. This feeling was heightened by shimmering snow crystals which were floating in the air all around us, like tiny mother-of-pearl sequins. Because of their size and lightness

242

they were carried on the wind, dancing freely in the air, almost transparent, their rainbow colours sparkling in the sun's dying rays. Their backcloth was grey storm clouds over the mountains of Pakistan, but when we turned to look out over the thousands of Chinese peaks topped by a clear blue sky they took on a new energy, a life of their own, and as if to check that they were really there, we both unconsciously reached out to touch them.

We stood pensively looking down the huge drop to the Gasherbrum Glacier more than 10,500 feet below us. Was it really only the previous summer that I had learnt the thrill of exploring these wild places? It seemed a lifetime away since we had been down there, the first people in the world to enter this spectacular glacier, and see Broad Peak's secret side. The enormous scale of the mountains and landscape seemed to belong to a different timescale too.

It was half past six and the light was beginning to fade. 'Come on Julie, we must hurry up and take our summit photographs.' Kurt's voice jerked me back to the present.

I went as close to the summit edge as possible and in the pose of an intrepid mountaineer held my ice axe aloft. Click went the camera shutter. We had made it! For Kurt a journey back in time – for me my first 8,000-metre summit. I was very happy.

It was on the way down that we were caught in the avalanche which we amazingly survived. Thankfully our injuries were only superficial. Even a minor damage like a sprained ankle could have proved fatal for both of us. We needed each other's strength and support if we were to survive the dangerous conditions still between us and the foot of the mountain.

We were both very calm after the accident but decided to shelter under another large serac and make some tea to help alleviate any delayed shock. Kurt's insistence on spending a few more minutes to rescue our stove, sleeping bags and some food from the avalanche-buried bivi tent certainly helped us to survive the next totally exhausting part of the descent to Camp 3.

Cautiously we set off to find our way back to the proper route. It was a slow and agonising descent across never-ending snowfields, sinking time and again deeply into the soft new snow, having to extricate our bruised and now stiffened limbs slowly and painfully, only to sink in again a few steps later. The weather had changed again and between heavy snowfalls and white-outs which blanketed all visibility, rendering the large white snow plateau featureless, it was only Kurt's expertly accurate route finding which saved us from getting lost.

Our slowness made us even more aware of our vulnerability to the danger of further avalanches, and our smallness on such a vast mountain. Kurt led us unerringly to the point on top of the long ice wall above Camp 3 that we had climbed up to in order to join the plateau on the ascent: quite a feat as you could not see anything of the tiny tent thirty feet below. My relief at finally arriving, after more than fourteen horribly tiring hours since leaving our bivi-tent refuge so hurriedly, was quickly dispelled, as all the fresh snow prevented us from descending to the safety of the tent at that point.

'We will have to go back up for a little way in order to get down,' Kurt said in a very tired voice, and we trudged wearily back up the steep slope which we had just descended. My legs were leaden. I just wanted to go to sleep – I didn't really care where. It took all of my willpower to drive myself on. How easy it would be to just curl up in the snow and close my eyes – but I knew too well that if I did I would never wake again.

For the past hour I had been worried about Kurt, who was reaching the limit of his strength. He had used so much energy to make the tracks for the whole long descent, to make it easier for my damaged leg. He was also suffering badly with his eyes, as he had to go all day without any protective snow goggles after losing his in the avalanche. If he fell into a deep snow pocket, he would just sit there, unable to get up until his body had recovered some energy. The stops were getting longer and longer until I was worried that he might just give up. But Kurt's inner determination is far stronger than any outer tiredness. Now he seemed to be getting a second wind, and it was my turn to be almost at the end of my endurance.

In the gloom of the night we finally collapsed into the tiny tent at Camp 3 and fell into a deep sleep – after several brews of tea, soup, Ovaltine and anything else interesting that we could find abandoned by the Polish, French, Swiss, German or Italian expeditions.

'Julie! Oh God, Julie! Wake up! My eyes, hell, my eyes!' I switched on the torch and shone it at Kurt. 'No, no! Switch it off again, quickly!' Poor Kurt, in a quick glimpse I had seen his eyes: the eyelids were black and blue and heavily swollen. He was suffering from snow blindness and was in a lot of pain.

I found some drops and dripped them carefully onto his inflamed eye-balls, but they only made matters worse. We tried soothing them with wet, warm and cold tea bags of different kinds, ordinary black tea, camomile tea, even peppermint tea, but nothing seemed to help to relieve the dreadful, intense pain.

When day finally broke it was more unbearable, as the inside of the orange tent was so bright, and even a glimmer of light made his eyes more sensitive. Nothing seemed to help. Outside it was snowing hard again, and there was no question of any further retreat.

For two days we lay in the dome-shaped tent waiting and praying for Kurt's eyes and the weather to improve, worrying more and more about the amount of fresh snow that was continuously falling, bringing renewed avalanche danger.

On the afternoon of the third day, the weather finally cleared and we decided to make a dash for the safety of the lower camps. Kurt's left eye was still very sore and swollen but thankfully we had found a spare pair of snow glasses in the tent and covered the left lens with elastoplast to black out the still-damaged eye. Going down to Camp 2 was a nightmare. Both of us still felt very weak, and the snow conditions were atrocious as a deep layer of soft powder snow covered everything. We wallowed and fell over time and again, longing to reach the comparative safety of the fixed ropes several hours below. Down the long snow slope we floundered, along the ridge we ploughed, always aware of further avalanche dangers . . . continuously looking upwards for signs of fast-moving snow.

When we did finally reach the fixed ropes, there were new problems as they were buried deeply under the snow and had to be pulled strenuously out, sometimes foot by foot as we went down. 'I can't find the next rope!' a tired anxious cry came from Kurt below me. Either it had been swept away or it was buried so deeply under the new snow that we simply couldn't find it. Five or six times this happened and we had to take out our safety rope and move one at the time, the other safeguarding with an ice piton belay. This slowed us down even more.

An eternity later we arrived at a flattened Camp 2. All the remaining tents left by the various expeditions who were still battling with the mountain had been collapsed and buried by the new snow. We stopped only to pick up the little depot of gear we had left there and hurried on down.

We reached Camp 1 in the early evening. After we had rested and drunk a lot of tea, Kurt went round to the back of the tent to find the bunch of keys which he had hidden under the stones on the way up to save us the weight of carrying them. I heard the ice axe scraping away at the icy snow and small stones below. The digging went on ... and on ... and became more frenzied, accompanied by curses in various languages. Kurt re-emerged, sweating and obviously very puzzled. 'They are not there! They have gone! How will we get into all our gear at Base Camp, everything is locked!' I went with him back round the tent, and together we searched. It appeared to be the same tent that we had slept in on the way up, and it was pitched in the same place.

It seemed as if Broad Peak was playing with us on the way down ... first the avalanche, then Kurt's snowblindness, after that the missing fixed ropes which had caused so much extra time and effort, all the fresh powder snow we had almost had to swim through, and now, the missing keys.

'Perhaps someone found them when they were going down and took them to their Base Camp,' I suggested as we settled in our sleeping bags after giving up the search, and drifted into sleep.

God! What was happening? I struggled for consciousness. Something was trapping my head in an iron grip. I struggled furiously to free myself. Where was I? In a tent ... with Kurt ... Kurt! It was Kurt who was pressing my face against his chest so hard that I couldn't breathe. Was he having some sort of fit? I had gone to sleep completely mummified inside my sleeping bag, the hood drawn right over my head.

I must free my arms. I fought and squirmed until I was able to force his hands away. 'What the hell's going on?' I demanded angrily, still unnerved by the sudden awakening from such a deep and pleasant slumber.

'Didn't you hear it? By the amount of noise it made it was a very large stone fall. All I could do was try to protect your head, but you were so wrapped up in that sleeping bag, I didn't know which way up you were. Anyway, luckily all the stones fell past us, but it certainly looks as if Broad Peak is giving us a hard time.'

The next day seemed to re-confirm this. A warmer, brighter day, which created fresh problems. Above Camp 1 stones began to be dislodged as the snow melted around them and came whirring down towards us. One hit me just above the knee and I almost cried with the pain.

We were about halfway down when we met five of the French expedition coming back up to make another attempt on the summit. They seemed relieved and very pleased to see us. 'We were very worried about you when we saw all the bad weather. You were the only people left on the mountain,' they told us.

Following their advice we tried a different way down the last thousand feet to Base Camp, but we must have traversed too far onto the glacier and we got lost amongst a mess of crevasses and unstable sloshy snow. The final section, which would have taken us two hours on the normal route, took over four hours and in the discomfort of the heat of the burning mid-day sun we got very tired, dehydrated and extremely frustrated.

At the foot of the mountain we drank from the clear spring until our tummies were swollen with the water. Then we set off across the maze of ice pinnacles of the glacier earnestly discussing all the food we were going to eat when we reached the central moraine, where the other Broad Peak expeditions had their camps.

Not long ago only one expedition was allowed on a mountain at a time – and when Kurt had first climbed Broad Peak his had been the only expedition in the whole of the Baltoro glacier. Now several expeditions can be climbing on the same route, which, although it can be good for international relations generally, can cause basic mountaineering problems. Everyone expects the first expedition to arrive at the mountain to fix the ropes, which doesn't always happen. Consequently, as happened on Broad Peak this year, a hotch-potch of ropes resulted, as no one had enough new ropes to cover the route, and old ropes, some of them very ancient and tattered from past storms and winters, were knotted together. Several of these broke and Peter Habeler and Voytek Curtyka, the top Austrian and Polish climbers, had dramatic falls as a result. Happily both were unharmed.

When we reached the Base Camps we planned to start with the French and gradually eat our way down through the two German camps to the Italians at the far end, and our minds were full of smoked ham, salami, spaghetti, cakes and chocolate as we climbed up and down, round and through the rows of mini ice mountains which form a broad band between the mountain and the stony highway of the moraine of the Godwin Austen Glacier.

We climbed down the last ice tower, and had just one more fast-flowing small river to cross before we could start our feasting. Kurt found a good crossing place, which involved climbing onto a twelve-foot boulder that sloped down towards the opposite bank, and he went over. I climbed onto the block and sat down to take off my crampons before jumping down. I threw them onto the stones six feet below. 'Here's my ice axe too,' I called to Kurt, but as the special lightweight titanium axe hit the bank it bounced, and jumped straight into the churning, rushing waters of the blue ice-lined river and swiftly disappeared towards Concordia and the Baltoro Glacier. I was upset, for although I had cursed the lightness of the axe so many times for its ineffectiveness on the hard icy conditions of Broad Peak, it had been with me up to the 'magic' 8,000 metres on K2 and I had developed a certain sentimentality about all the equipment that had survived with me on that climb. Well, at least it was the last bad thing Broad Peak could do to us. Now we were safe.

The French Base Camp was a lively place, and the mountaineers were so relieved to see us alive and well that they personally escorted us to each expedition camp in turn to show them that we had returned, relatively undamaged! A few days earlier an ice pinnacle at the foot of the glacier had broken. Inside, preserved in the icy coffin, was the body of a Polish climber who had fallen from close to the place of our avalanche several years before.

We didn't even have time for a cup of tea until we arrived, some two hours later, at the Italian camp. Then the feasting began. We had been on the mountain for nine days and we were starving.

We stayed another day with the friendly French, talking, eating and sleeping, resting and restoring our minds and bodies as we still had to return to K2 to rescue our abandoned equipment. While we were there we solved the mystery of the lost keys. The tent we had slept in at Camp 1 on the way up had been taken down but replaced by an identical tent a few days later. As both were new, we did not spot the difference. The second tent, put up in almost the same place, must have covered the hiding place of our keys by a few inches. We never did get them back and had to patiently saw through all the locks.

K2 was in a calm mood when we returned to retrieve our filming equipment from the abortive Swiss expedition. Even as we struggled to dig out our things from the snow-buried tent at Camp 2 in a windy storm, we could feel that the mountain meant us no real harm. Whoever says that mountains have no character can only have been involved with them at a superficial level.

On our way back down the Baltoro Glacier we called in to the French Camp to say our farewells. 'Here, Julie, I think this is yours,' Jacques said, and from behind his back produced my errant ice axe. 'I found it when I was wandering down by the river the other day; it was caught up on a large stone.'

I hugged him in delight. 'There you are,' I said to Kurt. 'I told you that Broad Peak was only playing.'

🐍15🐍

Keeping fit

Climbing the world's highest mountains is one of the most continuously demanding of all sports, both physically and mentally.

Because expeditions take up such a large chunk of the year, when I am at home I do not feel that I can keep abandoning Terry further to maintain my mountain fitness and training in the British hills three hundred miles away from our home in Sussex, or in the Alps, which are even farther and more expensive to reach. Most of my companions on expeditions are professional mountain guides, mainly in the Alps, and climb and ski all year round. At my level of mountaineering I am a rare part-timer.

Fortunately the martial arts which gave me the philosophy and developed my physical ability to take on the challenge in the first place, also keep me fit between expeditions, even though I can usually only attend classes two or three times a week and often have long gaps in between because of filming and other commitments. Practice exercises the whole body and gets the heart and lungs working to full capacity. When I started going to the *dojo*, for the first time in my life I understood the importance of warming-up exercises and how to do them properly. They were taught in a logical order, stretching before stressing, and co-ordinating movement with breathing. By breathing out when I wanted to stretch I found that I was relaxed and soon became more supple. Ankles, toes, fingers and wrists are stretched and strengthened, peripheral parts which are usually neglected, as is the mind which needs to be relaxed and made more flexible just like the body.

Body movement and co-ordination have helped develop my

sense of balance and control, and many commonsense aspects of health that I had never thought about before have fallen into place, radically changing my approach to a lot of things. Perhaps the simplest is realising that any tension inhibits movement as does breathing in or holding the breath. Best of all I have lost the self-conscious attitude of mind that stopped me trying new actions and experiences. I was forced to learn to relax.

In the *dojo* we use a form of massage to relieve muscular pain and soothe damaged parts and to treat the body generally after a particularly hard practice. Few injuries actually occur on the mat, and most aches and pains needing treatment stem from other activities. *Shiatsu* is a finger-pressure therapy which is widely used in Japan as a health-keeping art encouraged by their Ministry of Health. It uses the same key points (*tsuba*) on the body as acupuncture, but instead of needles applies pressure to these points by thumbs, fingers and palms, and can be used for a revitalising massage or to cure a wide variety of disorders including insomnia, bedwetting, neuralgia and high blood pressure. It is sad that we are so shy about touching others, even members of our own families. This form of contact is an important means of human communication and can give great comfort especially in times of stress. A peck on the cheek does not bring about the same closeness as a hug between friends or relatives. Many experiments have now confirmed that touch can stimulate the brain, but we still do not encourage children to feel textures, shapes, or even their own bodies. Many, particularly older boys, will not have been cuddled by their parents for several years and yet when they grow to sexual maturity we expect them to have enjoyable balanced relationships in which touching and being caressed by their partners are so important. In a tiny village in Pakistan I was given a massage as a courtesy shown to a guest after a nice meal, a lovely custom which soothed away all the aches and pains of travelling and drew me immediately into the family circle. I was a bit disconcerted at first when they announced they wanted to 'press' me, but very pleased when I understood what they meant.

I have not always been as fit as I am now. In 1975 I developed sciatica from helping pupils over the years at Harrison's. The first ten feet of most climbs are difficult because the soil has eroded from the base of the rocks, making the first holds difficult to reach. As the safety rope has built-in elasticity to absorb any shock-loading in the event of a fall, someone who slips off on the first few feet of a climb will hit the ground, so I often give them support or a helpful push from below. As we mainly teach young people of over fifteen years, the strain of supporting their weight in a twisted position – and many of them are far heavier than me – had taken its toll. My lower back and right leg had a constant nagging ache and at times I got pins and needles, and numbness, right down to my toes.

I went along to the special Sports Clinic at Guy's Hospital and was X-rayed and given a cortisone injection to suppress the inflammation. Unfortunately many doctors still treat the symptoms and not the cause. This did not help and I was admitted to hospital, given a spinal injection to coat the damaged nerve with a special fluid and told to lie immobile for seven days. By day two I was impossibly restless and longed to go home.

'If my husband drives very slowly and I lie flat in the car, may I go?' I pleaded. 'I'll go straight to bed at home and not move a muscle,' and to my relief they agreed.

On the gentle drive back from London to Sussex Terry casually mentioned that the hot water at home had suddenly ceased to flow. 'Don't worry, I'll look at it when we arrive,' he reassured me.

I lay in bed and heard him scuffling around in the loft. 'Bloody hell!' he suddenly swore. 'Julie, can you get me a ladder and a hose? I've got a big problem.' Imagining that he had a leak which he had plugged with his finger I leapt out of bed to his aid. It was not until he climbed back down the ladder that I learnt what had happened. The roof space in the Bothy is very small, and it is not possible to see into the cold water tank. Terry had put his hand in to check that the outlet pipe was clear and felt a piece of string. He pulled at the obstruction and when he looked at what was in his hand, discovered he held the tail and back legs of a mouse. The front end of the poor animal had been sucked down the pipe and into our hot water system. That was the end of my bed rest. I rushed around getting hoses and things to poke down the pipe, draining off the water and telephoning plumbers. It seemed that we could only wait until the mouse gradually disintegrated and filtered out through the taps. None of us could face taking a bath for weeks.

I went back to the Clinic. It was not their fault that the treatment had not worked, but they decided the next stage was to operate to remove the offending disc and fuse the adjoining vertebrae. The day before I was due to go into hospital John Turner, a friend from the early High Rocks days, happened to telephone.

'How are you?' I asked him. We had not been in touch for several months.

'Terrible,' he said, and sounded very despondent. 'I've just had a disc removed because I was suffering from sciatica and now I'm crippled and can never climb again. I must not even jump down any distance.'

I cancelled my appointment with the hospital, despite a warning that I could lose the use of my right leg. The only choice was alternative medicine. It was a difficult and expensive time. Over the months I tried osteopaths, acupuncture, a chiropractor and eventually Stuart Korth, a registered osteopath with a very gentle approach, finally sorted it out. It was not easy as I tried to give each therapist time to help me before moving on to try something else. I think they all contributed a little to the eventual cure, which took almost three years and a lot of patience on their part and mine. But in 1978 I was able to go to Peru with Norman Croucher and only suffered pain in the leg during the long climb on Huascaran. Since Peru, in spite of carrying heavy rucksacks long distances on my many expeditions I have had no further trouble.

I am certainly no fitness freak. I feel rather claustrophobic in health clubs, hate running any distance and have seen too many people's lives ruled by keeping fit to keep fit myself. I do however firmly believe that it is necessary to feel good to enjoy and live life to the full. 'Look after your body, it's the only one you've got' was the excellent slogan of a health club where I once worked, and when I teach young people, I always stress that it does not matter how many exams they pass, or how much money they accumulate in later life, if they do not have good health nothing can help them get full pleasure from life.

Unfortunately many orthodox sports taught in schools are difficult to continue after leaving. Football or hockey, for example, need many people and a sports field. Also because they are competitive sports they tend to give preference to younger players. Sports such as tennis, golf and squash are all fairly addictive, but, given long-term dedication, they can cause joint and even spinal damage as they over-stress one side of the body. It is not often suggested that it is a good idea to balance such one-sided sports with a total body activity such as swimming. I am lucky; both my passions exercise the whole body and are very compatible. With so much extra leisure time, and as many people of sixty and seventy are still very active, we need to re-educate ourselves about general fitness, which is an important part of preventive medicine. Age is a matter of how you feel, and not a question of years.

I personally have two major problems to overcome. The first is a little outside my control as it concerns smoking. Ever since my childhood asthma attacks I have been allergic to cigarette smoke. It makes my eyes run, my throat sore and constricted and my chest wheezy. Unfortunately in public places it is not easy to avoid breathing in exhaled smoke, and because of the discomfort it causes it is one of my pet aversions. The other major problem is my feet. My enlarged toe joints make it difficult to wear correctly fitting shoes, and they become inflamed and painful. I cannot push with my big toes as they now lie at the incorrect angle and the swelling around the joints affects my balance. Last year I went to see a surgeon, as a friend had undergone a highly successful operation for the same problem.

'Are you a private patient?' was one of his first questions.

I explained that no private insurance scheme would accept me, I was supposedly a bad risk. I have the same problem with Life Insurance, which seems crazy when they are prepared to insure vulnerable young motor cyclists who are in danger every day.

'Well, I don't consider that you need an operation under the National Health scheme,' he told me, 'but if you can find £2,000 I am prepared to do it for you.'

I was shattered. Did I have to be completely crippled before he thought it necessary? If they are left untreated it seems likely that my deformed feet, which affect my whole body balance, will force me to give up mountaineering – and many other things – a prospect that I find extremely worrying.

The rest of me is in good working order, as the pre-expedition medicals have shown. The first one I had to undergo was at the French Sports Clinic in Paris. I made my first acquaintance with my expedition companions in the long hallway, where we all sat in our underwear filling out a pile of complicated questionnaires. I was called into various rooms to be inspected, tested and measured, and finally ended up in the basement with a cat's cradle of electrode wires stuck on my bare bosom, pedalling an exercise bicycle for fifteen minutes. Despite my lack of training, my results were some of the best.

The next one, in Italy, was rather more casual, but again I passed with flying colours. It was the last one, in England, that made me question the necessity to play the games that these tests required. Kurt and I were sent by our film production company to be checked over by a private doctor as a medical was necessary for the film insurance. I went into his consulting room first. He tested my pulse and blood pressure, asked me about the projected expedition, and signed the form. When Kurt went in, the doctor queried why he had not completed the form himself.

'You're supposed to fill in those parts,' Kurt told him.

The doctor sat at his desk and wrote something down.

'Don't you want to take my pulse?' Kurt asked when he saw him signing the bottom.

'Oh, that's not necessary,' his examiner told him. 'I can see that you're perfectly healthy.'

Kurt's experience with British doctors had been a little confusing on a previous occasion too. Three years before he contracted a mystery illness which he spent a year trying to get diagnosed. I arranged an appointment for him with a specialist at the new Charing Cross Hospital, and sat in on the initial interview in case he needed an interpreter. His English is very good, but he was not familiar with our medical terminology. All went well until the doctor asked, 'And what about your bowels?'

Kurt looked surprised. 'What do you mean?'

'Are they working well?' the doctor explained.

'Well, er . . . Yes!' Kurt looked embarrassed. 'I think so.'

I was a little surprised by his shyness; he is normally pretty open about bodily functions. Later I understood when he said. 'That is the first time any doctor has asked about my testicles. I didn't know what to say!'

Specific feminine problems seem to interest many people, although they are not often brave enough to ask me outright. Yes, I do menstruate, with monotonous regularity, but the inconvenience is really no greater than at home. Women can have problems with acute mountain sickness through fluid retention before a period or by taking the contraceptive pill, but I have never experienced this and have made strenuous climbs to high altitudes at all times of the month. Living together on expeditions in such close proximity is a bit like being in hospital: you accept the lack of privacy at the time, but as soon as I come back to civilisation, my inhibitions return. The main thing is to retain a sense of humour, then nothing seems so bad.

I use approach marches to get fit and find my mountain feet, rather than thinking of the long walk-in purely as an obstacle between civilisation and the mountain. Every step I take along the unstable mountain goat tracks, jumbled scree slopes, boulders and stones of dry river beds and finally the stone and ice hills of the glacier moraines needs the same sort of concentration as on the climb. No one wants to fall sick or be injured getting to Base Camp. Dysentery is another worry, and Kurt and I are very careful in the towns and villages to drink only boiled or treated water and milk, eat only cooked vegetables and generally observe the normal traveller's rules where food is concerned. *En route* to the mountain and at Base Camp we try to use our own mugs, plates and cutlery as infections within such a close community spread rapidly and sore throats, coughs and colds, chest infections and tummy bugs are often transported from Europe. It is doubly important that we do not get sick as no one else can do the filming.

When we reach Base Camp acclimatisation is the next problem. The amount of time this takes and how it should be done is very much an individual matter and fitness and training guarantee no protection. Generally it needs about three weeks of slow steady exercise and height gain, constantly returning to the lower altitude of Base Camp to allow the body to adjust to the diminished amount of oxygen available at higher levels. The balance of four parts nitrogen to one part oxygen in the air does not alter; it is their density which becomes thinner and the pressure to force the oxygen into our lungs becomes less. On the top of Mont Blanc at 15,780 feet the oxygen pressure is just over half that at sea level, and above 26,000 feet it is only about one-third. The body has to make drastic adjustments to keep its cells supplied with oxygen, and produces more red corpuscles to transport an increased amount of it around the body. As the blood consistency becomes thicker and more viscous, the heart is put under strain pumping the sticky fluid around the body and the circulation slows, hence the need to drink so much, five to six litres a day. The danger also is that thromboses can form and lodge in the fine vessels of the lungs or brain.

An unhurried approach march and relaxed first few days at Base Camp are crucial as too much rapid height gain or strenuous activity can cause acute mountain sickness with its unpleasant symptoms of pounding heart, thumping headaches, loss of appetite, nausea, dizziness and difficulty in sleeping. The cure is to rest and not go any higher until the body has adjusted properly, otherwise the risk of pulmonary or cerebral oedema is great and death can rapidly follow. These discomforts can start as low as 10,000 feet and at first I wondered how it was possible to live and survive at more than double that height. Our bodies have a complex chemical make-up of interacting cells. The *Penguin Medical Dictionary* explains oedema well:

> About 60 per cent of the body weight is water, making some 40 litres. The water is divided between the blood (3 litres of plasma), the body cells (25 litres) and the tissue fluid (12 litres). The tissue fluid permeates all the minute spaces and crevices of the body; it is the environment in which the cells live like fish in the sea.
>
> Tissue fluid is derived from the blood. The arteries and veins are waterproof, but the microscopical capillary vessels that carry blood from the arteries to the veins allow water to leak from blood to tissue fluid and back. The pumping pressure from the heart drives

water out of the capillaries. But protein dissolved in the blood cannot easily escape from the capillaries, and it draws water in, from the tissue fluid, by osmosis. These two opposing forces balance, so that the amount of tissue fluid remains more or less constant. Oedema or waterlogging of the tissues occurs either when the mechanical pressure in the capillaries is too high, or when the osmotic pressure is too low. In either case the balance is upset and water is forced out of the blood faster than it can return.

The brain and the lungs have a great concentration of capillary vessels, hence the greater danger of brain or lung oedema. Fluid retention from not passing urine, or too much salt in the body add to the problems. A pulmonary oedema can come on in minutes, characterised by breathlessness, hacking cough and wheezing chest, and frothy, often blood-stained phlegm. Cerebral oedema causes irrationality, drowsiness and confusion over a period of hours as the fluid collects in the brain. In both cases rapid descent is imperative for survival.

Impatience to get on with the climb often tempts people into convincing themselves that they have acclimatised too early, and it is easy to confuse the symptoms of acute mountain sickness with fatigue. That is when having a climbing partner who knows you well can help to prevent disaster, and Kurt and I are always checking each other unobtrusively for early signs which could lead to serious trouble.

Vitamins are important at this time as haemoglobin, which makes up about a third of the mass of red cells, needs iron to be formed and vitamin B_{12} to enable the cells to mature. A supplement of vitamin C is also necesssary as it cannot be stored by the body and is not normally readily available in mountain diets.

Eating well, drinking enough, getting a good night's sleep, not getting too cold, going too fast or carrying too much are all vitally important, but so is breathing through the nose, which moistens and warms up the air before it reaches the lungs, and protecting the exposed areas of the face with suncream to prevent burning, particularly from the increased ultra-violet rays. I have lost layers of skin off my face which pulls itself into a hard dry mask as it heals, making eating and talking painfully difficult. On K2 I had to resort to using a cream deodorant when I ran out of suncream; it was quite effective as it contained lanolin but smelt and tasted foul. It is particularly painful to be burnt under the nose or chin and on the lobes of the ears by the reflection of the sun on the snow. Eyes too can suffer from the effects of the sun and proper glacier glasses are imperative even in gloomy conditions, as we discovered to our cost when we left them off for a few hours on a mountain in order to see the snow slide avalanches more clearly. Both Kurt and I became snowblind, which is an agonising affliction. Any discomfort such as chapped lips, or the small cuts which open up on the fingertips from the cold and take an eternity to heal, or any illnesses, take on exaggerated proportions away from the comfort and security of civilisation; but generally Kurt and I have been lucky, and having a good high altitude doctor such as Urs Wiget to consult for prevention and cure is one of the most important considerations for any expedition.

I am glad that I was not on Hermann Buhl's Broad Peak expedition in 1957 when Kurt was informed two months before departure that he was to be the expedition doctor.

'You have a doctorate,' Buhl explained.

'But I know nothing about medicine,' Kurt protested. 'I am a doctor of business studies.' Nevertheless he had to accept the responsibility and spent the next few weeks pestering his own doctor and local hospital for information and advice. He managed to treat the porters' and local villagers' ailments, mainly with aspirins, and as the expedition members did not dare to get badly sick his short career as a doctor was a success.

It is essential for all mountaineers to learn mountain first aid and enough about drugs and medicines to be able to use them correctly if an emergency arises. You have to take responsibility for your own wellbeing and educate yourself to survive in the wilderness of high mountains.

I get very worried about the discarded equipment, food, drugs, litter and excreta left behind by expeditions which not only pollute the base camps and those on the mountains but affect the local people. At Nanga Parbat Base Camp a lovely young horse which represented a large part of someone's wealth, died because it swallowed a polythene bag. On the return march along the

Baltoro Glacier from K2 a porter was popping pills which he had found thrown away and was offering them to his friends as sweets and another was about to suck a tube of analgesic cream assuming that it was condensed milk. If we are prepared to carry in all the paraphernalia of home comforts we should equally be under an obligation either to transport it out and leave the place as we found it or to teach the local people how to adapt it to their needs. We do not even observe the normal rules of hygiene that are commonplace when camping in this country. Unfortunately on the glaciers the faeces freeze and remain intact under the winter snow until the following year. On the Godwin Austen Glacier below K2 they were everywhere, and although we joked about the vintage and nationality of the numerous brown piles it was very unpleasant and a serious health hazard. I believe firmly in personal freedom and the minimum number of rules and regulations, but this unnecessary spoiling of such beautiful and unique places needs to be stopped before the ever-increasing influx of mountaineers and trekkers ruins them for ever.

Keeping fit cannot be just a question of being in top form to perform a specific task like climbing a mountain; it extends far beyond to the wellbeing of others and keeping our world in a fit state for future generations to live in and enjoy.

❧16❧

Everest from five directions

In 1985, my fitness was really tested. Completely out of the blue, I received an invitation beyond my wildest dreams – to go to Everest. On our way back from K2 and Broad Peak, Kurt and I had met Mal Duff, the leader of a successful British expedition to the Mustagh Tower, an impressive 23,860-foot peak which lies on the watershed between the basins of the Baltoro and Sarpo Largo Glaciers. Mal had been offered the permit for Everest when he got back to Rawalpindi, in the dining room of Mrs Davis's hotel. Norwegian mountaineers had authorisations for both sides of the mountain and had planned a traverse over the top. However, they could not raise the money or enough mountaineers for such an ambitious project, and so they sold the permit for the North Face to Mal. It is not easy to buy permits for Everest; most of the routes are booked for years ahead. The climb by the Western Cwm is reserved until 1997.

Kurt had accompanied Mal to Peking to help him to sort out the contract with the Chinese Mountaineering Association, and to get the route permission changed from the North Face to the North East Ridge, the route we really wanted to climb: the last big unsolved problem on Everest. Kurt has had considerable experience of dealing with the Chinese, having sorted out three previous expedition negotiations in Peking – but this one proved to be the toughest. The Chinese official designated by the Chinese Mountaineering Association was not at all flexible over the cost of changing the route. 'He was like a Panzer tank,' Kurt told me. 'He would not deviate from his line and Mal and I had to put our heads together to work out how we could make him fall into a hole, otherwise the expenses in China were way above the expedition budget.'

After several days of stalemate, they managed to demolish the 'Panzer' by juggling with the figures, but leaving off the final total. They then got him to agree each single item in turn and when he finally added up the total, and discovered that it was much lower than his original figure, it was too late. Kurt and Mal also managed to arrange that the expedition could use the North Col route as an alternative way down the mountain, and for filming.

The Press soon discovered that I was the first British woman to be invited to climb on an Everest expedition and showed a lot of interest. We were extremely lucky with our sponsors, Pilkington's, who had generously backed us with £80,000 and a lot of practical assistance with computerised warehouse facilities, shipping, sunglasses, etc., and it was important to them that the expedition gained a lot of publicity. I was glad I was used to being interviewed by the media: being faced by a barrage of photographers, cameramen and reporters at press conferences can be quite daunting.

Terry and Lindsay had their privacy invaded too. Lindsay answered the phone one morning. It was a man from Radio 4.

'How do you feel about your mother going to climb Everest?' he asked her.

'Does your mother climb mountains . . . and put up tents in the kitchen when she is cooking the Sunday lunch?' she blurted out.

'Thank you very much,' the caller said, after several more questions.

'When will you do the interview?' Lindsay asked.

'We just did. It went out live, and I thought you were very natural!' came the reply.

Even though this was a British expedition, I had not previously met many of the members, although I had heard of their mountaineering achievements, which were very impressive. 'It'll be great to understand what my companions are saying for once,' I said to Terry.

'Don't be too sure,' he said with a grin. 'Most of them are Scots!'

It was a very genial group that left Heathrow on 7 March for Peking. Once again we had to cross the breadth of China, but this time down to the south-west and fabled Tibet. We flew in two stages to Lhasa, stopping overnight at Chengdu, an agricultural town famous for its good cuisine. We could feel the difference in altitude as we walked across the tarmac at Lhasa Airport. We had entered Tibet at 4,000 metres.

Lhasa itself was bustling and colourful. Thirty-five years after the Chinese occupied the town they are busy renovating it. They have realised that it should be rebuilt in the old style and that it does not make sense to erect ugly skyscrapers and modern buildings if they want to develop it as a tourist attraction. It was an enormous building site of rubble and dust when we arrived. During the occupation many of the monasteries were destroyed, but the spirit of the Tibetans is so strong that the Chinese infiltration has not swamped the people, and it is they who give the place its atmosphere. In some ways the new regime has helped them, as they have always been traders and the bustling street market is a jumbled mixture of old and new.

Despite the Dalai Lama's exile, Lhasa remains the Mecca for Tibetan pilgrims and everywhere they were prostrating themselves at body length before stepping forward two or three paces to where their heads had touched the ground. They made slow progress along the streets like human caterpillars. It looked very hard on the knees and hands as they slid forwards to a face-down prone position time and again. The sparkling white edifice of the Potala, the palace of the Dalai Lama, its multi-coloured pelmets fluttering from its hundreds of windows, was beautifully mirrored in the still waters of a lake below. It sits on a hill looking out over all the changes that are taking place. It was fascinating to wander around the highly decorated rooms with their many fabled murals, but the building is a museum now and empty of the life for which it was built; I preferred the still active monasteries we visited later, where young and old monks spent hours praying. These places were a kaleidoscope of colours and sounds, the swaying figures of the monks wearing magenta robes under faded saffron cloaks, intoning like buzzing bees from the brilliant red and gold covered prayer books, surrounded by wall paintings of strong shades and intricate design and golden statues glowing in the warm light of the rancid-smelling butter-lamps.

While we were in Lhasa Kurt and I celebrated our birthdays. We climbed a small double-peaked mountain which formed a backdrop to the town during the afternoon of 15 March, and in the evening we had our joint 99th birthday party! We had bought various Chinese wines, some which tasted like sweet sherry and others like gut rot, but washed down with plenty of Chinese beer the party went with a swing. We even had ninety-nine candles to blow out and, together, managed it with just one puff.

We travelled in lorries and a film jeep over the hills of the Tibetan Plateau. On the third day of travelling, from a sixteen-thousand-foot pass high above the barren landscape, we got our first glimpse of our goal. Chomolungma – Mother Goddess of the World. Spread out sixty miles away was an enormous wall of snow-capped peaks, the most impressive panorama of Himalayan mountains to be seen anywhere in the world. From Shisha Pangma to Cho Oyu to Gyachung Kang and, on the other side of Everest, Chomolungma and Makalu, Everest totally dominated the scene, her head and shoulders floating above the other mountains. It gave an awe-inspiring scale of audacity to our intentions to try to climb this spectacular giant. It was only when I saw the enormousness of Everest with my own eyes that I fully appreciated that it *is* the highest thing on earth.

We had been warned that Base Camp was a cold, bleak place. Chris Bonington had led the first expedition to try to conquer this ridge in 1982, and information from Chris and his expedition book were a great help in our endeavours. His team had consisted of just four mountaineers. Sadly, two of the best climbers Britain has ever had died on the climb. Peter Boardman had stayed with us at the Bothy several times on his way to the Alps or lectures. He was an easy-going, Peter Pan-like person, who like his companion Joe Tasker had many talents and great depth of character. Joe was making his first film, and the footage he shot showed his sensitivity and love of the mountains. Peter and Joe disappeared between the first and second Pinnacles on the ridge, and what actually happened to them still remains a mystery.

Our Advance Base Camp was twelve miles distant up the East Rongbuk glacier, at an altitude of 21,000 feet. It was much colder there than at Base Camp. The constant wind made it very uncomfortable to live anywhere, at Base Camp, Advance Base Camp and on the mountain. It takes a long time to pluck up the courage to have a strip wash on expeditions. Fortunately, one's sense of smell is affected by the altitude and cold, and is not as sensitive as at sea level, so cleanliness is a matter of comfort rather than worrying about BO. Often it is not possible to wash for a week or so, and then I find foil-wrapped cleansing tissues invaluable. The expedition had some moistened with eau-de-cologne, but these were not a success as they stung the 'delicate' places unmercifully. I only managed to wash my hair three times in nine weeks and the first time I tried the hairs became rigid with ice and I was scared that if I combed the frozen strands they would snap off.

Taste too is affected by living so high and on the mountain I crave for salty, savoury foods like salami and cheese and can eat a whole tin of anchovies at one go, something I could never do at home. After I returned home I could not face chocolate – we had six thousand assorted chocolate bars on this expedition, enough for seventeen each, every day, and hundreds of sticks of Everest rock. Generally the food was good and as we had no official cook at Base Camp everyone took a turn, which ensured a variety of meals. We also had a good supply of Scotch whisky to help keep the chill out of our bones.

Kurt and I were in the unusual position of being commissioned to film for both commercial television and the BBC, the rival channels even sharing the cost of hiring the large Arriflex camera. Our news reports for ITN brought in funds and financed the jeep runs to the nearest town of Xegar to collect the expedition mail and any extra necessary supplies.

Fortunately, the Chinese had constructed an amazing road over the stony moraine of the Rongbuk Glacier all the way to Base Camp for their 1960 expedition to Everest.

The Chinese petrol cookers constantly broke down and at least one had to be replaced every trip. Each new type seemed more potentially lethal than the last although they were all rather Heath Robinson constructions. One had a round pressurized tank, welded to which was a thin copper rod leading to a watering-can type rose. To keep it going, and we needed endless hot water for cooking, drinking and washing, this contraption had to be pumped furiously and constantly. The last type was a large blowlamp which heated the pots from the side and threw out such a heat that it melted the solder on the kettle.

Our film vehicle, a Toyota Land-Cruiser, also ferried two part-time members to Lhasa. Pilkington's had not only sponsored the expedition, but they had allowed their Company Secretary to join us for several weeks. David Bricknell is a dedicated long-distance runner and was very fit and acclimatised easily. It was interesting to hear his impressions of expedition life, as he had no previous experience of how mountaineers live. He even managed to inject some organisation into us – climbers are notoriously casual about the domestic side of things.

For this expedition we had a young film porter, Danny. As the BBC filming for Pebble Mill which would finance his participation was not finalised until just before we left, he endured several weeks of uncertainty as to whether or not he would be joining us. He is a very mature lad of over six feet and looked and behaved as if he were about twenty-five, so I never queried his age. It was quite a shock to discover, when I asked for his details, that he was only nineteen years old. However, having said that we would take him, and he was very strong, we could not let him down at the last minute, but I always felt a motherly responsibility for him; after all, he was younger than Christopher.

Kurt and I were very happy that, on our recommendation, Urs Wiget, our Swiss doctor from the 1984 K2 and Broad Peak expedition, had been invited to join us. On K2 he had cured many members of a wide variety of medical problems, among them toothache and a dislocated shoulder. I had pneumonia in the early days at Base Camp there and then Peter Habeler had to have his head stitched after a fall on the mountain. Urs is not only the best high-altitude doctor I have ever met, but he is an

excellent mountaineer which gives him an even greater understanding of the specific problems encountered on big mountains.
He has tremendous energy and is a commonsense, practical
person with a winsome lively personality.

Urs was understandably concerned about Danny's youth. 'You
do not acclimatise well until you are over 25; it has to do with
the growth of bone marrow where the new blood cells are
formed,' he warned us. So we gave Danny extra time at Base
Camp to adjust while Kurt and I went for a ten-day exploration
and filming trip to the Karma Valley.

All day we drove along dusty, bumpy, tracks. We had to travel
one hundred miles to reach the village of Karta where the road
ended and our long walk would begin. Our driver, who had come
from the smooth roads of Peking, had now got his confidence on
these unsurfaced, uneven roads and our speed rarely dropped
below 40 kph regardless of conditions. This drive was a real test
for the Toyota; we forded rivers, drove along bouldered glacier
moraine, negotiated narrow tracks of sand over high drops,
climbed steep mountain roads and its four-wheel-drive facility
was really necessary time and again to keep us out of trouble.

We were ravenous when we arrived at the stone-built village of
Karta, set on a hill above the grassy meadow by a stream where
we put our small tent. The locals came to investigate us and the
children besieged us. They did not see many strangers. Even when
I retreated into the tent, they lay on their tummies and peered
under the front extension. Beneath the grime they had lovely
faces, but one little lad stood out from the rest in character and
intelligence. Dorje was about seven. He soon organised all the
children, understanding our sign language far quicker than the
others. We made a circle with our fingers and clucked like hens,
flapping our arms. 'Eggs!' we mouthed. 'Bring us some eggs.'
Dorje rushed off up to the village. Ten minutes later he returned
with his hat full of eggs. We hard-boiled them, burning our
fingers as we peeled off the shells in our hurry to satisfy our
immediate hunger and craving for fresh eggs. They tasted so
good. 'More?' we asked, and another ten arrived nestling in
Dorje's homespun headgear. That day we demolished forty eggs
between us, but soon burnt off the cholesterol crossing the

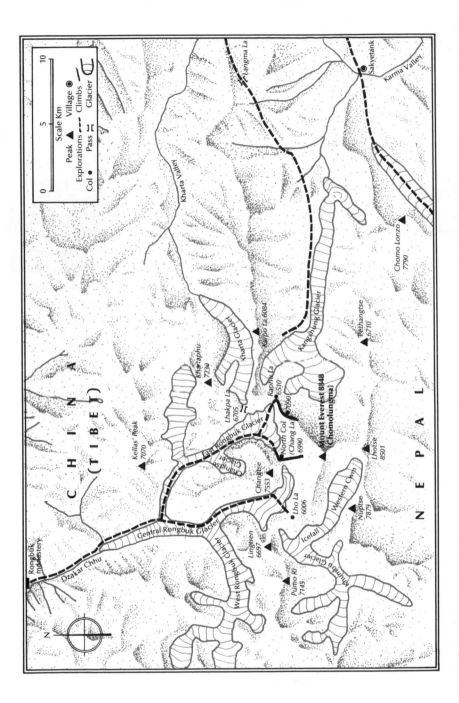

Scale Km

Peak ▲   Village ⊙
Explorations - - -   Climbs
Col ●   Pass ⌒   Glacier

N

C H I N A
(T I B E T)

N E P A L

Rongbuk
monastery

Dzakar Chhu

West Rongbuk Glacier

Central Rongbuk Glacier

Lingtren
6697

Pumo Ri
7145

Khumbu Glacier

Icefall

Western Cwm

Nuptse
7879

Lho La
6006

Changtse
7553

East Rongbuk Glacier

Changtse
Glacier

Kellas' Peak
7070

Lhakpa La
6705

Khartaphu
7230

Kharta Glacier

Kharta Valley

Karpo La 6084

Raphu La

Rapiu La
6510

North Col
(Chang La)
6990

Mount Everest 8848
(Chomolungma)

Kangshung Glacier

Langma La

Sakyetaink

Karma Valley

Chomo Lonzo
7790

Pethangtse
6710

Lhotse
8501

16,400-foot Shoa La Pass, a three-thousand-foot climb twelve miles away.

As we dropped down into the Karma Valley on the other side of the Pass, I could not believe my eyes. Whole mountainsides were covered in rhododendrons and azaleas and far below, in the bottom of the valley, tall cedar and pine trees stuck up through the dense undergrowth of an impenetrable jungle. No Tibetans have their houses in this amazing valley, but in the few short months of the summer they cross one of the two high passes to graze some yaks and collect building timber for the whole of the Tingri province of Tibet.

Only a few of the rhododendrons were flowering; they were late this year, but they were not our wild mauve variety. Brilliant reds, yellows and pinks were starting to burst from their green buds and we felt a little sad that we could not return two weeks later when the whole valley would be a breathtaking *mélange* of colour.

We investigated two valleys. To explore one we had to fight our way through the rhododendron jungle to reach the glacier at the foot of Makalu. It was a wonderful adventure in this secret remote place with its wealth of plant life and unclimbed peaks. We had been told that monkeys and bears lived in the dense woods, and there were rumours about the yeti. I certainly could imagine him living there. This green valley with its massive rock walls hung with cotoneaster, ferns and mosses is sandwiched between high snow peaks and enormous glaciers, a beautiful unexpected freak of nature, a green oasis in an icy Himalayan world.

It took us two days to reach the end of the moraine where the plant life stopped and the ice took over. Makalu (8,481 metres) towered above us, its huge beautiful white form studded with rock buttresses of rust-coloured granite, and it closed off the end of the valley. Kurt had stood on its summit on 21 May 1978. It was the start of his second 8,000-metre Himalayan life. Eighteen years before he had climbed Dhaulagiri (8,176m) and three years before that Broad Peak (8,047m). During the break he had spent his life exploring and filming many other parts of the world: Greenland, Africa, America, Peru and the Hindu Kush. It was quite a challenge at forty-six to return to climb the highest peaks of the world. His success on Makalu made him realise that age was no barrier. After that he climbed Everest (8,848m) and Hidden Peak (8,065m). Fate was kind; there I was at the same age, standing next to him, so close to the mountain that had made it possible.

On our way back down to the main valley it started to snow and we took refuge under the primitive tree-branch lean-to shelter of some woodcutters. The smiling Tibetans gave us tea which was greasy and salty and tasted like soup, and handfuls of roasted barley grains, which were delicious. They split all their wood into five-foot planks, with very primitive tools. They did not appear to have any saws. These lengths would be carried on their backs out of the valley.

We worked our way round to the other valley which Kurt had visited in 1981 when he went with the Americans to climb the East Face of Everest. We not only retraced his footsteps up the side of the long Kangchung Glacier, but those of Mallory in 1921 when he was searching for the best way to climb Everest. It took us three days and was well worth every step. The East Face is vast, 3,500 metres high, and with its stupendous fluted ridges and curving cornices is the most impressive sight I have ever seen.

We were in the middle of an amphitheatre of enormous mountains: Chomolenza, Makalu, Pethangtse, Shartse, Lhotshe and Everest. We had a superb view of our North East Ridge but could not spot any of our mountaineers moving along it.

We returned to Karta over the other high pass, the Langma La (5,300 metres), climbing above a clear, stunningly blue, holy lake with a picture postcard view of Everest. We were the first people to cross the Langma La that year, as the Tibetans thought that it was still covered in deep snow from the winter.

On 22 April we returned to Base Camp, fully understanding why the Karma Valley had so excited the British pioneers.

Danny had acclimatised in our absence and had also learnt to bake excellent bread in a pressure cooker. We went with him up to Advance Base Camp and up on the North East Ridge to film. The expedition had managed to get as far as the first buttress, and while they were fixing ropes and stocking the snow caves at

Camp 1 and Camp 2, we were busy setting up various film points. We had one on the Raphu La and another on what we called the White Mountain on the other side of the Raphu La col from the ridge.

When filming a climb, it is necessary to show the mountain from as many sides and perspectives as possible and, although this is a lot of work, it is very interesting and gives us a real excuse to explore our surroundings. Making the regular news reports and the documentary kept us very busy even when we went down to relax at Advance and Base Camps. Film logs had to be kept up to date, sound tapes listened to and listed, films changed, equipment checked, batteries changed, cameras cleaned . . . a hundred and one jobs which left us little leisure time.

On 10 May we went up to the North Col, an adjacent route at right angles to the North East ridge, from which we got an excellent view of the higher section of the climb. We wanted to set up a film tent and hopefully film the first members of our expedition reaching the Pinnacles. These are the really serious problem on this route and the reason why this ridge has not yet been conquered. They are mini-mountains which start just below 8,000 metres and present some very difficult climbing at a very high altitude. Even after seeing them from most sides and many angles, Kurt and I could not decide exactly how many there are, or judge whether some of them could be traversed at the base or if they would all have to be climbed. The route to this point is not very difficult by high mountain standards. It is relatively safe, especially with fixed ropes, and the angle is not severe. However, the foot of the ridge is already at 6,500 metres and any exertion at this altitude and above, fixing ropes and carrying loads, takes a lot of effort, and the weather was fickle with strong winds and always bone-chillingly cold.

Apart from the difficult climbing on bad broken rock, the Pinnacles present a logistics problem. To climb them quickly it is almost certainly necessary to use oxygen, which helps to keep the body functioning as it would at sea level and lower the dangers of pneumonia and frostbite. But the oxygen cylinders are very heavy, each one weighs 11½ pounds (about 5¼k) and it is not possible to carry more than two at a time. Each Pinnacle has two

271

sides, one up and one down. It is fine to go over the first one with oxygen, but then you have none left to get back again, or to help climb the rest. If a mountaineer did manage to get over the whole lot, it is very doubtful that he would be strong enough to return over them, even if he did not go on to the summit, which is still a very long way away. There are solutions to the problem, but Kurt and I felt that these lay with the North Col which joins the summit ridge just past the last Pinnacle. If a tent, food and oxygen could be taken up this way, the climbers would have a chance of survival whatever they ultimately decided to do.

The route up to the North Col is steep and dangerous, with many delicately balanced seracs on the ice wall which blocks the end of the glacier like the wall of a dam. It was 1,650 feet high. We decided not to put Danny at risk by taking him with us and so we carried very heavy packs as we slowly worked our way up to the top of the col at 23,000 feet. I had expected a wide plateau of snow, but as we stepped over the top into the full brunt of the galeforce wind, there was a pathway a foot wide along which we had to balance, with a drop of two thousand feet either side.

Further along the col broadened out and we dropped down a little before we found a suitable flat place to pitch our tent. Although we were feeling good at altitude, we were starting to tire more easily. We had been living above 21,000 feet for sixteen days on this visit to Advance Base Camp and working and carrying a lot. We filmed all the next day.

That night, by torchlight, I wrote to Terry:

> . . . 6.55 pm and the wind is still trying to rip the tent asunder. Ten out of ten to Ultimate for making this little tent so strong. I would not sit in another so calmly in such an exposed place. The Basque climbers are somewhere up above us, poor sods. They must have got to a camp before the storm broke today, but the top of Everest looks dreadful. I do hope they are OK. We will wait here until tomorrow in the hope that we see them either going up or coming down.

The Basques were a brave expedition of just four friends led by Mario Apprego. They were hoping to climb Everest without oxygen and did not have a doctor in the party. They had been

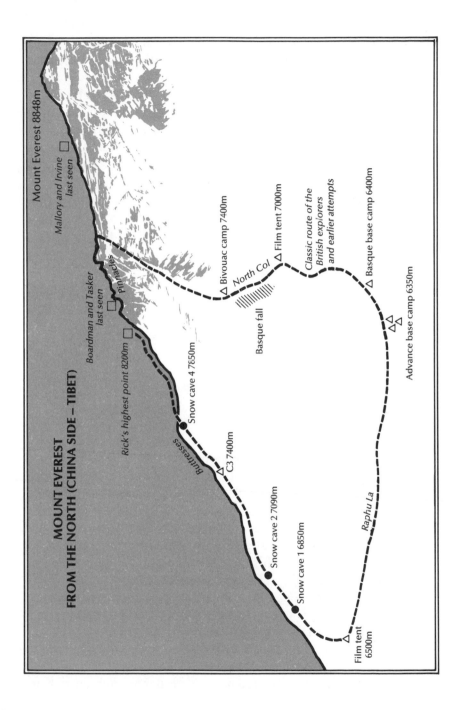

MOUNT EVEREST
FROM THE NORTH (CHINA SIDE – TIBET)

Mount Everest 8848m

Mallory and Irvine
last seen

Boardman and Tasker
last seen

Pinnacles

Rick's highest point 8200m

Snow cave 4 7850m

Bivouac camp 7400m

North Col

Film tent 7000m

Classic route of the
British explorers
and earlier attempts

Basque base camp 6400m

Basque fall

Advance base camp 6350m

Buttresses

C3 7400m

Snow cave 2 7090m

Snow cave 1 6850m

Raphu La

Film tent
6500m

above the North Col for three days, but we did not know where as bad storms had racked the mountain and clouds obliterated the view.

On 12 May we saw no sign of them until two in the afternoon. I was working with the camera in the tent when Kurt, who was outside, gave a shout. '*Gott sei Dank!*' I heard him say as he saw the Basques appear at the top of the snow ramp leading down to the Col. 'I can see all four, and they are moving well. They are all right!'

We had finished our filming and I was taking the last film out of the camera in the black bag. It was a relief to be sitting in the shelter of the tent out of the battering of the strong, very cold, wind constantly blowing over the Col from the direction of the Lho La Pass.

Suddenly I heard Kurt cry out. 'They're falling! Oh God. Two are falling!'

I thrust my head out of the tent entrance. Two climbers, obviously roped together, were sliding down the 2,000-foot white tongue of snow, desperately out of control. I felt sick as they slipped and tumbled from one side of the 40-foot-wide slope to the other. At each edge there were horrifying drops. They seemed to fall endlessly as we watched, totally helpless. Eventually, some 800 feet further down, they stopped at a band of rocks bordering the drop to the sheer North Face. There was a brief moment of stillness, and then something slid on down the slope. I gripped Kurt's arm. It looked so much like a body as it bounced and slid a further three hundred feet. Seconds later another object fell, down into the abyss of the North Face.

We strained our eyes to see if there was any movement, but they were a good half-mile and seven hundred feet in height away from us. Kurt strapped on his crampons and set off up the slope.

He moved up steadily. Halfway up he made a detour to the object lying on the slope. Thankfully it was only a tent which had fallen out of a rucksack, and the object that had fallen down the North Face was the rucksack itself.

Slowly, carefully, the two unscathed mountaineers descended and when they reached the spot where their friends had ceased falling I could make out three forms. Half an hour later Kurt joined the little group. Afterwards he told me. 'They were completely shattered and stunned with shock. It was Anxthon and Juan-Jo who had fallen. Juan-Jo was lying on the rocks, and they had already covered his body with stones. 'Are you sure he's dead?' I asked them, but they just shook their heads, unable to speak. I ran my fingers along his hand. It was solid and cold. 'Juan-Jo hit the rocks with his head, half his face is missing!' Mario told him, in tears.

I watched them until they started to move on down. The weather clagged in and clouds blocked my view. I went back into the tent and began to melt snow to make hot drinks for them. We had no food left as we had stayed up on the Col longer than we had planned, waiting for the Basques. It was always a difficult decision for us to choose between carrying food or film. One can of film weighs roughly the same as a tin of fish or meat. I had three one-cup packets of hot chocolate and two tea bags left and it took an hour to heat enough snow to fill a litre bottle. I could not settle to do anything else and kept looking anxiously out of the tent, hoping to get a glimpse of them, but even with the strong wind there was no gap in the clouds which blanketed the slope.

It was five-thirty when I heard a shout outside and two figures loomed large in the mist. I hugged the first one, Josemar, and he burst into tears on my shoulder. 'Está muerto!' he sobbed. Mario, the leader, was on the other end of the rope and he was so exhausted with grief that it took him five minutes to take the last twenty steps.

Kurt arrived with Anxthon half an hour later and we laid him gently in our tent. He was stunned with shock and the trauma of the fall. I could not check his injuries properly as it was too cold to open his clothing to examine him. I did not want to let out what body heat he had accumulated during the struggle down. However, there was no blood on his clothing, and he was able to tell me that he did not feel any excessive pain in any one spot. I noticed his wrist was swollen and removed his watch. His pulse and breathing were erratic and he drifted in and out of consciousness.

I forced Anxthon to swallow as much liquid as possible. I had learned from the others that they had lived at 7,700 metres for three days in such bad storms that they had not been able to melt enough snow to make hot drinks. The only other comfort that I could give him was to stroke his head and hold his hand. Sudden death is a terrible shock, and a cold, cramped tent, battered by fierce winds on an exposed Col at 23,000 feet, was no place to come to terms with it. We all went down to Advance Base Camp the next day.

When Urs examined Anxthon, he found only a broken wrist, but he was very badly bruised and shocked. A couple of weeks later at the Basque Base Camp I had a chat with him. He had come to terms with the accident in a very mature way for a young man of twenty-five.

'In spite of everything, I don't hate the mountain, Julie,' he told me. 'In fact I have come to love it more. I must come back and try again.'

If I could choose a place to die, it would be in the mountains. When we were falling in the avalanche on Broad Peak, I knew that I would not mind dying that way. There have been a number of other occasions in the mountains, when just to sit still and drift into an eternal sleep would have been an easy and pleasant thing to do, but hopefully the circle of nature will not close for me too soon. I have a lot to live for. Injury worries me far more, especially being damaged in a senseless accident. More of my friends have been badly injured and crippled in road accidents than in the mountains.

After the Basque accident Kurt and I went back down to Base Camp for a much-needed rest. It was difficult to know when to go back up to Advance Base Camp again. We did not want to return before the expedition really attacked the Pinnacles as living at 21,000 feet and above for so long over the weeks had a cumulative draining effect on our physical condition. In order to be fit enough to film so high on the mountain, we planned to go up at the very last moment and use all our stored energy to stay with the lead mountaineers as long as possible. Unfortunately, the expedition radios did not work between the lower and the upper Base Camps as they relied on 'line of sight' to function, so there was no regular communication with our friends at Advance

Base and on the mountain. Usually we could only study the weather and guess how much progress had been made, although occasional messages arrived when someone came down to recuperate.

In the meantime we did our exploration to the Lho La. Instead of turning left off the main Rongbuk Glacier into the East Rongbuk Glacier which led to our Advance Base Camp, we continued straight up it. There was no well-trodden path to follow as no expedition had visited the North Face of Everest for several years, and it was towards this uninviting-looking side of the mountain that we had to go. The glacier was complex to follow and it took us two eight-hour days to negotiate it and work our way up the long upper snow slope bisected by many hidden crevasses. We reached the col quite close to the long West Ridge and traversed across to the other side, where we found the deserted Base Camp with a large underground snow cave which must have served as a Mess Tent for an American expedition that had tried the West Ridge a few weeks before. They had an unusual approach situation. They came to the mountain via Nepal and climbed the Lho La to establish their Base Camp just over the border in Tibet. We also saw the incredible gear winch erected by an earlier Spanish expedition 700 metres below where the Khumbu Icefall started, its jumbled blocks forming a chaotic road to the Valley of Silence leading up to the Western Cwm. I felt happier with our side of the mountain, but it was good to make even a brief acquaintance with the other faces of the 'Mother Goddess'.

After our return to Base Camp, while we were preparing to go back up to Advance Base, one of our youngest members, Tony, came down. He looked very tired.

'There's been a terrible storm, we were lucky to get off the mountain safely,' he told us. Then he added, 'The expedition's over!'

It was shattering news. We had all hoped so much to succeed on this last unclimbed ridge, or at least to solve the mystery of what had happened to Peter and Joe. It was hard for our little group at Base Camp to accept. Kurt and I were feeling revitalised after three days of eating and sleeping well. It was very different for the lads who had been struggling on the mountain when the storm raged.

We all decided to write a letter to Mal at Advance Base suggesting that the expedition be extended a further week to give us time for one more try, but the suggestion was rejected. The mountain camps had already been cleared of any valuable equipment on the assumption that with the storm the monsoon had arrived. Kurt and I went back up immediately. The first time we had walked up with yaks it had taken us three days; now we were fit and acclimatised it was possible to cover the long glacier in eight hours.

Almost as soon as the decision was made to go home, the weather improved and was better than it had been for the whole duration of the expedition. The sun shone and the sky was clear and blue. But most people's thoughts were with returning to their families. We had been away from home for three months, and it had been a tough existence. In two days most of the Advance Base Camp was packed up ready for the yaks to carry down six days later.

One mountaineer felt that he could not give up. Rick Allen has a tenacious character and he decided to take advantage of the fine spell and make one more try to get high on the ridge. 'I'd rather be up there giving it a go than drinking coffee at Base Camp,' he commented as we filmed his lonely start back up the fixed ropes.

Kurt and I were in a difficult situation. We would dearly have loved to accompany him, but our expedition contract stated that the leader's decision was final and binding. Had Rick suffered an accident somebody might have surmised that we had asked him to make the attempt for the sake of the film. Even though this was not the case, it could have created serious insurance problems.

After we had watched Rick safely arrive at the first snow cave, Kurt, Danny and I packed up our film camp on the Raphu La and while I went back to Advance Base Camp to start clearing up our tent there, the other two rescued the movie gear from the White Mountain. The next two days Kurt filmed Rick gradually working his way up the long ridge through the telephoto lens, and we also filmed a lot of other scenes which we had not had time to shoot previously. Apart from ourselves and Danny, there was only one other young mountaineer at this camp. Jon Tinker stayed on to give Rick moral support, even though he was very tired. Through regular radio contacts we followed Rick's progress. It takes a special sort of person to maintain the mental ability to keep pushing on alone in such committing circumstances. My admiration for Rick is tremendous, for he climbed halfway up the broken rock of the first Pinnacle, higher than anyone else had achieved on this expedition, before turning back. He even discovered Joe Tasker's movie camera, which he had obviously abandoned to lighten his load before climbing the rest of this Pinnacle with Peter Boardman. Regrettably there was nothing on the film, but Rick came closer than anybody to solving the mystery of their disappearance.

As far as the documentary filming was concerned, Kurt and I were in a similar difficult position to that on the Swiss K2 expedition. Sadly our expedition had not succeeded in climbing either the Pinnacles or Everest, but thankfully they had no great drama or tragedy. Once again we had no satisfactory ending for the film.

Before returning to Advance Base Camp we had thought carefully about what we could do to solve this problem. It costs a lot of money to make such a film, and it was our responsibility to bring back a transmittable pictorial story. To solve this problem we decided to follow the continuing fortunes of the Basque mountaineers. Mario and Josemar had to go back up to the North Col to finish burying their friend, as after the accident they had only temporarily covered his body with stones. Later they bravely decided that they would try to make one last attempt to reach the summit. 'Would you come with us?' they asked Kurt and me. 'We are feeling very low, and any support for our morale would be a great help.' We also had to return to the North Col as we still had valuable cameras and equipment in our film tent on the saddle, and so, with Mal's agreement, we decided to stay on alone for one extra week after our expedition had gone home.

The two Basques did not want to wait until we had finished filming Rick's ascent in case the weather changed again. On 26 May we watched them climbing slowly up the ice wall leading to the North Col. We planned to set off ourselves the following day, but during the night Kurt woke me urgently. 'Oh hell! Julie, my eyes! The pain is unbearable!' He was again suffering from snow blindness, the result of looking through the 800mm telephoto lens of the movie camera for long periods without his sunglasses while filming Rick on the ridge. I spent the rest of the night getting cups of cold water for Kurt to bathe his poor swollen eyes. A few weeks later, after retreating in terrible conditions from Nanga Parbat, I was to experience for myself this cruel affliction. Like sunburn the pain starts suddenly hours after the damage is done, and the eyes sting as if they are full of soap and grit. All the next day and the following night Kurt had to endure this torture, and he still had double vision when we did set off for the North Col on the morning of the 28th.

We were about halfway up the snow cliff when we met the two Basques coming down. 'It's no good, we can't go on!' Mario said totally dejected. 'The wind is so strong, it took all our effort to make the grave, our spirit has gone.' We felt very heavy-hearted that we had been unable to help them in their sad task, and give them the moral support they so badly needed to go higher. As we continued on up to our camp on the Col, I thought about them a lot. The sun had gone and an icy chill ate up its warmth in no time and made me shiver.

It was as windy as ever on the ridge, and we lay in our noisily flapping tent and debated the possibilities open to us. We felt that we should at least try to go higher. We had a responsibility to the film and the expedition's sponsors to do everything possible. I was the first British woman to make an attempt on Everest, and so far circumstances had not given me a chance to prove my worthiness for that privilege. If only we could get high enough to film the Pinnacles from this side, it would be so useful to any future expedition making an attempt to conquer the North East Ridge. But the weather was atrocious. It would be far safer to pack up our rucksacks and go down. We still had time to catch up the rest of the expedition and go home with them. In the back of my mind a quotation I had seen somewhere nagged at me: 'Only those who risk going too far can possibly find out how far they can go.'

Luckily Kurt and I have always been in agreement on our major decisions. At nine in the morning we were again ploughing our way slowly upwards. We had to battle into the full force of the wind. It was like pushing against a resisting door which would not open. We reached Juan-Jo's resting place and filmed the lonely grave, which was surrounded by bamboo sticks carrying the Basque colours, fluttering in the wind like prayer flags. It was a good place with magnificent views out as far as distant Nepal.

The wind increased and it got bitterly cold. Removing my gloves for a few minutes to take photographs made my fingers go white and numb. There seemed no sense in going on, so we made a depot and returned to the comparative warmth of our tent down on the col.

On 30 May we tried again. This time we got higher than the point from which the two Basque mountaineers had started their tragic fall. A woolly hat lying in the snow brought a lump into my throat; it was easy to visualise the accident. It was not an easy climb. The wind was unrelenting and the old fixed ropes were a mess and not always anchored to a snow stake or piton. At just above 24,000 feet the pattern of the wind changed and instead of blowing fairly constantly, which I could cope with by leaning with all my weight into it, started to gust. It was so powerful that it blew me off my feet. Standing up again took all my energy; my rucksack felt like a lead weight on my back. The fifth time I was blown over I was beginning to despair. The bloody wind, would it never give up? If only I had not lost so much weight!

'I can't go on much farther,' I shouted up to Kurt, who was pulling in the safety rope. We were lucky. About thirty yards from us, right on the edge of the ridge, was the only possible campsite. There were not many places that could be levelled enough to take a tent.

We spent the rest of our strength carving out a platform with our ice axes and then had to struggle for an hour and a half to slide the tent poles into the narrow sleeves to form the hoops which gave the tent its tunnel shape. We did this with the tent collapsed on the snow, kneeling on it to hold it down, but the moment we tried to stand it up and fix it to the mountain the wind blew into it; even with the entrance to the lee-side, it filled like a balloon and it took a supreme effort to hold.

Kurt used everything he could find to anchor the tent, our ice axes, part of some old fixed ropes, the largest stones he could manage to move. I had just started to sort out our sleeping bags inside, using my weight to help keep it down, when the front end began to sag. I looked out of the wildly flapping door and saw a section of pole sliding away down the almost vertical slope at the very edge of which the tent stood. I looked at the pole pocket. It had a hole. The strong vibration of the wind had caused the fibreglass stick to drill straight through. I wondered how long it would take before the other two hoops did the same thing. Then we would be left with a collapsed tent which would give us little protection from the wild below zero elements. Kurt struggled on to move more stones to act as plates under the ends of the poles, and amid his frenzy of effort he gave a bellow of joy.

'Here, take this,' he shouted as he passed into the tent a chunk of rock. 'I think it's a fossil.' In the gloom I felt its strange concentric oval lines and the unexpected gift of nature gave me comfort through my fingertips. Even though I knew that Everest was born under the sea, it was marvellous actually to hold something created many millions of years ago that had been lifted up so high.

That night was the most frightening I have ever spent on a mountain, the wind unrelentingly hitting the tent with such ferocity that I was convinced that either the poles or fabric would be destroyed, or the anchoring strings would tear out.

I fought a battle in my mind, for I knew that we should put on our boots and all our spare clothing and have our rucksacks packed in case the worst should happen. But I was warm in my sleeping bag and very tired. Kurt was sleeping peacefully; he did not seem to share my fears. We had been caught in bad storms much higher on K2 and I had not been so scared. I tried to rationalise my fears. We should most probably be blown away inside the tent anyway, and I wondered how it would feel to be carried on the wind like a wave-tossed dinghy. For several hours I tried to give extra support to the curved poles by holding the front one with my hands and the middle one with my bent-up knees but gradually, thankfully, sleep took over.

The wind raged on in the early light of dawn, and stormclouds blew in layers across Everest's mighty flank. We wanted so much to go higher, even a little way would have satisfied, but by the time we were dressed in our bulky clothing and ready to move, the gales above intensified, warning us against such folly. We abandoned our tent and everything that was not absolutely necessary, and slowly, carefully, remembering how easily a false step could mean disaster, we started the long climb down.

Returning to England ten days after the main expedition, I crept in quietly. It would have been difficult to explain publicly how I felt about this adventure. Mountaineering is a sport, and in all sports you cannot always expect to win. Climbing mountains, I have found that I have always gained something from the special experience of the many facets involved, and even without a summit have come home satisfied. This time something was missing, hunger pains still remained. The whole thing seemed inconclusive, and I felt frustrated. I had never come back home feeling this way before.

Now that I have had time to reflect quietly I am happier. It was a good first meeting. I had seen not just the East, North, West and a glimpse of the South of Everest, but also viewed it from the fifth direction – which I discovered in an old Tibetan song – up! We had followed the historic footsteps of Mallory and Irvine part of the way up the North Col route and had climbed on the North East Ridge. I had shared many good adventures on and around the mountain in good company. My frustration lay with myself. I had worried only about what I had not seen or achieved instead of truly appreciating what I had experienced, possibly in my great desire to know more about this mountain. Life does not normally give many second chances, and I have been exceptionally lucky with both K2 and Nanga Parbat. I long to go back to Everest, and can only hope that the opportunity will arise while I am still capable.

☙17☙

Nanga Parbat – to be or not to be?

On my return to England from China on 15 June, I was thrown into a fever of preparation. It was Terry's fiftieth birthday eight days after I got home and, as it meant a lot to him (it's strange how some ages have a great importance in life), I wanted to give him a special party. At first I planned the celebration for the Saturday night and began telephoning our friends, inviting them to join us but without telling Terry as I wanted it to be a surprise. However, the seventh person I called gave me the surprise. 'Are you sure this party's on Saturday?' he asked. 'Terry's already asked me, but for Sunday!'

When Terry came home we sorted it out. 'I thought you'd be too busy to organise a party, so I invited just a few friends for drinks,' he explained. We decided to hold the party on the Sunday, but to invite our friends to come and help us celebrate throughout the day and evening, whenever they had time. This idea worked very well, with the first guests arriving at ten in the morning and the last going home at three the following morning, but as they were spread out over so many hours we had time to spend with them all and it was a very happy relaxed birthday party. It also went on a little longer than we had planned as, in the confusion of trying to organise all I had to do, I forgot to tell the change of date to the original people I had invited for the Saturday night!

They were very hectic days. I had to unpack and wash all my Everest clothes; plan and prepare the food for the party; and repack all my mountain equipment again, because two days after Terry's birthday I was off to Pakistan to have another try at climbing Nanga Parbat. This was an unexpected expedition as, although Kurt and I had known that it was a possibility before we left for Everest, while we were away we were led to believe that it would not happen. Some Austrian mountaineers had come to visit our Base Camp in Tibet and told us that Peter Habeler, the Nanga Parbat leader, had cancelled the trip. When Kurt got home to Italy, there was a letter waiting for him. 'We have left for Pakistan on 2 June. Please catch us up as soon as possible!' Peter had written.

It was not an opportunity to be turned down: a second and this time a real chance to climb Nanga Parbat, in such good company and, with our present level of fitness and acclimatisation from Everest, we could make it the shortest expedition possible. The only problem was finding a way to finance it, as we would obviously have to pay our share and each contribute a fifth of the cost of the mountain fee and the Liaison Officer, as well as finding our air fares, food costs, porter's fees, etc. I estimated that I would need about £1,500 for my share. Normally I finance my expeditions from my filming fees, but for this trip there was no time to try to find a television company that might be interested in making a documentary. Kurt would get a small amount from Austrian television for some footage to be included in a film about his life, which would help, but I needed an instant fairy godmother. I racked my brains; there had to be a way. I had never needed to find a personal sponsor before, but knew it was difficult and time-consuming. Then I remembered the Alison Chadwick Trust. Alison was a brilliant mountaineer and had been Britain's highest woman for many years, after reaching 26,098 feet on Gasherbrum III in August 1975. Tragically she had died in an avalanche on Annapurna in 1978 and a trust fund was set up to commemorate her courage and to help other women who wanted to try to reach such heights.

A year previously I had received a letter from the Trust offering me assistance to finance an expedition, but I had written back, with grateful thanks, explaining that I had a film commission for Everest and I felt that a more worthy cause should benefit. Now I could really use their help. I finally tracked down John Fowler, the Trust secretary, who was very kind and extremely efficient, and before I left I knew that I would be able to repay the £1,000 that I had borrowed from various sources. Many times on the mountain I sent my heartfelt thanks to the Alison Chadwick Trust and those generous people who had donated funds which made my return to Nanga Parbat possible.

We had booked ourselves onto the first available flight and, just ten days after leaving Peking, we arrived in Pakistan. I think we had travelled so far so fast that we caught up with ourselves and I did not suffer from jet lag.

We wasted no more time than necessary in hot Islamabad, buying supplies and completing the official requirements. As an Austrian, Kurt had to register with the police and we had to get insurance for our approach march porters. We were held up an extra day as Friday – their Sunday – intervened and everything was shut, but in four days we were on our way, driving the six hundred miles to the start of the walk-in Base Camp in a taxi. Kurt and I were to be a self-sufficient mini-expedition within another mini-expedition consisting of Peter Habeler, Michel Dacher, another famous German climber who has climbed eight of the world's highest mountains, and Udo Zehetleitner, a friend of Michel and Peter.

Crammed inside and on top of the taxi we had everything we would need to eat, live in, film with and use to climb the mountain. It was a great contrast to the truckloads of gear that had accompanied us to Everest Base Camp. It felt very exciting to set out this way.

The Karakoram Highway is no motorway, but it is an incredible achievement for the combined Chinese and Pakistan road builders, and has many hazards of switch-back bends – often with mind-blowing drops to the Indus river far below – frequent stonefall from loose cliffs above, jay-walking herds of goats, and unexpected road works marked only by a few stones lying in the road. Many of the drivers are very tired after driving in the heat and dust for long distances and most vehicles would never pass an MOT test. Consequently it is a dangerous road, but a fascinating one to travel.

Coming back we hitched a ride on a petrol tanker to Islamabad. After travelling for about an hour, the driver offered me the wheel. It was quite an experience to handle such a truck on this road. I felt very important as I swung it round bend after hairpin bend, hooting furiously. It was the newest, smartest lorry in the Pakistan Oil Company's fleet, and had DANGER written in very large letters across the back. I had always nurtured an ambition to drive a vehicle with air brakes, but never imagined that I would do so with such an impressive vehicle on the Karakoram Highway.

At four in the morning we arrived in our taxi at Bunar Bridge, a desolate little row of one-roomed shops, like a tiny Western outpost on a deserted road stretching for uninhabited miles in either direction. By six o'clock we had organised seven porters and started the walk-in to Base Camp. Our route followed barren brown mountainsides, a steep river gorge and finally a long valley, with Nanga Parbat sitting like a king on a throne at the end.

We tried very hard to cut the approach march down to two days, or three at the most; but although it was no problem to make it shorter, our porters refused to allow this, even though we promised to pay them for four days' work however long it took. It was very frustrating trying to keep them going, especially when they insisted on stopping at twelve noon in order to get ready to pray at three o'clock. We knew that Peter and his friends might have already climbed the mountain, or be very close to doing so, and then we would be too late to join in. I found the walk-in much easier and more enjoyable than it had been with the French expedition, and it seemed shorter, but I had a lot of unused energy and fitness left over from Everest.

When we arrived at the Base Camp, our friends were still up on the mountain, and we spent what was left of the day unpacking and sorting out our food and equipment. Two of our porter loads consisted of food and fuel sufficient for four weeks. We had brought only the most essential dehydrated food from Britain, and discovered that we could buy most things in Rawalpindi at more or less the same price. Without the cost of excess baggage, it was a big saving. For Base Camp we had tins of meat, vegetables and fruit, rice, spaghetti, even olive oil.

For carrying to the mountain camps we had packet soups, Oxo cubes, tea, coffee, chocolate, salami, powdered potato, muesli and dried fruit, a simple but sufficiently varied diet.

We put our tent on the same spot that we had used in 1982. New grass and forget-me-nots covered the site. Several other expeditions were climbing the mountain at the same time this year. Mountaineers from Japan, France and the four Polish women, Wanda, Krystyna, Anna and 'Mrufka', who had been with us on the Swiss K2 expedition in 1984, had tents scattered about the meadows. When we arrived they were all away climbing on Nanga Parbat.

At four o'clock in the morning of the day after we had reached Base Camp we set off, hoping to go straight to Camp 2 at 6,000 metres, a climb of 7,000 feet. Of all the 8,000-metre peaks, Nanga Parbat has the greatest distance from the Base Camp to summit: more than thirteen thousand feet of climbing to reach the top. A local legend explains the attraction of this mountain for climbers from all over the world. There is a beautiful lake on the summit, the story goes, and in the centre of the lake a very special tree which is bedecked with precious jewels. The second half of the legend explains why so many people have died on Nanga Parbat – it has now claimed 56 lives, more than any other mountain. Many strangers from all over the world come in search of the jewels, it is said, but the tree is guarded by evil spirits which live on the mountain and they try to kill anyone who is audacious enough to try to reach these treasures. Echoing this legend, we had called our first film on Nanga Parbat with the French expedition *Les Envoûtés de Nanga Parbat*, The Bewitched of Nanga Parbat – very appropriately.

We were to have plenty of experience of those evil spirits later, but on our first attempt it was over-ambition that slowed us down. We were carrying very large heavy rucksacks, with enough camping equipment and food to survive for eight days on the mountain. We had a crazy dream of climbing the mountain in Alpine style on our first attempt. Although we were in good physical shape from Everest, we had both lost a lot of weight and had had little time to catch up with our eating before setting off again. This made us weaker and slower carrying such big loads, and the melting heat, which we had not had to cope with in Tibet, made us tire even more.

As darkness fell we reached the foot of the Kinshoffer Wall, a steep, almost vertical, rock section which you climb using awk-wardly placed wire ladders. We abandoned one rucksack there to make us faster to reach the camp which is just above this difficult obstacle, and we arrived in total darkness seventeen and a half hours after leaving Base Camp.

Nanga Parbat is an unrelentingly steep mountain. The climbing was interesting and varied, but that day snow conditions had been like sticky porridge continually balling up our crampons and on one section we had been bombarded with stones falling from above. Later the following day we retrieved our rucksack from the bottom of the Kinshoffer Wall and the day after caught up with Peter, Michel and Udo at Camp 3 at 6,800 metres.

All the expeditions were retreating back to Base Camp. Some of the French and Japanese had reached the summit after two and a half months of trying, but Peter's group and the Polish women were on their way down for a rest. Perhaps they were wise, for the next day bad weather prevented us from going higher. On the following day, Kurt and I decided to carry on and spent our fifth night on the mountain at Camp 4 at 7,200 metres. During the hours of darkness a storm blew up and we got no sleep. We had to spend the night punching and kicking the heavily falling snow off our tiny tunnel tent in case its weight broke the thin fabric. The following morning was very windy and we stayed put, hoping that conditions would improve. We both began to suffer from strange headaches, the like of which neither of us had experienced before, but as aspirins and sleep cured them, we did not worry. Later in the day it snowed again and all night strong winds rattled and tore at the tent.

After that traumatic night sunshine woke us, and we had almost repacked everything when Peter Habeler arrived. He and Michel had gone back up to Camp 2 the previous day in just four and a half hours, and planned to go straight on to Camp 5 the following day, which they did. As all their gear was already in the camps on the mountain they did not have to carry much, but nevertheless it was an incredible feat to climb so far, so fast, on such a steep mountain. It was an exceptional speed which had never been achieved before. We followed Peter's lithe figure along the featureless ascending traverse leading into the Bazhin cwm, in the centre of which, below the summit roof of the mountain, was Camp 5, at 7,400 metres. It was good to see that someone had taken the trouble to mark the best route with some flags. But where were the tents? We could see no sign of them. Eventually Peter stopped in the distance. Then he started digging into the snow slope.

'The whole camp has been buried by a huge snow slide,' he explained when we caught up with him. It must have been a heartbreaking discovery, but he was luckier than Michel and the Polish girls as he did manage to find his sleeping bag and foam mattress after uncovering part of his demolished tent by digging four feet down in the hard-packed snow. The women, when they arrived several hours later, could not even ascertain where their tents were, as the whole slope had changed in appearance.

Peter and Michel were determined not to have their summit bid thwarted and dug themselves a snow hole to shelter in for the night. The smallest Polish girl, Mrufka, fitted herself in as well. The other three women had to go back down to Camp 3. The next day the two men reached the summit in record time. Peter and Michel are both extraordinary mountaineers. Mrufka tried too, but after getting quite high had to give up and make a frightening and dramatic solo retreat in a storm.

Kurt and I also made a summit bid that day, but were still weak and tired from the sleepless nights of storms at Camp 4. We realised that we were moving too slowly to reach the summit and get down to the safety of the camp in daylight, so at 25,000 feet we made a depot by fixing a rucksack to a rock and went back down the long slope to our tent.

On the morning of 13 July, we awoke to discover that a foot of fresh snow had fallen during the night. This gave us a good reason to have a rest day. Living in a tiny tent high up on a mountain is not as romantic as it might sound. It is cramped, uncomfortable and condensation from the frost which forms at night inside the tent drips on everything as it thaws. Living at such close quarters for hours on end can make or break friendships. A tidy person can be driven mad by sharing a tent with someone who is not, and a companion who fidgets or snores all night is infuriating. Social barriers and conventional inhibitions are quickly broken down because climbing situations make this imperative. Things that niggle are better discussed. The façade we try to protect ourselves with socially crumbles and you are exposed as yourself – warts and all!

Sex is one of the last things that you think about, and young mountaineers get worried when even thinking about their girlfriends fails to excite them. Of course there are some 'superman' exceptions, but I once heard Urs warn someone it could be extremely dangerous to exert yourself physically to such an extent above twenty thousand feet, while the poor girl could easily die of suffocation!

On the 14th we tried again for the summit and left our tent at the early hour of four-thirty. It was a bitterly cold morning. By the time we reached the depot place my feet were freezing. When I took off my boots to check them, they were an ominous white and I spent two hours trying to massage some life back into them. Kurt, too, was feeling strange. He felt disorientated, as if his head were split in many directions. Later we found that he had taken two vascular dilators, used by mountaineers to improve circulation, by mistake for aspirins when he felt a headache coming on before dawn. Michel had given him the packet of aspirins but forgot to warn him that the dilators were tucked inside. At least his feet were warm!

It was disappointing to have to go down from our high point, just 1,500 feet below the summit, especially as it was Lindsay's birthday and I had wanted to reach the top as a special present for her. But we had been living high on the mountain for ten days, and it had taken its toll. (We had lived above 20,000 feet for 52 days this year.)

On our way back down to Base Camp we decided to depot a rucksack of gear by tying it to a sheltering rock below Camp 4, ready for our next try. We did not want to risk losing all our equipment in another avalanche at Camp 5. I sat on top of the seven-foot-high rock as Kurt fixed the pack to a piton. This contained everything we did not need to carry for the way down. Wanda, the leader of the Polish women, joined us at this exposed place as we were carrying out this manoeuvre. She was on her way back up to Camp 5.

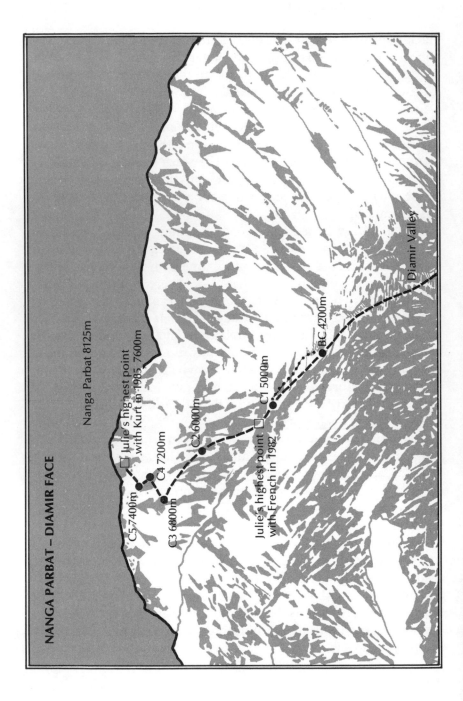

NANGA PARBAT – DIAMIR FACE

Nanga Parbat 8125m

Julie's highest point
with Kurt in 1985 7600m

C5 7400m

C4 7200m

C3 6800m

C2 6000m

Julie's highest point
with French in 1982

C1 5000m

B.C. 4200m

Diamir Valley

'I'm ready for the other rucksack now,' Kurt said, as he had kindly volunteered to carry this load on down. I handed it down to him but, just as I thought he would take it, Wanda spoke to him, and at the same moment it fell from my glove-encased hand, hit him on the head and bounced slowly, once ... twice ... three times across the snow-covered ledge and fell over the edge of the mountain out of our sight. Thank goodness Kurt was tied on the rock or he might have followed it. The rucksack had fallen over a point where the mountain dropped for 6,000 feet down to the glacier. I cannot explain how or why I let go of it. Normally we are both so careful when handing things to each other, especially film equipment.

'Have you got it?'

'Yes, I've got it!'

'Are you sure?'

'Yes, it's OK,' is the standard dialogue between us before we let go of anything we are passing. The evil spirits of the legend had partially won that round. In the rucksack were our two sleeping bags, down jackets, my down trousers, a headtorch, a Leica camera and all the movie film we had taken on the mountain.

At first we felt devastated, but when we analysed the true loss it was only the movie film that was irreplaceable; everything else we could most likely borrow from other expeditions at Base Camp. I was far more upset about dropping the rucksack than losing the gear inside it. On a mountain there is no excuse for carelessness.

Back down in our tent on the meadow which was now flooded with flowers of all colours and lush green grass, we slept and ate and ate. We were still underweight from the Everest expedition. I had shed a stone and a half and my bones had lost enough padding to make it uncomfortable to sleep on hard ground. Kurt always loses a standard twenty kilos. He blames his normal 90-kilo rotund bear-like physique on the good Italian pasta he eats so much of when he is at home, but apart from the inconvenience of having to carry different-sized trousers the extra weight does not appear to have any detrimental effect on his physical abilities. High-altitude mountaineering is not a good slimming method, however, as when we get back to civilisation we are always ravenous and eat twice as much as normal, never feeling full up or satisfied for long.

We had hoped to go back to the mountain after two days' rest, but incessant rain made this impossible. We were now again in the same difficult position as we had been the previous year with the Swiss K2 expedition and on Everest. Peter and Michel had climbed the mountain and wanted to go home. Udo had already left earlier. Three of the Polish women, Wanda, Krystyna, and Anna, had made the top the day after our second try and they too were ready to leave. The French and Japanese expeditions had departed ten days before. So even if we could persuade our Liaison Officer to allow us to stay on by ourselves, if only to re-film some of the climb and try to find our lost rucksack, we would be totally on our own with no chance of any help if we got into trouble on the mountain.

Peter, Michel and the Austrian Liaison Officer went back first and the nice young Army captain who was acting for the first time as a Liaison Officer, for the Polish, adopted us and our problem. He was very understanding. Once again we wrote undertakings to take responsibility for our actions, to help to calm the authorities in the Ministry of Tourism who would obviously worry about our not having a Government representative to look after us and make sure that we adhered to their rules.

Before they left Peter and Michel lent us enough gear to replace what we had lost in the rucksack, and the Polish girls very kindly left one tent and some depots of food for us on the mountain. In the short time we spent with Peter and Michel, I came to like them enormously. This was their first expedition together and they got on so well that they formed a partnership for future climbs which should make them world-beaters in this area of the toughest mountaineering. Their previous individual success has not made them aloof or arrogant; they are both honest, sincere, talented men who I feel are climbing mountains for the right reasons and not just for exploitation and fame.

We had left Camp 5 on 15 July for our short rest at Base Camp, and on the 24th we set up our tent again on the high snow plateau beneath the summit peak. We felt very fit and strong and looked forward with great hope to tackling the summit the next day.

There was a lot of strong wind during the night which made it difficult to tell whether snow was actually falling or whether it was spindrift blowing down from the Bazhin Gap and piling up against the walls of the tent. It was not possible to unzip the door for long enough to look for the stars, which would answer the question, as the whirling snowflakes blew inside in a flurrying cloud, making a wet mess on our sleeping bags and clothing.

Another sleepless night was spent trying to prevent the heavy snow from piling up against the mountain side of the tent. This could collapse our shelter or push us off the slope into which we had dug the tent platform. The consistency of the snow had changed. It was impossible to go outside with such a storm raging to dig out our refuge, and we had constantly to push from the inside and try to channel the icy beads of snow along the side of the tent to the gap at the end where they could funnel down the slope.

A quick glimpse out at first light told us the worst. The summit rocks were barely visible beneath a blanket of white. It had been snowing during the night, and heavy white flakes were still falling.

There was no decision to be made; the only choice was to go down, and as quickly as possible. We stuffed only the most essential things into our rucksacks and, abandoning everything else, and the tent, set off across the steep side of the snow plateau. We would be in danger of avalanches for the whole length of the descent. It is at times like this that knowing your companion is a great help. I trust Kurt's judgement implicitly and know his strengths and weaknesses as well as my own, just as he does mine. We took it in turns to lead this featureless section, which took us five hours. All our tracks had been obliterated and a step either side of where our previous trail had solidified the old snow left us floundering thigh deep. To extract ourselves was like trying to get out of a bog, and very exhausting.

We were in the silent fog of white-out which would clear now and then for a second giving a glimpse of the next marker flag in the distance. When I was leading I would fix my eye in the direction I had seen it, but instead of walking in a straight line I would constantly drift uphill. When Kurt led he did the same thing. It was very frustrating for the person behind who could see what was happening, and we started guiding each other with shouts from the rear.

Making our way along the fixed rope traverse leading to Camp 3 was laborious. The angle of the slope was severe, and the stretchy ropes strung across in long arcs did not give much helpful support as our legs sank into the deep snow. We reached the tent left at Camp 3 at two in the afternoon, seven hours after leaving Camp 5. We sat in the welcome sanctuary and made ourselves tea and soup. It was still snowing. During the afternoon the snowfall got heavier and at four we decided to make a dash for Camp 2, which was a better place to stay the night. This section of the route is endless and the gradient is steep. Rope after rope had to be pulled out from under the snow and once a small avalanche shot down, burying my legs in seconds. For the rest of the day I looked up constantly, but even if I had spotted another avalanche descending there was little I could do in such an exposed place.

It was dusk when we stumbled into Camp 2 at seven-thirty. We had abandoned our Camp 5 tent twelve and a half hours earlier. Here we were very thankful for the tent left by the Polish women, which sat on a minute ledge on the edge of rocky rib. That night we slept well.

A fine morning greeted us when we emerged from the tent, but eight inches of fresh snow covered everything and the snowfalls of the past few days had extended a long way down the mountain, far farther than we had expected. Precipitation often falls as snow on the higher sections and as rain lower down, and sometimes clouds only empty themselves at certain levels. It was bad news for us that there was so much avalanche-prone unstable new snow sitting on the side of Nanga Parbat which, on this fine morning, could be triggered to slide off by the warmth of the sun. However, we could not move on down until the sun reached the long ladder sections on the Kinshoffer Wall, as we knew that all the ropes would be heavily iced-in and unusable. We started down at nine-thirty, and I could hear Kurt grunting with effort and worry below as he struggled to dig the ropes out of the thick waterfalls of ice that encased them. When he did free them they were unmanageably stiff and the coating of ice that remained made the 'figure of eight' difficult to control. My gloves were soaking wet and inside my fingers were numb with cold by the time I reached the foot of these sheer rock walls.

We took no rest, just kept on going down and down. The sun was getting higher and hotter and the slopes of the Great Couloir below were the most dangerous place for avalanches.

Kurt was twenty feet down the second rope on the Face when, silently, the first avalanche slid down. He was in its path. It rode over him and then carried on down and he was left as a white lump until he shook himself free. 'Don't worry,' he called up to me. 'If they're all like that one they will not harm us. As long as the ropes don't break we can survive. But watch carefully while I go down and give me a shout if you see another one coming.'

When I caught up with Kurt at the end of the third rope we had a short rest under a rock overhang. 'I think that most of the new stuff must have already come down this part,' he observed. 'Look, there are wide avalanche channels everywhere.' Just ten feet away from me the top surface of the snow had been swept off to a depth of nine inches leaving a broad gully, as flood water does in mud.

'At least we can see where they will come, if they do,' I commented.

We moved on slowly, one watching, one moving. The ropes were even more difficult to pull out from under the snow here. These steep 70° slopes had metamorphosed in the warmer temperature of the lower altitude and the snow was more compacted. Every few minutes a snow slide would shoot down, like chunks of white coke down a coal shute, but they were not big enough to worry us. Half an hour later it was very different.

Whoosh! An enormous waterfall of snow fell over a tall rock pillar five hundred feet above us. By the time it had gathered all the snow in its path it was like a torrent ready to engulf anything in its way. Then there was another like a billowing cloud, then another. They kept coming. The smaller ones sounded like rumbling explosions as they came over the rocks. The noise was in stereo sound as they fell over all sides of the rock amphitheatre at full volume. The larger ones spilt with an ominous silence. There was no way to judge when they would come. From 6,000 feet above us vast quantities of snow were starting to slide down the mountain. The Great Couloir is shut in on three sides by huge rock walls over which these rivers of snow were cascading to funnel down the 200-foot-wide snowfield. We were caught in the perfect trap. We had to traverse long sections of these dangerous chutes three times during the descent.

Often, to make it faster for me to come down, Kurt dug out the intermediate anchors on each rope length. These minimise the stretch in the rope on the way up, but take precious seconds to change from one side to the other on the way down. It was an agonising wait as he made his way slowly down. Schhhht! Another avalanche shot past him on one side. Whoosh! That one came so close to me that I was wet with the spray.

We had another brief rest under the next big rock and sucked thirstily at some icicles which hung down like transparent stalactites. The beneficial effect of drinking that ice was soon negated by the water which had dripped from the icicles and refrozen. Our ropes were set in the middle of the solid mass. Kurt chipped them out, taking care not to damage the fibres with his ice axe. Inch by inch he tapped patiently away. It was too risky to go even ten feet down without the security of the rope.

We had traversed the face twice under sporadic fire and I was about to start on the third and final crossing when all hell broke lose. I had watched Kurt safely cross all three rope lengths and he was sheltering under the rocky cliff on the other side. Now it was my turn. I clipped my carabiner onto the first rope which hung in a too-loose arc across a short gully just fifteen feet wide. This gully was constantly swept by fast-moving rivers of snow. At first I tried to set off immediately a big one had passed, working on the idea that no more snow would be ready to come down for a while, but this theory was rapidly disproved. As I sat huddled under a protecting rock and studied the situation I felt totally isolated. There was little chance that I could get all the way across without at least one avalanche hitting me, and the longer I waited the more stones would be mixed in with the snow, loosened by the heat of the sun.

There was no best time to move as the floods of snow fell with no pattern, so I might as well go now.

I took a deep breath and, as I swung on to the rope, exhaled deeply. I was halfway across when a chute of snow took my feet away. The sight of the fast-moving small chunks made me feel dizzy as they rushed down with the urgent movement of a torrent in full spate. I swung sickeningly with all my weight on the rope; if it broke with the weight of the snow, I would fall thousands of feet to the glacier below. After I had struggled up fifteen feet of slippery ice, I reached the rock island where the next rope was anchored. My legs were shaking. I stood marooned on my sanctuary for several minutes to recover. There was no lull in the avalanches. It seemed as if the whole mountain was alive, was moving. The evil spirits were everywhere around us.

The next bit was the most exposed and strenuous and it took all my control not to rush, which would only make me run out of steam halfway. I concentrated on each foot in turn and inched my way across, subconsciously switching off the noise of the falling snow all around me. I had a short distance to go to the next rock refuge when I saw the stones bouncing down towards me. I stood still and the first four zipped past, but the fifth changed direction and, as I jumped out of the way, hit my trailing left leg.

It was a block about six inches in diameter and the blow made me wince. When I reached the rock I looked at my leg. Luckily the stone had hit me on the fleshy part of the calf which was protected by two pairs of socks and trousers and two pairs of thick overgaiters. Had it caught me on the shin bone I am sure it would have broken my leg. A very large bruise came out several days later and it hurt for a long time.

The rest of the descent was not easy, but was tame by comparison. As we finally came up the dust incline leading out of the glacier to the welcoming green meadows, I looked back at Nanga Parbat sitting peacefully in the late afternoon sun and uncontrollable tears rolled down my cheeks.

I recorded my feelings on my little tape recorder: 'It's like coming back to the world, and life. The flowers seem brighter, the sun warms me to the core, and inside I am myself again, able to smile from the heart.'

That evening as we sat by our tent amongst the forget-me-nots and buttercups, with the birds singing and the marmots whistling to each other in the background, I felt content. 'I don't mind not getting to the top,' I confided to Kurt. 'It really doesn't matter.'

'No, I feel the same way,' he said quietly. 'You see, it was like reaching the summit, just to get down safely. This time this is our summit . . . to be here.'

I turned and looked back up at Nanga Parbat, painted mauve and red by the rays of the dying sun. I had reached the clouds and climbed through them, going up and coming down. We had met the evil spirits of Nanga Parbat and had survived; we had a future. This time I was content. 'There are no winners or losers,' is a martial arts philosophy. 'The challenge is only within yourself.'

18

The final summit

by Peter Gillman

When Julie came home from Nanga Parbat, arriving at the Bothy at Leyswood on August 9th, she was already talking of her next project. She and Kurt wanted to make a film for Austrian television about the life of Tashigan, a village in one of the high mountain valleys of Nepal. It was, as ever, an immensely busy period: Julie was buzzing with new ideas and the phone would ring constantly – usually several times a day from Kurt in Vienna. For Terry, there was little to do but stand aside, offering encouragement and assistance where he could. Julie visited Kurt in Vienna several times and in November went with him to Nepal to shoot the first part of the film, which was intended to portray Tashigan at two different seasons of the year.

At Christmas, 1985, Julie and Terry flew to New York. At first Julie had been unable to enjoy the pure indolence of a holiday but after a few days she relaxed. She and Terry took a Greyhound bus to Las Vegas where they hired a car and spent Christmas Day in Death Valley. They moved on to California and Colorado, returning to Leyswood in early January. Life for Julie promptly resumed its usual frenetic pattern. She was planning lectures, talking of future schemes, and trying to complete her book. To Terry, who had provided her with a large measure of financial support over the previous six years, it seemed as if they were reaching a plateau of security at last.

Then Julie broached a new project: she and Kurt were planning a third visit to their 'mountain of mountains', K2. Kurt was negotiating with an Italian expedition hoping to climb K2 in July and with a Frankfurt production company interested in filming the Italians' attempt. The arrangements remained fluid until the last moment, but finally Julie told Terry that after making the second half of their film in Nepal she and Kurt would be travelling direct to Pakistan and K2.

Parting, in the Tullis household, was a frequent event; but somehow Julie and Terry never got used to it. It was Terry who left the Bothy first, as he was helping to escort a school group on a skiing trip to Austria three days before Julie was due to depart for Nepal. Early that morning Julie drove him to Eridge station. 'We were always very emotional when we said goodbye,' Terry recalls. They both cried.

Julie left London on March 22nd. Seven days later she and Kurt flew north from Kathmandu to the tiny grass airstrip of Tumlingtar where the five-day trek to Tashigan began. In the following month they made a colourful record of life in the area. They filmed the farmers planting maize on the steep hillsides, weaving fibre from nettles, and making butter, flour and the corruscating local brew known as *chang*. Although it rained or snowed almost every day, Julie maintained her customary enthusiasm for the task in hand, while also relishing her dramatic surroundings. As she told Terry, in an account composed for his benefit, she began writing her diary sitting on a rock warmed by the early morning sun, with 'towering granite cliffs, topped by snow-capped mountains,' all around.

At times Julie's thoughts strayed elsewhere. She and Kurt could not resist the tempatation to visit the base camp below Makalu, which Kurt had climbed in 1978. After a two-day walk they were rewarded with a perfect view of Everest 20 miles away, where they had been only a year before. From Everest, Julie looked ahead to K2. She was disconcerted to find that as the result of an insect-bite at Karachi airport during the flight to Nepal she had lost the sensation in two of her fingers. 'I am now very worried about my chances on K2,' she confided.

By May 1st, with filming almost complete, Julie's thoughts were back with Terry. 'This place is like a huge wild Leyswood garden, the rhododendrons are fantastic, red, pink and yellow and so big,' she told him. 'I wish you could see it.' She also wished she could come home before going on to K2. 'But there is no way it works.'

Julie and Kurt joined the Italian expedition in Rawalpindi on May 15th. To her delight, Julie found that she knew five of the climbers from the 1983 expedition to K2. 'This expedition seems to be the best we could have joined,' she wrote. For two film-makers hoping to record an ascent of K2, the Italian team indeed seemed ideal. It included several strong climbers from other European countries and formed part of an enterprise known as 'Quota 8000' which was aiming to climb all fourteen 8,000-metre peaks in the Himalayas within five years. They had climbed several of the peaks already and two – the Italian leader, Agostino da Polenza, and a Czech named Josef Rakoncaj – had even climbed K2 before. Julie found them splendid company and particularly admired their devotion to the task of searching for alcohol in a Moslem country. 'They enjoy themselves whatever they are doing.'

The journey to K2 had an inauspicious beginning. First there was a breakneck 24-hour ride to the town of Skardu in a bus which, Julie observed, seemed to have been designed for midgets, while Kurt's discomfort was aggravated by flu. Skardu was crowded with other climbers and they were compelled to spend their first night on the floor of a hotel lobby. Then they learned that at least eight other expeditions were bound for K2, creating an immediate shortage of porters. The Italians were keen to get ahead of a large German team and so Julie and Kurt left Skardu at 3 A.M. on May 25th. A jeep took them 40 miles to the village of Dassu where the long approach march began. The next day Julie opened a new diary with the words: 'So we are on our way to K2.'

Julie enjoyed the next two weeks. She and Kurt had five porters of their own and with Kurt still recovering from flu, they let the Italian party forge ahead. 'It's strange how the urge is to rush to Base Camp like a bunch of lemmings,' Julie observed. Despite a catalogue of minor ailments, from a sore achilles tendon to the persistent numbness in her fingertips, she considered it the most enjoyable approach march she had made. They passed the foot of the Baltoro glacier, 44 miles below the K2 Base Camp, on June 2nd. The next day they decided to wait for 24 hours at a grassy slope named Urdokas in the hope of filming the German expedition as it passed. On the far side of the glacier soared the Cathedral and the Trango Towers, two of the most majestic peaks in the Karakoram. Julie and Kurt had filmed there in 1984: 'I love this place,' Julie wrote.

Julie and Kurt reached the Base Camp on June 7th. The weather had been grey but beyond Concordia, the confluence of the Baltoro and Godwin-Austen glaciers, the clouds parted and K2 rose before them with enticing clarity against a brilliant blue sky. When they rounded the final bend and saw a line of tents ranged along the glacier moraine, Julie wrote, 'It felt like arriving at a second home.' The Italians greeted them with exuberant hugs and led them into their dining-tent, an 'Aladdin's cave' lined with hams, cheeses, pastas, vegetables, fruit, exotic biscuits and sweets. That evening, after living off tea and chapatis for two weeks, Julie ate far too much. 'I was sick all night and slept all the next day.'

By mid-June no fewer than ten expeditions were camped below K2, aiming to reach the summit via four different routes. There were four teams – from Austria, France, South Korea and the Basque region of Spain – who were hoping to climb the Abruzzi Ridge, which Kurt and Julie had attempted in 1984. A further four – the Italian group to which Kurt and Julie were attached, an American group, a Polish team of men and women, and the Italian solo climber Renato Casarotto – were to attempt K2's South-South-West Ridge. The ninth, an international expedition led by the veteran Dr Karl Herligkoffer, was trying the South Face. The tenth, a strong British party, was attempting the immensely long and difficult North-West Ridge, which forms Pakistan's border with China. Of the four routes, only the Abruzzi Ridge had been climbed before.

For Kurt and Julie, the international gathering brought happy reunions with climbers they had encountered elsewhere, such as the Basques they had met in tragic circumstances on Everest in 1985, and three Polish women they had met on K2 in 1984 and again on Nanga Parbat in 1985. Despite the possible rivalry over the routes on K2, the atmosphere at Base Camp was remarkably free of any competitive edge. Yet there was a chilling undertone that some of the climbers sensed, most notably among the British expedition which had camped slightly apart from the main group. Close by was the memorial cairn to Art Gilkey, the American who had died on K2 in 1954, and Nick Estcourt, the British climber killed by an avalanche in 1978, which also served as a reminder of the inevitable risks of Himalayan mountaineering.

'It was a thought that occurred to most of us,' says Jim Curran, a climber and cameraman with the British team. 'There were 60-odd climbers there and we would be remarkably lucky if there wasn't a death. It was as if we were waiting for the first one to happen.'

Julie and Kurt spent their first week at K2 in frustrating inactivity. The weather closed in again and with nine inches of snow falling at Base Camp they were unable to film higher than Camp 1 on the SSW Ridge. Both succumbed to further ailments – Julie developed a racking cough, Kurt had stomach pains and diarrhoea – and among the waiting climbers the delay bred short tempers and the occasional row.

On June 19th, the weather cleared and Julie and Kurt decided to film on the Abruzzi Ridge. Despite a heavy load and the unaccustomed sun, Julie was encouraged to find that she was reasonably fit. At Camp 1 they met the Basque team who were delighted when Julie said she was confident they would succeed.

The Basques set off on their summit bid on June 20th. Julie and Kurt followed them to a ledge below House's Chimney, the principal obstacle on the lower section of the ridge, where they deposited a load. They returned to Base Camp that night to learn that four members of the Italian team had climbed Broad Peak, opposite K2 across the glacier, which Julie and Kurt had climbed in 1984. They celebrated with tea and biscuits, and that night Julie slept 'like a log'.

The morning brought grim news. At ten-to-six, the slope below Camp 2 on the SSW Ridge had been raked by a massive windslab avalanche, the consequence of the heavy snowfall over the previous week. Four Italian climbers had been at Camp 3 and had escaped. But the Americans had been moving up behind them and two, John Smolich, the expedition leader, and Allen Pennington, had been killed. Pennington's body was buried at the Gilkey cairn the following day and Julie wrote: 'The glacier village is a mixture of emotions – extreme sadness, and worry for those still up.'

Among the Italians, the accident prompted a change of plans. Concluding that the SSW Ridge was too dangerous, they decided to switch to the Abruzzi Ridge, launching their first attempt on the 8,611-metre summit the next day. They reached 7,850 metres before turning back in the face of fresh storms and on June 25th reached Camp 1 where Julie and Kurt were waiting. But they had more distressing news to impart.

On June 23rd the entire French team, comprising the married couple Maurice and Liliane Barrard, Michel Parmentier, and the Polish woman Wanda Rutkiewicz, had reached the summit, followed soon afterwards by the Basque pair Mari Abrego and Josema Casimiro. However, on June 24th, in the same storms that drove the Italians back, the Barrards had fallen behind and disappeared. Liliane's body was eventually discovered at the foot of the face but her husband's was never found. Julie was stunned: 'A major tragedy,' she tautly recorded. Earlier, in one of the prescient asides she was given to make, she had noted the Barrards' determination that Liliane should be the first woman to climb K2. 'I only hope they don't kill themselves in the attempt.'

On July 3rd, after five more days of storms and snow, the Italians launched their next attempt. Julie and Kurt moved up the Abruzzi Ridge with their climbing and filming equipment too and on July 5th pitched their tent on a broad snow shoulder at 8,000 metres. From there they watched six members of the Italian expedition climb the final 600 metres to the summit. They included the Czech, Josef Rakoncaj, who thus became the first person to make two ascents of K2, and the Frenchman, Benoît Chamoux, who accomplished the entire climb in an astonishing 23 hours, and they were followed by two Swiss members of the international expedition led by Karl Herligkoffer. As they came down, Julie plied them with soup and tea: 'We were brewing until after 9 P.M., they really appreciated it.'

306

The next day – 'a little cheeky', Julie admitted, as they had not previously gone above 6,300 metres – she and Kurt made their own summit attempt. They left at six o'clock and made steady progress through the narrow rock and ice funnel known as the Bottleneck. But above the Bottleneck, on an awkward ice traverse below an enormous overhanging serac, they 'wasted about an hour,' according to Julie, when they strayed from their route and had to place two pitons for protection. By the time they reached the final 300-metre snow slope below the summit it was four o'clock; the sun had disappeared and it was suddenly bitterly cold. After the briefest of discussions they turned back, and survived an anxious three-hour descent, belaying each other on the steepest sections. 'Kurt started to get slower and slower going down the Bottleneck,' Julie wrote, 'and on the interminable slope to the tent was walking a little like a drunk, his legs felt wooden.'

Julie and Kurt waited for 24 hours in their tent in the hope of making a second attempt. Instead, on July 8th, they found themselves fighting for their lives. As they descended in a gathering storm, the wind tore at their clothing and they had to wait for up to ten minutes in the frequent white-outs for the visibility to improve. Kurt was immensely relieved to pass the section where the Barrards were assumed to have fallen and they sheltered for a while in a tent left by the Italians at 7,750 metres. Then came a long, featureless slope scoured by the wind and made more hazardous by a sudden 'desperately slippery' patch of blue ice that was obscured by snow. They came upon three tents at Camp 3 at 7,350 metres and gratefully slid into the sleeping bags they found inside.

The morning, with the storm blowing at full fury, brought further trials. The fixed ropes below Camp 3 were tangled and shrouded with ice, and it was increasingly hard to unravel them with fingers becoming 'worryingly numb'. They found Camp 2 at 6,700 metres half-buried by snow and so continued down House's Chimney. At its foot they found another tent – 'thank God' – and crawled inside. Even now they were not safe, for the snow piling up around them threatened to engulf them as well as creating an avalanche risk. But in the middle of the night, Julie wrote, there was nothing to be done. 'There are certain points in mountaineering where all you can do is wait.'

With dawn came relief at last. Outside lay a new world – 'calm, beautiful, quiet' – and Julie and Kurt were able to descend in comparative peace. At Camp 1 they met a group of Koreans who told them there had been considerable anxiety over their safety and at Base Camp climbers poured out of their tents to greet them: 'a very warm home coming,' Julie wrote. But in her diary she admitted that the harrowing descent was giving her considerable food for thought. There were moments, she revealed, 'when I convinced myself that that was it. I was not going all that way back up again. Who really cared if I climbed 300 metres higher on K2 or not?'

Julie's doubts soon deepened, for at Base Camp she learned of yet another death. On July 8th two members of the international expedition attempting the unclimbed South Pillar, the Poles Tadeusz Piotrowski and Jerzy Kukucza, reached the summit. During their descent in the storm that Julie and Kurt had endured, Piotrowski lost both his crampons and then, as Kukucza watched in impotent horror, tumbled down a steep ice slope and disappeared. 'Everyone was devastated by Teddy's death,' Julie wrote.

Six days later came what was for Julie the most painful blow of all. On July 12th the Italian Renato Casarotto set off for the third time up the SSW Ridge, promising his wife Goretta, who was with him in the Base Camp, that it would be his final attempt. On July 16th he turned back less than 400 metres from the summit, intending to reach Base Camp that night. At 7 P.M. Julie heard Goretta shouting hysterically. Barely half an hour from Base Camp and safety, Casarotto had fallen into a crevasse and had radioed to his wife that he was dying.

Kurt, Julie, and five other climbers immediately went to Casarotto's aid. They found him at the foot of a 40-metre crevasse and when an Italian climber abseiled down to him, Casarotto cluched him desperately, 'very relieved but very frightened,' Julie wrote. He had a head injury and by the time he had been extricated from the crevasse he was unconscious. When Julie shone a light into his eyes shortly afterwards there was only the slightest reaction from his pupils. Fifteen minutes later he was dead.

It fell to Julie to console the grief-stricken Goretta. Julie cuddled her throughout the night and tried to comfort her in her improvised Italian. In her next letter Julie told Terry that she had no wish to go through those twenty-four hours again and that she had firmly decided against making another summit bid. 'To get three hours from the top and go down safely means more to me than standing on the summit,' she assured him. 'I have no more pleasure to climb my mountain of mountains.'

In the aftermath of the successive triumphs and disasters, Base Camp, for the next ten days, had an end-of-term atmosphere. Those expeditions which had succeeded were packing up to go home; those which had failed were considering whether they should do the same. Julie and Kurt continued to film but as the Base Camp gradually emptied it began to resemble, in Julie's simile, a ghost town. Among the last to leave, on July 28th, was the bulk of the British expedition, who had given up with little more than half its route climbed. Just two of them stayed behind: their leader, Alan Rouse, and the climber/camerman Jim Curran who remained determined, he said later, 'to see things through.'

No sooner had the British turned the first corner in the glacier than the weather dramatically cleared. The climbers' altimeters showed that the barometric pressure was soaring and that a settled spell was on its way. Now Julie hastily addressed another letter to Terry. 'Chaos is reigning,' she wrote. 'We are rushing off for one more try.'

It was a curiously improvised group which prepared for the new attempt on the Abruzzi Ridge. There were the well-organized South Koreans, with their oxygen and high-altitude porters, who had been assiduously fixing ropes up much of the ridge. Next were the seven Austrians, regarded by the other climbers as tough and determined, if also somewhat taciturn. Then came Alan Rouse who had teamed up with the Polish climber Dobroslawa Wolf, nicknamed for her diminutive size as 'Mrufka', the ant. Finally there were Julie and Kurt. In addition to these teams, the

Polish expedition, sticking to its original objective, was making a summit bid via the SSW Ridge.

Despite Julie's note to Terry, she and Kurt were coy about revealing their true goal, even to each other. Julie told Jim Curran they were merely going to Camp 2 in order to film. According to Kurt, he and Julie had a 'silent agreement' which neither dared articulate. 'We moved up with the equipment for filming,' he says, 'but also with all the necessary gear for a summit attempt.'

Julie and Kurt left Base Camp on July 28th and spent that night at the advance Base Camp at the foot of the ridge. The morning brought 'splendid sunshine', Kurt recalls. After filming the Austrians climbing above them on the ridge, they packed their rucksacks to depart. By now, says Kurt, the ambiguity has been resolved: they would go for the summit. Julie, he adds, acknowledged her own change of heart by saying: 'I know I did not want to go up again, but I have changed my mind'. Most decisively of all they resolved to leave all their filming equipment at Camp 1: the summit was their overriding goal.

Moving as cautiously as ever, they made steady progress from camp to camp, using tents left by previous climbers on the ridge. On July 29th they slept in a Swiss tent at Camp 1 at 6,150 metres; on July 30th, in a Basque tent at Camp 2 at 6,700 metres; on July 31st a French tent at 7,000 metres. They had been carrying their own small bivouac tent but they swapped this for the French tent which they used as their Camp 3 at 7,350 metres on August 1st. On August 2nd they headed for Camp 4, designated the 'assault camp', which was to be at 8,000 metres on the broad snow shoulder below the final summit pyramid.

It was, however, with a sense of foreboding that they approached the site of Camp 4. Before descending from their previous summit attempt in July they had left behind a rucksack which contained a tent, sleeping bags, mattresses, gas cylinders and food. At Camp 3 they had met three of the Koreans' high-altitude porters who had warned them that the shoulder was devoid of equipment. When they reached Camp 4 the warning proved all too true: no sign of their rucksack was to be found. They spent half an hour probing the snow with their ice-axes, but even the ski-poles they had used to anchor the rucksack had disappeared. Other climbers later speculated that the rucksack must have been buried by the three weeks of storms and snow; Kurt darkly wondered whether it had been removed by one of the high-altitude porters.

A greater shock awaited Julie and Kurt at Camp 4. Precisely what occurred there, and how far it bore on the subsequent tragedy, was to become a matter of acute controversy. Almost inevitably, the accounts of the surviving witnesses differ in crucial respects, with each attempting to make the best sense of the harrowing events in which they were involved. At its heart is a dispute over a radio conversation that took place between the Korean and Austrian teams two days before.

When the four sets of climbers left Base Camp on their summit bids via the Abruzzi Ridge, the Austrians had soon forged ahead. They too faced problems over their equipment for they strongly suspected – from the discovery of various items among avalanche debris at the foot of the mountains – that their own Camp 3 had been destroyed. Instead, for their final camp they had been intending to use two tents left by the Italian climbers at 7,750 metres. But when they approached the site of the tents they saw that they too had been swept away.

There was, however, one tent still standing at Camp 3. It belonged to the Korean team which had erected it during its first summit attempt a month before. On July 31st, therefore, the Austrians radioed to the Korean team below them on the ridge. According to the Koreans' leader, Chang Bong-Wan, the Austrians made an offer that was hard to refuse: 'If you lend us your tent at Camp 3 we will set it up at Camp 4. After we reach the summit we will leave the tent as it is.' The Korean team, Chang adds, 'accepted the Austrians' offer'.

By August 2nd there were just three Austrians left on the ridge, their leader, Alfred Imitzer, and his colleagues Hannes Wieser and Willi Bauer, the remaining four having decided to retreat. When Kurt and Julie arrived at Camp 4 that day they could see the three Austrians apparently going for the summit. They had passed the Bottleneck and were fixing ropes on the dangerous ice traverse above. But when the Austrians reached 8,400 metres they turned back and descended to Camp 4. That evening, says

Kurt, 'there was a big argument between everybody'. It turned on whether the Austrians, having made their summit attempt, should descend to Camp 3 and leave the Koreans free to use their tent.

The Austrian Willi Bauer denies that there was an argument and says that the matter was settled amicably enough. 'We arranged it and discussed it with the Koreans,' he says. 'We agreed that the Koreans should go for the summit the next day and we would give them back-up. Then we would swap. When they came back, we would go up. And that's what happened.' Bauer says that the Austrians had fixed the ropes on the ice traverse above the Bottleneck at the Koreans' specific 'wish and request' and denies that they were obliged to descend to Camp 3 that night. 'That would have made no sense.'

But the Koreans' leader, Chang Bong-Wan, confirms Kurt's account. 'After failing to reach the summit the Austrian team asked if they could sleep in our tent,' he says. 'We refused their request as we had to try to reach the summit the following day. But they repeated their request. They begged us. There was no way to escape so two members of the Austrian team slept in our tent. It was very overcrowded. Another Austrian slept in another tent.'

The third Austrian was the expedition leader, Alfred Imitzer, and the tent he slept in belonged to Alan Rouse. Imitzer had first asked Julie and Kurt if he could stay with them, but they refused. Against Julie's protests, since she felt that Rouse was being placed in an impossible position, Imitzer then descended to Rouse's tent some 100 metres below and squeezed in there.

How far these events contributed to the subsequent tragedy is a further matter of controversy. The Koreans had planned to embark on their summit attempt at five o'clock on August 4th. According to Kurt, they did not leave until eight o'clock – and Kurt believes that it was the difficulty of preparing for their departure in an overcrowded tent which caused the delay. The Koreans were using oxygen and Julie and Kurt had planned to follow them, taking advantage of their tracks. Julie and Kurt also planned to climb with Alan Rouse, but he said later that he could not have climbed that day after spending a sleepless night. In any

312

case, says Kurt, by the time the Koreans left, 'We decided the day was lost.'

This time Chang Bong-Wan disputes Kurt's account. Chang says that although the Koreans *did* fall behind schedule the delay occurred not because of the overcrowding but because his companion, Kim Chang-Son, was feeling unwell. Chang adds, crucially, that in any case the Koreans left Camp 4 at six o'clock. They had been expecting Julie and Kurt to follow them, Chang says – 'and we didn't know why they did not.' Whatever the reason, the loss of that day was to prove disastrous.

The three Koreans reached the summit at four o'clock that afternoon. They were joined shortly afterwards by three members of the Polish team which had been advancing steadily up the SSW Ridge, and the six men began to descend together. Then came the seventh death on K2 that summer, when the Pole Wojciech Wroz fell from the ice traverse. (The eighth death occurred the same day, when the leader of the Koreans' porters, Mohammed Ali, was killed by a falling stone near Camp 1.) One of the Korean summit party was benighted and did not reach Camp 4 until the following morning. But the arrival of the four remaining climbers in Camp 4 that night made conditions even more cramped. The two Polish climbers joined Alan Rouse, so that he spent another wretched night, half in and half out of the tent.

In the morning it was Rouse and Mrufka who left for the summit first, at six o'clock. They were followed by Imitzer, Julie and Kurt, and finally Wieser and Bauer. Wieser returned after only 100 metres as his gloves were wet and he was afraid of frostbite. Before long Julie and Kurt, climbing slowly and with their usual caution – they were the only pair who were roped – found themselves last in line.

Bauer reached the summit at 3.15 P.M., followed soon afterwards by Imitzer and Rouse. As they headed back down Rouse met Mrufka, who was visibly flagging, and persuaded her to give up. At around 4.30 P.M., some 100 metres below the summit, Julie and Kurt met the two Austrians, who asked whether they were certain they should go on. The weather was patently deteriorating, with clouds welling up from below and the mountains around becoming grey. As Kurt recalls, 'I said to Julie, "we are very close to the top. It's a question of one hour, shall we do it or shall we not?" The summit was so close and we were feeling good and we went on.'

Soon after 5.30 P.M., Julie and Kurt stood on the summit of their dreams. 'We hugged each other,' says Kurt. 'It was clear, both of us thought it was the most desired peak we could ever get to, we said it was "our K2."' They photographed each other and Kurt picked up a small British flag that Alan Rouse had deposited on the summit and handed it to Julie. By now the light was fading fast and Julie said: 'It's high time we started our descent.'

Two hundred metres below the summit came near-catastrophe. Kurt was in the lead when he heard Julie shout, 'Oh Kurt!' and in the next moment she slithered past at gathering speed. Kurt was wrenched from his stance and as they slid towards a 3,000 metre drop he was convinced they were doomed. By some miracle they stopped, Kurt sitting upright, Julie sprawled in the snow above. 'We were very relieved,' says Kurt. 'It was almost death.'

Their predicament was acute: night was almost upon them, and they had left their bivouac equipment in a rucksack at the top of the fixed ropes. They dug a shallow snowhole at the edge of a crevasse and passed an 'endless night', Kurt says, sucking sweets and hugging each other in an attempt to stay warm. When an ominous dawn broke, bringing with it clouds and a rising wind, Julie was suffering from frostbite on one hand and her nose. 'But she did not complain,' says Kurt, 'and we were in relatively good spirits.' With considerable difficulty, in what soon became a complete white-out, Julie and Kurt found their way back to the fixed ropes and headed for Camp 4. At the foot they stayed roped up and moved in zig-zags to improve their chances of finding the camp. They also started to shout in the hope that someone in the camp would hear.

There were now five climbers left in Camp 4. The Korean and Polish climbers who had reached the summit on August 3rd started their descent the next day, and eventually reached safety. But Alan Rouse, Mrufka, and the three Austrians had been unable to leave on August 5th because the gathering storm had reduced visibility to a few yards. By eleven o'clock that morning they had virtually given up Julie and Kurt for dead. Then the Austrian, Willi Bauer, heard Kurt's shouts and called in response.

When Kurt and Julie heard Bauer they were, says Kurt, 'quite relieved'. Julie, who told Kurt she could not see properly, sank to the ground and crawled the last part of the way. Bauer came out to meet them and helped Julie back to the camp where he took her into his tent. 'Her fingers were frostbitten, as was her face,' he says. 'We gave her hot drinks to try to get her going again. We lit the stove to get the temperature going and after a while she was fit enough to leave the tent.'

At the foot of K2, meanwhile, the climbers in Base Camp were watching the mountain with increasing trepidation. The weather had been breaking down visibly for two days and by August 5th, when four inches of snow fell on the glacier, K2 had disappeared from view. That night the most ferocious storm of the summer broke, and with the wind roaring constantly from K2's higher reaches, Jim Curran felt 'a well of sorrow' for the climbers marooned near the summit.

In Camp 4, the seven climbers were enduring the storm's full fury. Julie rejoined Kurt on the night of August 5th but seemed worried and distracted. She and Kurt awoke to find their tent was on the point of collapsing from the weight of snow. Yelling above the wind, they aroused Rouse and Bauer, who helped them to struggle out. Julie now returned to the Austrians' tent while Kurt joined Rouse and Mrufka. The separation was especially painful to Kurt: the wind was so powerful, he says, 'that even by yelling you could not make yourself heard from tent to tent'.

Later that day, Julie struggled across to Rouse's tent. She told Kurt she had just come to say hello but added, disturbingly, 'I feel rather strange.' Kurt could not see her properly from inside the tent and asked her to bend down. Even then he only glimpsed her hair. 'Be strong,' he told her. 'I think of you.'

In the Austrians' tent, the weight of snow pressing from outside was restricting the space more and more. Julie lay quietly in her sleeping bag – 'she was very undemanding,' Willi Bauer says. But Bauer, who had trained as a nurse while undertaking military service, was painfully aware how every extra hour they were trapped by the storm was putting Julie – and everyone else – more and more at risk.

Julie had already spent four nights at 8,000 metres.. At that height, to compensate for the lack of oxygen, the blood forms extra red corpuscles which causes it gradually to thicken, with potentially lethal results. At the same time the brain accumulates extra liquid which leads to a form of stroke known as a cerebral oedema. Dehydration increases these dangers and Julie had been weakened further by the frostbite and hypothermia she had suffered during her enforced bivouac. Bauer knew that one of the symptoms of this perilous syndrome was impaired eyesight, which Julie had shown since August 5th. 'When we gave Julie drinks she kept missing the cup,' he says. 'We knew then she had no more chance.'

That evening Julie kept drifting asleep. Bauer was watching her and talked to her, he says, 'to try to perk her up'. At one point, believing that there was a lull in the storm, Julie asked if they could go down. Later, says Bauer, 'she asked me several times to make sure that Kurt got down safely. An hour or so later I looked at her again and she had died.' Gently, Bauer closed her mouth and eyes.

For Kurt, almost as distressing as Julie's death was the manner in which he learned of it. When morning came on August 7th, Willi Bauer shouted from his tent: 'Kurt, Julie died last night.' For Kurt, the news came as a hammer-blow. 'It was totally unexpected for me. I couldn't understand that nobody had called me over. Maybe I couldn't have helped her. But when you have been with someone for so long, you can give her spiritual help.' Later that day, Bauer moved Julie's body into the French tent she had originally shared with Kurt.

For the next three days the six climbers in Camp 4 declined inexorably towards the same fate. By August 8th all supplies of food and cooking gas was exhausted. After his two sleepless nights and the energy he had expended leading most of the way to the summit, Alan Rouse was the most vulnerable. At times he became delirious, beating his hands on his sleeping-bag; at times, murmuring 'water, water', he lapsed into unconsciousness.

Mrufka, by contrast, closed in on herself, as if entering a state of near-hibernation. Kurt meanwhile wrestled with his grief.

In the Austrians' tent, Bauer observed with disquiet that his two companions seemed to be suffering from dizziness – another telling high-altitude symptom. They waited by the hour for the storm to ease so that they could start their descent, but in vain. 'Visibility was nil,' says Bauer. 'It was only on August 10th that we could see to go down.'

By then Alan Rouse was too weak to move. Kurt tried to cajole him into action, without success. He was still asking for water and Kurt moistened his lips with snow. 'I had no choice but to leave him,' Kurt says. Bauer pulled his two companions to their feet and pushed them out of the tent. Bauer set off first, breaking the trail through snow that was waist deep in places, followed by Mrufka. Kurt waited until they had gone and then looked into Julie's tent for the last time. 'I could touch her but I could not see her face.'

As Kurt began his descent, he came upon Imitzer and Wieser lying in the snow barely 100 metres below Camp 4. One was face-down and motionless, the other on his back, his arms waving feebly. When Kurt tried to speak to them they appeared to neither see nor hear him; concluding that they were beyond all help, he pressed on. Bauer was still leading with Mrufka close behind, and she helped to extricate Bauer when he sank, chest-deep at times, into the snow. Then Kurt caught them up and all three helped break the trail for a while. Below Camp 3 they found that many of the fixed ropes were encased in ice and had to be pulled free. They were also handicapped by not having proper *descendeurs* for abseiling and of the three it was Mrufka who found it hardest to cope. She gradually fell behind Bauer and finally was overtaken by Kurt too. That night Bauer and Kurt stopped at Camp 2 but Mrufka did not arrive. In the morning they waited until midday in the hope that she had camped higher up but she was never seen again.

In Base Camp, Jim Curran was convinced that all seven climbers were dead. On August 11th, at the Pakistani liaison officer's request, he opened Kurt and Julie's tent to look for their passports and other documents. He also came upon some lager that Kurt had been brewing and he and the remaining climbers drank a sorrowful toast to absent friends. But as dusk fell, a silhouette appeared on the glacier half a mile away, stumbling towards Base Camp. It was Bauer, his hands and feet frostbitten, his clothing in tatters. He managed to convey the news that Mrufka was missing and that all other climbers but Kurt had died.

Curran and two Polish climbers left at once for the Abruzzi ridge. Just before midnight, on the snowfield at the foot of the ridge, they came upon Kurt, moving down so slowly that he seemed to be barely alive. Curran told him that he was safe at last. Kurt replied: 'I've lost Julie.'

Six weeks later, on September 27th, 1986, Terry held a 'remembrance' for Julie at High Rocks, where they had met and first climbed together. Five hundred people came, from all the diverse aspects of her life: fellow teachers of the handicapped children she had encouraged to climb; members of her local martial arts club, who performed a *musogi*, or cleansing ceremony, to help express and purify their collective grief; climbing friends from around the world. Kurt was there too. Terry spoke briefly and emotionally about Julie's life and many who came brought trees and shrubs to be planted in her memory. Some will grow at High Rocks and Harrison's, some by the duck-pond at Leyswood. They will bear no plaque, but those who knew Julie will know why they are there.

Acknowledgments

For their information, assistance and advice, I am immensely grateful to Willi Bauer, Chris Bonington, Chang Bong-Wan, Chang-Rae Park and the *Dong A Ilbo* newspaper in Seoul, Dr Charlie Clarke, Jim Curran, Kurt Diemberger, Xavier Eguskitza, Simon Freeman, Heather Jeeves, Ingrid Leili, Rudi Maier, Doug Scott and Terry Tullis.

◈ INDEX ◈

Index